Social and Psychological Dynamics of Collective Action: From Theory and Research to Practice and Policy

Issue Editors: Aarti Iyer and Martijn van Zomeren

INTRODUCTION

Introduction to the Social and Psychological Dynamics
of Collective Action — 645
Martijn van Zomeren and Aarti Iyer

COLLECTIVE ACTION BY LOW-STATUS GROUPS

Metaphors of Protest: A Classification of Motivations
for Collective Action — 661
Martijn van Zomeren and Russell Spears

Pathways to Collective Protest: Calculation, Identification, or Emotion?
A Critical Analysis of the Role of Group-Based Anger
in Social Movement Participation — 681
Stefan Stürmer and Bernd Simon

Collective Psychological Empowerment as a Model of Social Change:
Researching Crowds and Power — 707
John Drury and Steve Reicher

Collective Action—and Then What? — 727
Winnifred R. Louis

Collective Action in Modern Times: How Modern Expressions
of Prejudice Prevent Collective Action — 749
Naomi Ellemers and Manuela Barreto

COLLECTIVE ACTION BY HIGH-STATUS GROUPS

Why Do the Privileged Resort to Oppression? A Look at Some
Intragroup Factors — 769
Tom Postmes and Laura G. E. Smith

Why Do Men and Women Challenge Gender Discrimination
in the Workplace? The Role of Group Status and In-group
Identification in Predicting Pathways to Collective Action — 791
Aarti Iyer and Michelle K. Ryan

BEYOND STATUS: COLLECTIVE ACTION AROUND OPINIONS AND POLICY OPPOSITION

Context Matters: Explaining How and Why Mobilizing Context
    Influences Motivational Dynamics   815
  *Jacquelien van Stekelenburg, Bert Klandermans,
  and Wilco W. van Dijk*

Collective Action as the Material Expression of Opinion-Based
    Group Membership   839
  *Craig McGarty, Ana-Maria Bliuc, Emma F. Thomas,
  and Renata Bongiorno*

COMMENTARY

The Next Generation of Collective Action Research   859
  Stephen C. Wright

Issues in Progress
   Impact Validity as a Framework for Advocacy-Based Research
      Ricardo E. Barreras & Sean G. Massey
   Social Stigma and Social Disadvantage
      Manuela Barreto & Naomi Ellemers
   Scaling the Higher Education Pyramid: Research Addressing Academic and Career Success of Minorities and Women in Science and Engineering
      Martin Chemers & Moin Syed
   Immigrants and Hosts: Perceptions, Interactions, and Transformations
      Kay Deaux, Victoria Esses, Richard Lalonde, & Rupert Brown
   The Changing Landscape of Intergroup Relations in South Africa
      Gillian Finchilescu & Colin Tredoux
   The Reality of Contemporary Discrimination: The Consequences of Hidden Bias in Legal, Employment, and Health Care Context
      Jason A. Nier & Samuel L. Gaertner
   75 Years of Social Science for Social Action: Historical and Contemporary Perspectives on SPSSI's Legacy
      Alexandra Rutherford, Frances Cherry, & Rhoda Unger
   Latinos and Latino Immigrants in the United States
      Carey S. Ryan & Juan F. Casas

Editorial Advisory Board
   Harold L. Arnold, Jr., Temple University, United States
   B. Ann Bettencourt, University of Missouri, United States
   Herbert H. Blumberg, Goldsmiths College, University of London, United Kingdom
   Marcella H. Boynton, University of Connecticut, United States
   Heather E. Bullock, University of California, Santa Cruz, United States
   Susan Clayton, College of Wooster, United States
   Gillian Finchilescu, University of the Witwatersrand, South Africa
   I-Ching Lee, National Chengchi University, Taiwan
   Sara McClelland, City University of New York, United States
   Rupert W. Nacoste, North Carolina State University, United States
   Noraini M. Noor, International Islamic University, Malaysia
   Louis A. Penner, Wayne State University, United States
   Stephanie Rowley, University of Michigan, United States
   Johanna Vollhardt, University of Massachusetts, Amherst, United States

Reviewers of Selected Articles, This Issue
  Matthew Hornsey, University of Queensland, Australia
  Jolanda Jetten, University of Queensland, Australia
  Winnifred Louis, University of Queensland, Australia
  Joanne Smith, University of Queensland, Australia

Past JSI Editors
  Irene Hanson Frieze (2001–2005)
  Phyllis Katz (1997–2000)
  Daniel Perlman (1993–1996)
  Stuart Oskamp (1988–1992)
  George Levinger (1984–1987)
  Joseph E. McGrath (1979–1983)
  Jacqueline D. Goodchilds (1974–1978)
  Bertram H. Raven (1970–1973)
  Joshua A. Fishman (1966–1969)
  Leonard Solomon (1963)
  Robert Chin (1960–1965)
  John Harding (1956–1959)
  M. Brewster Smith (1951–1955)
  Harold H. Kelley (1949)
  Ronald Lippitt (1944–1950)

Introduction to the Social and Psychological Dynamics of Collective Action

Martijn van Zomeren*
University of Groningen

Aarti Iyer
University of Queensland

Collective action is one of the core mechanisms of social change, and thus of major importance to social scientists, practitioners, and policy-makers. Our goal in editing this issue is to bring together recent advances on the social and psychological dynamics of collective action among members of disadvantaged as well as advantaged groups. This article introduces the contributions to this issue after a brief review of the major psychological perspectives on collective action (social identity, relative deprivation, and resource mobilization theories), and a discussion of the considerable diversity in collective action research in terms of contexts, populations, and measures. We hope that this issue contributes to a more multi-faceted and integrative understanding of the social and psychological dynamics of collective action in terms of theory, research, policy, and practice.

Social inequality and injustice have been documented in societies around the world. Institutionalized status differences between social groups (based on categories such as gender, race/ethnicity, and sexuality) have created and maintained systemic disparities in wealth, health, and educational opportunities. Moreover, throughout history, groups have perpetrated crimes and injustices against others (i.e., a country may invade and occupy another, or a company may impose harsh working conditions upon its employees). Disadvantaged individuals, however,

---

*Correspondence concerning this article should be addressed to Martijn van Zomeren, Department of Social Psychology, University of Groningen, 9712 TS Groningen, The Netherlands [e-mail: m.van.zomeren@rug.nl].

We would like to thank all the contributors for their hard work, patience, and enthusiasm throughout the process of putting this volume together. We would also like to thank our colleagues who kindly provided useful feedback on the articles: Naomi Ellemers, John Drury, Matthew Hornsey, Jolanda Jetten, Winnifred Louis, Joanne Smith, and members of the *JSI* Editorial Board.

do not always accept the status quo. Rather, history shows that under particular circumstances they attempt to challenge social inequality and injustice through *collective action*.

Collective action is traditionally defined as any action that aims to improve the status, power, or influence of an entire group,[1] rather than that of one or a few individuals (Tajfel & Turner, 1979; Wright, Taylor, & Moghaddam, 1990). For instance, individuals take collective action to challenge systemic discrimination on the basis of ethnicity (e.g., Morris, 1984), gender (e.g., Kelly & Breinlinger, 1996), or sexuality (e.g., Stürmer & Simon, 2004). However, collective action can also seek to cease or prevent group injustice (suffered by ingroups or outgroups), as illustrated in ongoing protests against the American military occupation of Iraq and efforts to influence the 2007 G-8 summit. Note that collective actions do not necessarily require actual collectives. What matters is the aim of the action—to change the status of a group—rather than the number of people who are participating. The concept of collective action therefore includes mass political actions such as participation in demonstrations, but also individual-level actions such as signing a petition and voting (Brady, 1994; Klandermans, 1997). Moreover, people may organize and develop a social movement organization (SMO) whose sole aim is to create social change through orchestrating collective actions and recruiting others to join them (Klandermans, 1997).

What are the social and psychological factors that move people to collective action? Scholars have long been interested in this question because the societal consequences of collective action can be enormous: The disadvantaged rise to power, whereas the advantaged lose their high status position, although they may, in time, organize to regain it. Although such struggles may include violent and nonviolent collective actions, the contributions to the current issue all focus on nonviolent collective action. Furthermore, knowledge about when and why people engage in collective action has important theoretical implications for the study of group processes and intergroup relations. Research on this topic can also yield important practical strategies for those who seek to move people into collective action (e.g., union leaders, politicians), as well as for those who wish to prevent them from doing so (e.g., authorities).

The past 10 years have seen a resurgence of interest in the study of social justice efforts within social psychology and sociology. This work has primarily examined collective action by disadvantaged or low-status groups but has recently begun to investigate collective action by advantaged or high-status groups, as well as groups not strictly defined by a status position (e.g., opinion-based groups).

---

[1]We use the terms *group status, power,* and *influence* more or less interchangeably in this introduction. One reason for doing so is to acknowledge the use of different terminology in various theoretical and empirical approaches to the study of collective action while remaining neutral toward all approaches in an evaluative sense. Another reason is that collective action is not always based in intergroup status differences, as is illustrated by the papers in the third section of this issue.

This issue of *JSI* brings together multiple lines of theory and research on collective action from Europe, Australia, and North America. Our main aim is to identify the social and psychological factors that motivate collective action among members of low-status groups, high-status groups, or collectives built around a dimension other than status (e.g., political opinion). The issue further promises to translate theoretical and empirical insights to the domains of practice and policy. In this introductory article, we first review theory and research on collective action, and then connect it with the specific contributions to this issue.

An Overview of Theory and Research on Collective Action

The literature on collective action is large and heterogeneous (see van Zomeren, Postmes, & Spears, 2008, for an overview and meta-analysis), as work on this topic is conducted in different disciplines, including sociology, political science, history, and psychology. Theory and research thus reflect different levels of analysis, including the macrolevel (tapping into the strategic and political forces that facilitate or impede collective action; e.g., McCarthy & Zald, 1977), the mesolevel (tapping into the general conditions that affect groups and their members within society; e.g., Opp, 1991), and the microlevel (tapping into group members' psychological responses to collective disadvantage; e.g., Wright et al., 1990). Empirical studies reflect different research methods, such as laboratory experiments with groups created by the researchers (e.g., Ellemers, 1993), surveys of participants in real-world social movement (e.g., Klandermans, 1984), face-to-face interviews with social movement participants (e.g., van Aelst & Walgrave, 2001), ethnographic studies of political movements and SMOs (e.g., Scott, 1985), and analyses of media coverage of protest events (e.g., Koopmans & Statham, 1999). Furthermore, researchers have operationalized collective action in many different ways (Klandermans, 1997). Below, we outline the historical roots of theory and research on collective action.

Social and Psychological Explanations of Collective Action

Early work on collective action highlighted objective status variables as predictors of collective action (e.g., Blumer, 1939; Davies, 1962; Gurr, 1968; McCarthy & Zald, 1977; Olson, 1968). Such frameworks proposed that structural status differences between groups (as measured by various indicators such as wealth and health) explained low-status groups' participation in collective action to achieve social equality. In these approaches, less attention was paid to the role of individuals' subjective perceptions and emotions in motivating efforts to create social change.

However, as Marx and Engels (1848/2002) have suggested, the abstract conditions of historical and social structures do not automatically produce social change.

Indeed, the classic studies reported in *The American Soldier* (Stouffer, Suchman, DeVinney, Start, & Williams, 1949) demonstrated that structurally disadvantaged group members do not necessarily seek to improve their group's circumstances. Why should some cases of social inequality be challenged and not others? To address this question, various frameworks have proposed subjective explanations of collective action participation, which focus on individuals' psychological motivations to help achieve social equality and social justice. That is, these explanations suggest that how individuals perceive their social world profoundly influences how they respond to it.

Relative deprivation theory (RDT), for example, posits that only when individuals perceive their situation as relatively deprived will they experience anger and resentment, and seek to improve their lot (Crosby, 1976; Runciman, 1966; for a review see Walker & Smith, 2002). RDT has developed at least two key insights as to why individuals participate in collective action. First, the deprivation must be perceived as group based for this experience to predict collective action (e.g., Kawakami & Dion, 1995). Meta-analytic evidence (Smith & Ortiz, 2002) suggests that when disadvantage is perceived as individual based and unjust, the resulting sense of deprivation does not predict collective action. However, when the same disadvantage is perceived as group based and unjust, relative deprivation is a strong predictor of collective action.

A second insight from RDT suggests that individuals do not simply perceive social injustice or inequality, but are often emotionally aroused by it too (see Kawakami & Dion, 1995; Leach, Snider, & Iyer, 2002). RD theorists argue that it is this emotional response that motivates participation in collective action (van Zomeren et al., 2008). That is, the action-related experience seems most prototypically captured in the affective or emotional component of relative deprivation. This idea has paved the way for applications of group-based emotion (Leach et al., 2002; Smith, 1993) to the study of collective action. For instance, feelings of group-based anger and resentment motivate individuals' willingness to engage in collective action (e.g., Mummendey, Kessler, Klink, & Mielke, 1999; van Zomeren, Spears, Fischer, & Leach, 2004). Similarly, American and British citizens' feelings of shame and anger about their countries' occupation of Iraq has been shown to motivate a willingness to protest the occupation (Iyer, Schmader, & Lickel, 2007).

Social identity theory (SIT; Tajfel, 1978; Tajfel & Turner, 1979) offers another framework of collective action, proposing that it is individuals' perceptions of sociostructural characteristics that determine their identification with the group, which predicts the likelihood of their participation in social change strategies (Kawakami & Dion, 1995; Mummendey et al., 1999; Wright et al., 1990). First, group members should perceive the boundary between their (low-status) group and the comparison (high-status) group to be impermeable, such that they cannot join the high-status group and improve their individual position (Ellemers, 1993). This hypothesis parallels RDT's distinction between group and individual deprivation. Second, the group's low-status position should be perceived as illegitimate or undeserved (e.g., Mummendey et al., 1999). This means that people should be able to imagine alternatives to the status quo (Tajfel, 1978). And third, the inequality should be perceived as unstable, reflecting a sense of agency that the social structure can be changed (e.g., Wright et al., 1990). In this way, individuals' group-based perceptions of, and emotional responses to, inequality and injustice have been identified as important predictors of their willingness to engage in collective action.

Others have argued, however, that perceptions of, and even emotions based in, relative deprivation and illegitimacy may not be enough to predict actual collective action behavior (Stürmer & Simon, 2004). Building on SIT, they propose that a strongly developed and politicized sense of identification with a social movement is the best predictor of such behavior (Simon & Klandermans, 2001). Research has indeed shown that people are unlikely to engage in collective action when their group means little to them (see Ellemers, Spears, & Doosje, 1999). This is illustrated by the fact that demonstrations typically attract only a tiny fraction of all the individuals who are sympathetic to the cause (Oegema & Klandermans, 1994). Some authors have taken this argument even further to argue that people primarily identify with social groups for the purpose of mobilizing for collective action and social change (e.g., Reicher, 1996). Thus, a second important factor motivating collective action is individuals' (politicized) identification with their group.

A final perspective proposes that injustice and identity explanations do not take into account individuals' more instrumental concerns about the perceived costs and benefits of collective action. For example, resource mobilization theory (McCarthy & Zald, 1977) has been influential in proposing that relative deprivation elicits collective protest behavior only when individuals believe they have the resources to mount an effective challenge to the inequality or injustice. That is, individuals often do not participate in collective action because they do not expect (material or social) rewards for their efforts (Olson, 1968; Stürmer & Simon, 2004). Similarly, people may perceive their group to be too weak to enforce social change (in terms of the group's efficacy to achieve change; Mummendey et al., 1999; van Zomeren et al., 2004). Lastly, individuals may not have sufficient opportunities or networks to join social movements or collective actions, or they may face practical obstacles to actual participation (Klandermans & Oegema, 1987). Thus, a third important factor motivating collective action is individuals' instrumental expectations of costs and benefits.

In sum, at least three subjective explanations of collective action can be distilled from the literature: perceptions and emotions of group-based injustice, (politicized) social identification, and instrumental cost–benefit expectations of available resources (van Zomeren et al., 2008). However, at least two points should be noted that complicate this picture. First, collective action is often operationalized in different ways in studies employing a diverse range of methods, which may potentially produce conceptual confusion. Second, and directly related to the structure of this issue, collective action has been studied mainly among members of low-status groups, raising the question of whether the same social and psychological factors predict collective action among members of high-status groups, or groups undefined by status. We discuss each point in turn below.

Operationalizations of Collective Action within a Diverse Range of Methods

Collective action has been operationalized in different ways by researchers, including attitudes toward collective action, intentions and action tendencies to participate in collective action, reports of past participation in collective action, and actual collective behavior. Most social psychological research on collective action relies on survey research methods and laboratory experiments. Yet researchers also use more qualitative methodologies in studying collective action participation, such as interviews with collective action participants, participatory action, or observations of protest events. Still others have shifted their analysis away from individual participants, focusing instead on media coverage of protest events, or literature generated by SMOs.

As the ultimate goal of the field is to be able to predict actual participation in collective action, some have argued that behavioral measures are the most valid and useful dependent measures. However, "true" behavior may reflect only one aspect of the social and psychological dynamics of collective action. We propose there is much to gain from studying the social and psychological processes and constructs that are (at least) one step removed from actual behavior, as they may still influence behavior later in time.

In this respect Klandermans (1997) offers a useful four-step model to organize these dynamics (see also Klandermans & Oegema, 1987). In a first step toward actual participation in a social movement, people become part of the *mobilization potential* of a social movement by sympathizing with its political and strategic aim(s). Here only attitudinal support for the social movement is required. In the second step, people become *targets of mobilization attempts* by the social movement, and in the third step they become *motivated to participate* in specific social movement activities. It is likely that specific intentions regarding collective action become relevant at these stages as a consequence of social influence efforts by others in the social movement. The fourth and final step concerns *overcoming concrete barriers* (e.g., time, money, or other responsibilities) to actual participation. Here the key point is whether intentions will be translated into actual behavior.

These different operationalizations of collective action may correspond to the different steps outlined in Klandermans' model. To illustrate, consider the example of observing and interviewing participants at a demonstration or protest event (e.g., Drury & Reicher, 1999; Reicher, 1984). Given that participants are already at the demonstration, the conclusions from the obtained data should apply to the fourth step of Klandermans' model. In a similar vein, survey data about social movement members' action intentions should apply to the third step of the model (see Simon et al., 1998), because participants are already sympathetic (Step 1) and targeted as potential participants (Step 2). Lastly, some studies focusing on natural groups in the laboratory (e.g., Wright et al., 1990) have asked individuals from a disadvantaged group (e.g., women, or members of an ethnic minority) about their attitudes toward collective action. Such an approach allows for an investigation of the social and psychological processes that operate at, or even before, the first step of the model.

Conceptualizing the different measures of collective action as reflecting different steps of the social and psychological dynamics of collective action makes it apparent that the diversity of methods and operationalizations is actually a strength. Understanding the predictors of collective action attitudes, intentions, and action tendencies provides valuable information about the dynamics that underlie actual behavior later in time. From this perspective, knowledge about how people become sympathizers of social movements, how they are targeted and influenced by social movements, and how they are persuaded to act in the final step are all different but equally important aspects of individuals' pathways to collective action. Moreover, it is these dynamics (rather than the sole outcome of participation) that should be of considerable interest to activists and social justice organizations, because some collective actions may need to be organized from the grassroots level (e.g., before or at Step 1), whereas others may be more established (focusing more on Steps 3 and 4).

Structural Position of Collective Action Participants

As noted, the three social and psychological factors explaining collective action have been examined mainly among members of low-status groups. Indeed, for a long time, the prevailing view in the collective action literature has been that members of high-status or advantaged groups are motivated to maintain and strengthen group-based hierarchy (e.g., Simon & Klandermans, 2001; Tajfel & Turner, 1979; Wright et al., 1990). It is therefore not surprising that the historical focus of collective action research has typically been on the low-status group and its members.

Nonetheless, recent theory and research suggests that advantaged group members sometimes act to promote the outgroup's interests (e.g., Iyer & Leach, in press; Iyer et al., 2007; Leach et al., 2002; Leach, Iyer, & Pedersen, 2006). Drawing from work on attributions and group-based emotion, several empirical studies have now shown that emotions like anger, guilt, and sympathy can motivate advantaged group members' actions to compensate or help the disadvantaged (e.g., Doosje,

Branscombe, Spears, & Manstead, 1998; Iyer et al., 2007; Leach et al., 2006). This suggests that there is little reason to justify the neglect of advantaged groups in the study of collective action—rather, there lies a great challenge for collective action researchers to think of ways to motivate the advantaged to help the disadvantaged in their efforts for social change. For example, individuals may perceive themselves to be part of a superordinate category or group that has a common goal (e.g., environmentalism).

Therefore, this issue includes articles investigating collective action by members of high-status groups as well as low-status groups. In addition, a number of contributions focus on collective action by groups that may include members of both low-status and high-status groups.

Overview of Contributions to this Issue

All the articles in this issue explore the social and psychological dynamics that encourage (or inhibit) collective action among members of low-status groups, high-status groups, and groups undefined by status. The contributions develop their research questions and hypotheses from solid theoretical foundations (e.g., RDT, SIT, group-based emotion), often integrating principles from various frameworks in novel ways (e.g., Louis, 2009; van Zomeren & Spears, 2009). Each article addresses at least one of the three social and psychological explanations of collective action we reviewed, often empirically testing the independent predictive power of multiple factors. Some of the reported studies operationalize collective action as attitudes, whereas others measure intentions, action tendencies, or actual behavior. Several articles offer different methodologies to the study of collective action. Nonetheless, all articles begin from a general psychological perspective on collective action that suggests that how individuals perceive their social world profoundly influences how they respond to it.

Furthermore, each article grounds its analytic focus in real-world contexts of challenges to inequality and injustice. Some articles focus their analysis on efforts to dismantle inequality based on social categories such as gender (Ellemers & Barreto, 2009; Iyer & Ryan, 2009), sexuality (Stürmer & Simon, 2009), weight (Stürmer & Simon, 2009), and immigrant status (Postmes & Smith, 2009). Other articles analyze participation in movements to protest perceived social injustice, such as increases in university tuition fees (Stürmer & Simon, 2009), increases in local taxes (Drury & Reicher, 2009), the reduction of retired workers' rights (van Stekelenburg, Klandermans, & van Dijk, 2009), and poverty in developing countries (McGarty, Bliuc, Thomas, & Bongiorno, 2009). As a result, their analyses and conclusions are well positioned to inform policy and practice regarding ongoing efforts to challenge inequality and injustice.

The organizational structure of this issue reflects a long-standing division in theoretical and empirical approaches to collective action. Conceptual frameworks typically seek to explain action by members of low-status groups (RDT, SIT) or groups undifferentiated by status (resource mobilization theory), and others are being developed to explain action by high-status groups (e.g., group-based emotion). Similarly, empirical research has typically investigated collective action participation among individuals from only one status group (high or low), or with no mention of status. These distinctions make theoretical and practical sense given that a group's structural position can influence its members' experiences of inequality and injustice. For instance, members of low-status or disadvantaged groups typically take collective action in the name of justice to improve their group's circumstances. In contrast, members of high-status groups contemplating participation in social justice strategies must weigh their group interests against the interests of societal justice. Finally, collective action participants from a range of status positions are likely to have distinct experiences of inequality and injustice that motivate their participation, which may not necessarily mirror the concerns motivating low- and high-status group members' participation (see Iyer & Leach, in press).

Although status position should influence individuals' pathways to collective action, it is also likely that some similar factors will operate to facilitate (or inhibit) their participation in social justice efforts. As such, after providing an overview of each section, we consider points of convergence and divergence among the articles. Wright's (2009) final article offers an integrative commentary on the entire issue, as well as an agenda for future research based on points of convergence and divergence.

Collective Action by Low-Status Groups

The articles in the first section focus on collective action by members of low-status or disadvantaged groups who seek to improve their group's status, power, or position. In a theoretical review article, van Zomeren and Spears (2009) develop a set of metaphors to classify the range of motivations proposed for collective action and, in so doing, identify conceptual gaps in the extant literature. They argue that researchers have traditionally viewed collective action participants as intuitive economists (who weigh the concrete benefits of action for their individual and group interests) and intuitive politicians (who consider whether participation in action will help them maintain a positive social identity). Yet little attention has been given to participants as intuitive theologians, who are motivated to defend threatened moral convictions. van Zomeren and Spears thus propose a new line of research and offer practical guidelines for how SMOs may encourage individuals' different motivations for participating in action.

The next two articles in this section provide empirical evidence for low-status groups' motivations to engage in collective action, as well as a key obstacle they may face in this process. Stürmer and Simon (2009) compare two established psychological pathways to social movement participation (calculation of costs and benefits of participation, and group identification) with a third: anger. Their experimental data show that, unlike cost–benefit calculation and group identification, anger is a relatively weak predictor of collective action participation when there are other less costly means to reduce this emotion. Stürmer and Simon conclude with recommendations for how social justice organizations might more effectively mobilize their participants to take action.

In their article, Ellemers and Barreto (2009) highlight a key obstacle to the development and mobilization of collective action strategies: modern expressions of prejudice that tend to be more subtle and indirect. In their experimental studies, Ellemers and Barreto demonstrate that women who face subtle (rather than overt) expressions of prejudice are less likely to interpret this treatment as group-based discrimination. As a result, these women blame their negative treatment on their own shortcomings, thus helping to maintain the meritocracy ideology. Importantly, the women facing subtle prejudice also experience less anger and are less likely to engage in collective action, compared to those facing blatant prejudice. Ellemers and Barreto offer concrete recommendations to improve the recognition of, and concrete challenges to, modern expressions of gender prejudice.

The next article, by Drury and Reicher (2009), takes the study of collective action out of the laboratory by analyzing collective action by crowds. Crowd events reflect instances of collective action that are rarely scripted, and thus may quickly evolve in unplanned ways. Thus, research conducted in such contexts is perhaps best suited to observing the dynamics of collective action as it unfolds over time. In studies of crowds ranging from a student protest, to a mass demonstration against local taxation that turned into a riot, to football fans, Drury and Reicher argue that empowerment within these groups enhances the development of widely shared goals, and support for normative action. They conclude that a sense of emerging psychological collective empowerment is crucial in motivating collective action, because it instills a belief that the group can overcome the intergroup power differences that may otherwise seem too great.

In the final article of this section, Louis (2009) investigates another gap in social and psychological work on collective action. Although many have considered how to motivate people to engage in action, few have focused on how collective action might be used to create social change, and whether this is actually effective. Thus, Louis argues, there are few concrete strategies that activists and community organizers might take from the extant literature about how to achieve change (e.g., change social norms or level of identification) and the factors that might moderate the effectiveness of these strategies (e.g., the role of opponents or third-party observers). Building on SIT principles, Louis develops a model to address these shortcomings, discusses its practical implications, and calls for future research on this issue.

Collective Action by High-Status Groups

The second section illustrates two different forms of collective action high-status groups may take in the face of social inequality and injustice. First, Postmes and Smith (2009) investigate how members of privileged groups might act to maintain oppression. They report experimental evidence that ingroup norms—as an intragroup process—serve to normalize and encourage oppression against disadvantaged groups. Individuals in a condition where group norms are consistent with oppression are more likely to engage in oppressive acts. Postmes and Smith consider the theoretical implications of this analysis for the study of oppression and discuss the practical strategies that could be developed for use by those seeking to eliminate such behavior.

Iyer and Ryan (2009) explicitly compare advantaged and disadvantaged group members' (emotional) responses to a particular instance of gender discrimination (the "glass cliff"). Building on SIT principles and work on appraisal theories of (group-based) emotion, they suggest that men's and women's willingness to challenge the "glass cliff" is explained by different perceptions of the inequality (i.e., its illegitimacy and pervasiveness) and different emotional reactions (i.e., anger or sympathy), depending on the gender group to which they belong, and their level of identification with that group. This is because the two groups have different interests (i.e., challenging vs. maintaining the status quo), with higher identifiers more in tune with these interests, and lower identifiers less so. As a result, higher and lower identified men and women are likely to interpret and experience the same situation quite differently. This direct comparison between advantaged and disadvantaged group members' responses highlights the need for researchers to examine advantaged groups as well as disadvantaged groups in the study of collective action.

Beyond Status: Collective Action around Opinions and Policy Opposition

The last section focuses on collective action among members of groups not strictly defined by their status position, even while the aim of such actions is to further the interests of a disadvantaged or harmed group. For instance, investigations of political demonstrations (van Stekelenburg et al., 2009) include participants who may belong to high-status groups, low-status groups, or third-party observer groups. Thus, the social and psychological factors and processes being considered in such studies are applicable to members of all status groups.

van Stekelenburg et al. (2009) surveyed and interviewed individuals who participated in two large coalition-sponsored demonstrations, thus gaining information about who actually protests, and for what reason(s). They demonstrate that ideological motives are key predictors of participation in collective action, independent of instrumental motives (i.e., cost–benefit analyses). In addition, they find that the social movement context influences the motivational patterns of individual protesters. Instrumental concerns and beliefs about efficacy are more important for those among a power-oriented movement who are protesting a government reduction to early retirement plans (concrete outcomes), whereas ideological concerns are more important for those among a value-oriented movement who are protesting a more abstract neo-liberal value system. van Stekelenburg et al. close with a discussion of implications for social justice organizations.

In the next article, McGarty et al. (2009) propose that many instances of collective action are expressions of a specific (political) opinion held by the individual, rather than the social or demographic groups (e.g., based on race, gender, or nationality) they belong to. Similarly, other examples of collective action by groups cannot be equated to either social categories or institutions (e.g., rallies against the 2003 invasion of Iraq). As such, McGarty et al. consider the factors that motivate members of an opinion-based group (defined by a shared opinion or political position) to take collective action on behalf of this opinion. In arguably the best example of translating theory and research into practice and policy, they discuss an intervention aiming to create psychological commitment with various opinion-based groups (e.g., groups who disagree with the government). This intervention is reported to have long-term effects on participants' political consciousness and behavioral intentions, thus nicely demonstrating the key point that collective action research is not only theoretically relevant, but can also be socially consequential.

Points of Convergence and Divergence

As noted, this issue includes a range of empirical work on the social and psychological factors that motivate individuals from groups to engage in collective action. For example, some articles focus on the experience of group-based injustice (Ellemers & Barreto, 2009) and group-based emotions (Iyer & Ryan, 2009; Stürmer & Simon, 2009; van Stekelenburg et al., 2009), whereas others focus on the strength of identification with one's disadvantaged group (Iyer & Ryan, 2009; Louis, 2009; Stürmer & Simon, 2009; van Zomeren & Spears, 2009) or advantaged group (Iyer & Ryan, 2009), and still others focus on individual cost–benefit analyses (Stürmer & Simon, 2009; van Stekelenburg et al., 2009; van Zomeren & Spears, 2009). Various articles also introduce novel variables that should contribute to participation in collective action, such as moral conviction (van Zomeren & Spears, 2009), ideology (van Stekelenburg et al., 2009), perceived pervasiveness of inequality (Iyer & Ryan, 2009), ingroup norms (Postmes & Smith, 2009), opinion-based groups (McGarty et al., 2009), as well as empowerment and positive emotion (Drury & Reicher, 2009).

Many articles converge on the importance of social identity in collective action, be it based on group status or not. For example, Stürmer and Simon (2009) argue that social identification with a group or social movement is a key predictor of collective action participation among low-status group members, whereas McGarty et al. (2009) and Drury and Reicher (2009) argue that self-categorization and identification processes are key to opinion-based groups and crowd events, respectively. Iyer and Ryan (2009), as well as Postmes and Smith (2009), contend that even members of high-status groups may engage in collective action on the basis of their group membership.

However, there is also an important point of divergence across contributions, which concerns the role of group-based emotions in collective action. For example, van Stekelenburg et al. (2009) and Iyer and Ryan (2009) demonstrate that emotional responses to inequality and injustice predict individuals' willingness or intentions to take collective action. Drury and Reicher (2009) also argue for the importance of positive group-based emotions among crowd members. However, Stürmer and Simon's (2009) findings suggest that while emotions like anger may spark motivation for collective action, they do not necessarily translate into behavior at a later stage. Such divergence offers an opportunity for healthy scientific debate and offers a strong pointer for future research. Such research can identify, for example, the specific conditions under which emotions like anger predict collective action, and why they do so.

Concluding Remarks

Whether from the perspective of low-status groups, high-status groups, or groups undefined by status, the articles in this issue of *JSI* present theory and research on the social and psychological dynamics of collective action. Theoretically, the contributions consider which established and emerging factors (such as identity, instrumentality, and injustice) motivate collective action among these different groups. Methodologically, the contributions use different quantitative approaches (such as experiments, longitudinal studies, and field studies), and different operationalizations of collective action. And from a perspective of practical relevance, each article offers recommendations for the application of its findings and analysis in policy and practice. More generally, our aim was for these articles to contribute to a more multifaceted and integrative understanding of the social and psychological dynamics of collective action, in all its many shapes and forms.

We also hope that the present collection of articles will inspire new ways of thinking about the study of collective action. To date there have been too few attempts toward theoretical and methodological integration in the literature, leaving many apparent contradictions and unanswered questions. And, perhaps more importantly, there has been very little collaboration between scientists and practitioners in developing models of collective action that are valid in both theoretical and practical terms. We hope that this volume may serve as a rallying call for some scientific and practitioner "collective action" to start developing such frameworks.

References

Blumer, H. (1939). Collective behavior. In A. McClung Lee (Ed.), *Principles of sociology* (pp. 219–288). New York: Barnes & Noble.
Brady, H. E. (1994). Political participation. In J. P. Robinson, P. R. Shaver, & L. S. Wrightsman (Eds.), *Measures of political attitudes* (pp. 737–801). San Diego, CA: Academic Press.
Crosby, F. J. (1976). A model of egotistical relative deprivation. *Psychological Review, 83*, 85–113.
Davies, J. (1962). Toward a theory of revolution. *American Sociological Review, 27*, 5–18.
Doosje, B., Branscombe, N. R., Spears, R., & Manstead, A. S. R. (1998). Guilty by association: When one's group has a negative history. *Journal of Personality and Social Psychology, 75*, 872–886.
Drury, J., & Reicher, S. D. (1999). The inter-group dynamics of collective empowerment: Substantiating the social identity model of crowd behavior. *Group Processes and Inter-group Relations, 4*, 381–402.
Drury, J., & Reicher, S. (2009). Collective psychological empowerment as a model of social change: Researching crowds and power. *Journal of Social Issues, 65*, 707–725.
Ellemers, N. (1993). The influence of socio-structural variables on identity management strategies. In W. Stroebe & M. Hewstone (Eds.), *European review of social psychology* (vol. 4, pp. 22–57). Oxford: Blackwell.
Ellemers, N., & Barreto, M. (2009). Collective action in modern times: How modern expressions of prejudice prevent collective action. *Journal of Social Issues, 65*, 749–768.
Ellemers, N., Spears, R., & Doosje, B. (1999). *Social identity: Context, commitment, content*. Oxford: Blackwell.
Gurr, T. R. (1968). A causal model of civil strife: A comparative analysis using new indices. *American Political Science Review, 62*, 1104–1124.
Iyer, A., & Leach, C.W. (in press). When the advantaged work for social equality: The role of group-based emotions. In S. Stürmer & M. Snyder (Eds.), *Psychology of prosocial behavior: Group processes, intergroup relations, and helping*. Oxford: Blackwell.
Iyer, A., & Ryan, M. K. (2009). Why do men and women challenge gender discrimination in the workplace? The role of group status and ingroup identification in predicting pathways to collective action. *Journal of Social Issues, 65*, 791–814.
Iyer, A., Schmader, T., & Lickel, B. (2007). Why individuals protest the perceived transgressions of their country: The role of anger, shame, and guilt. *Personality and Social Psychology Bulletin, 33*, 572–587.
Kawakami, K., & Dion, K. L. (1995). Social identity and affect as determinants of collective action: Toward an integration of relative deprivation and social identity theories. *Theory and Psychology, 5*, 551–577.
Kelly, C., & Breinlinger, S. (1996). *The social psychology of collective action: Identity, injustice, and gender*. London: Taylor & Francis.
Klandermans, B. (1984). Mobilization and participation: Social-psychological expansions of resource mobilization theory. *American Sociological Review, 49*, 583–600.
Klandermans, B. (1997). *The social psychology of protest*. Oxford: Basic Blackwell.
Klandermans, B., & Oegema, D. (1987). Potentials, networks, motivations, and barriers: Steps toward participation in social movements. *American Sociological Review, 52*, 519–531.
Koopmans, R., & Statham, P. (1999). Political claims analysis: Integrating protest event and political discourse approaches. *Mobilization: An International Quarterly, 4*, 203–221.
Leach, C. W., Snider, N., & Leach, C. W. (2002). "Poisoning the consciences of the fortunate": The experience of relative advantage and support for social equality. In I. Walker & H. J. Smith (Eds.), *Relative deprivation: Specification, development, integration* (pp. 136–163). New York: Cambridge University Press.
Leach, C. W., Iyer, A., & Pedersen, A. (2006). Anger and guilt about ingroup advantage explain the willingness for political action. *Personality and Social Psychology Bulletin, 32*, 1232–1245.
Louis, W. R. (2009). Collective action—and then what? *Journal of Social Issues, 65*, 727–748.
McCarthy, J. D., & Zald, M. N. (1977). Resource mobilization and social movements: A partial theory. *American Journal of Sociology, 82*, 1212–1241.

McGarty, C., Bliuc, A.-M., Thomas, E. F., & Bongiorno, R. (2009). Collective action as the material expression of opinion-based group membership. *Journal of Social Issues, 65*, 839–857.
Marx, K., & Engels, F. (2002). *The communist manifesto*. New York: Penguin. (Original work published 1848).
Morris, A. (1984). *The origins of the civil rights movement: Black communities organizing for change*. New York: Free Press.
Mummendey, A., Kessler, T., Klink, A., & Mielke, R. (1999). Strategies to cope with negative social identity: Predictions by social identity theory and relative deprivation theory. *Journal of Personality and Social Psychology, 76*, 229–245.
Oegema, D., & Klandermans, B. (1994). Why social movement sympathizers don't participate: Erosion and non-conversion of support. *American Sociological Review, 59*, 703–722.
Olson, M. (1968). *The logic of collective action: Public goods and the theory of groups*. Cambridge, MA: Harvard University Press.
Opp, K. D. (1991). Grievances and participation in social movements. *American Sociological Review, 53*, 853–864.
Postmes, T., & Smith, L. G. E. (2009). Why do the privileged resort to oppression? A look at some intra-group factors. *Journal of Social Issues, 65*, 769–790.
Reicher, S. D. (1984). The St. Paul's riot: An explanation of the limits of crowd action in terms of a social identity model. *European Journal of Social Psychology, 14*, 1–21.
Reicher, S. D. (1996). Social identity and social change: Rethinking the context of social psychology. In P. Robinson (Ed.), *Social groups and identities: Developing the legacy of Henri Tajfel* (pp. 317–336). Oxford: Butterworth-Heinemann.
Runciman, W. G. (1966). *Relative deprivation and social justice: A study of attitudes to social inequality in twentieth-century England*. Berkeley: University of California Press.
Scott, J. C. (1985). *Weapons of the weak: Everyday forms of peasant resistance*. New Haven, CT: Yale University Press.
Simon, B., & Klandermans, B. (2001). Politicized collective identity: A social psychological analysis. *American Psychologist, 56*, 319–331.
Simon, B., Loewy, M., Stuermer, S., Weber, U., Freytag, P., Habig, C., et al. (1998). Collective identification and social movement participation. *Journal of Personality and Social Psychology, 74*, 646–658.
Smith, E. R. (1993). Social identity and social emotions: Toward new conceptualizations of prejudice. In D. M. Mackie & D. L. Hamilton (Eds.), *Affect, cognition, and stereotyping: Interactive processes in group perception* (pp. 297–315). San Diego, CA: Academic Press.
Smith, H. J., & Ortiz, D. J. (2002). Is it just me? The different consequences of personal and group relative deprivation. In I. Walker & H. J. Smith (Eds.), *Relative deprivation: Specification, development, and integration* (pp. 91–115). Cambridge, UK: Cambridge University Press.
Stouffer, S. A., Suchman, E. A., DeVinney, L. C., Star, S. A., & Williams, R. M. (1949). *The American soldier: Vol. 1. Adjustment during army life*. Princeton, NJ: Princeton University Press.
Stürmer, S., & Simon, B. (2004). Collective action: Towards a dual-pathway model. In W. Stroebe & M. Hewstone (Eds.), *European review of social psychology, 15* (pp. 59–99). Hove, UK: Psychology Press.
Stürmer, S., & Simon, B. (2009). Pathways to collective protest: Calculation, identification or emotion? A critical analysis of the role of group-based anger in social movement participation. *Journal of Social Issues, 65*, 681–705.
Tajfel, H. (1978). The achievement of inter-group differentiation. In H. Tajfel (Ed.), *Differentiation between social groups* (pp. 77–100). London: Academic Press.
Tajfel, H., & Turner, J. C. (1979). An integrative theory of inter-group conflict. In W. G. Austin & S. Worchel (Eds.), *The social psychology of inter-group relations* (pp. 33–47). Monterey, CA: Brooks/Cole.
van Aelst, P., & Walgrave, S. (2001). Who is that (wo)man in the street? From the normalization of protest to the normalization of the protester. *European Journal of Political Research, 39*, 461–486.
van Stekelenburg, J., Klandermans, B., & van Dijk, W. W. (2009). Context matters: Explaining how and why mobilizing context influences motivational dynamics. *Journal of Social Issues, 65*, 815–838.

van Zomeren, M., & Spears, R. (2009). Metaphors of protest: A classification of motivations for collective action. *Journal of Social Issues, 65*, 661–679.
van Zomeren, M., Spears, R., Fischer, A. H., & Leach, C. W. (2004). Put your money where your mouth is!: Explaining collective action tendencies through group-based anger and group efficacy. *Journal of Personality and Social Psychology, 87*, 649–664.
van Zomeren, M., Postmes, T., & Spears, R. (2008). Toward an integrative social identity model of collective action: A quantitative research synthesis of three socio-psychological perspectives. *Psychological Bulletin, 134*, 504–535.
Walker, I., & Smith, H. J. (2002). *Relative deprivation: Specification, development, and integration.* Cambridge: Cambridge University Press.
Wright, S. C. (2009). The next generation of collective action research. *Journal of Social Issues, 65*, 859–879.
Wright, S. C., Taylor, D. M., & Moghaddam, F. M. (1990). Responding to membership in a disadvantaged group: From acceptance to collective protest. *Journal of Personality and Social Psychology, 58*, 994–1003.

MARTIJN VAN ZOMEREN received his PhD in Social Psychology from the University of Amsterdam (2006). His main research interests concern the emotional processes involved in intra- and intergroup behavior such as collective action (van Zomeren, Spears, Fischer, & Leach, 2004; van Zomeren, Spears, & Leach, 2008; van Zomeren, Postmes, & Spears, 2008). His doctoral dissertation, which examined social-psychological paths to protest as ways of coping with collective disadvantage, received the APA Division 49 2007 Dissertation Award, and second prize in the 2007 competition for SPSSI's Dissertation Award. He is currently a faculty member at the Department of Social and Organizational Psychology of the University of Groningen.

AARTI IYER received her PhD in Social Psychology from the University of California, Santa Cruz (2004) and is currently a faculty member at the University of Queensland (Australia). Her research investigates challenges to group-based inequality on the part of individuals (e.g., through collective action) and organizations (e.g., through affirmative action programs). Another line of her work considers individuals' emotional and political responses to representations of terrorism. Her doctoral dissertation, which examined how White Americans and Australians come to participate in political action to achieve racial equality, won second prize in the 2005 competition for SPSSI's Dissertation Award. In 2008, she was awarded the Jos Jaspars Early Career Award by the European Association of Experimental Social Psychology.

Metaphors of Protest: A Classification of Motivations for Collective Action

Martijn van Zomeren[*]
University of Groningen

Russell Spears
Cardiff University

This article proposes a classification of motivations for collective action based in three of Tetlock's (2002) metaphors of social functionalism (i.e., people as intuitive economists, politicians, and theologians). We use these metaphors to map individual- and group-based motivations for collective action from the literature onto the distinction between individuals who are strongly or weakly identified with their social group. We conclude that low identifiers can be best understood as intuitive economists (supported by both early and recent work on collective action), whereas high identifiers can be best thought of as intuitive politicians or theologians (as recent work on social identity has started to explore). Interestingly, our classification reveals a remarkable lack of attention for the intuitive theologian's motivation for collective action. We therefore develop new hypotheses for future research, and derive recommendations for policy and practice from our analysis.

Many people may remember the World Press Photo 1989: A young Chinese man stands passively in Tiananmen Square to block the path of a Chinese tank. This powerful picture raises many questions, one of which is why people protest. Historically, most theory and research on collective action has been driven by individuals' pursuit of rational self-interest (e.g., Klandermans, 1984; McCarthy & Zald, 1977; Oberschall, 1973; Olson, 1968). However, this motivation does not appear to offer much help in understanding the Chinese man trying to stop a tank; in fact, it would be a substantial understatement to say that the risk of being overrun

---

[*]Correspondence concerning this article should be addressed to Martijn van Zomeren, Department of Social Psychology, University of Groningen, 9712 TS Groningen, The Netherlands [e-mail: m.van.zomeren@rug.nl].

We thank Hein Lodewijkx and Agneta Fischer for their comments on a previous draft of this article.

by tons of steel constitutes a big cost to the individual. Therefore, additional group-based motivations for collective action have been proposed to better understand and appreciate why individuals protest in terms of their social identity (Tajfel, 1978; Tajfel & Turner, 1979; see also Reicher, 1996, 2001; Simon et al., 1998). The main aim of this article is to provide a classification of individual-based and group-based motivations for collective action that identifies theoretical and empirical gaps in the literature, and to develop new hypotheses and recommendations for policy and practice.

We seek to meet this aim by applying three of Tetlock's (2002) metaphors of social functionalism to the collective action literature. We first identify theory and research on collective action that assumes humans to be intuitive economists (Edwards, 1962) who aim to achieve individual goals through collective action. Then we identify more recent theorizing on collective action that assumes people to be intuitive politicians and theologians (Tetlock, 2002) who aim to achieve group goals through collective action.[1] We will argue that low identifiers with a social group are more likely to resemble intuitive economists whereas high identifiers are more likely to resemble intuitive politicians and theologians.[2] Moreover, we will argue that progress and innovation in theory and research on collective action lies in the group-based metaphors in general, and in the intuitive theologian metaphor in particular. We therefore link recent theorizing on moral conviction (e.g., Skitka, Bauman, & Sargis, 2005; Tetlock, Kirstel, Elson, Green, & Lerner, 2000) to the collective action literature, develop new hypotheses for future research to explore, and apply our analysis to inform recommendations for policy and practice.

Metaphors of Protest

Social behavior is difficult to understand without some kind of social functionalist perspective (Tetlock, 2002). Even the most formal theories of social behavior already subscribe to some form of social functionalism the moment they assume that individuals (either implicitly or explicitly, either consciously or nonconsciously) are motivated to achieve particular goals. Indeed, most theories assume that there is at least some reason that people think, feel, and act the way they do. However, there are multiple perspectives on humans as motivated goal achievers. At the individual level, one can view humans as intuitive economists (Edwards, 1962) who seek to maximize subjective utility. People may protest

---

[1]*Group based* means here that intuitive politicians and theologians' motivations transcend intraindividual functions. Furthermore, it should be noted that although Tetlock (2002) also identified the metaphor of the intuitive scientist (who is motivated to reduce subjective uncertainty) and the intuitive prosecutor (who is motivated to hold others accountable), both are beyond the scope of this article.

[2]In line with the social identity and collective action literature we use "low" and "high" identifiers to differentiate the relative strength of group identification (i.e., "lower" vs. "higher" identifiers).

only when the individual benefits of taking action (e.g., lower taxes) outweigh its individual costs (e.g., time and effort). This metaphor is thus based in the individual, and assumes an intra-psychic function of social judgment, motivating people to focus on personal costs and benefits to achieve favorable individual change (i.e., changing the individual's relationship with external reality).

However, Tetlock (2002) also proposed group-based metaphors of social judgment and choice that are embedded in the larger social structure: intuitive politicians and theologians. In the context of collective action, these metaphors can be seen as motivations for social change (i.e., positively changing the group's relationship with external reality), which derive from the social identities that embed individuals in the larger social structure (i.e., being a woman, American, or gay). Whereas intuitive politicians' motivation for collective action is based in their accountability to different social groups (e.g., protesters symbolically burning U.S. flags in the face of the White House in front of television cameras), intuitive theologians' motivation is based in their defense of fundamental values that govern their social life (e.g., protesters against abortion or homosexuality). These two metaphors thus acknowledge the group-based nature of individuals' different motivations for collective action to achieve social change, and explicitly connect individuals through their social identities with the larger social context (that also includes social and economic conditions that may be associated with group membership).

The distinction between individual- and group-based motivations fits nicely with insights from the social identity approach on the difference between personal and social identities (Tajfel, 1978; Tajfel & Turner, 1979; see also Ellemers, Spears, & Doosje, 1999; Reicher, 1996, 2001; Turner, Hogg, Oakes, Reicher, & Wetherell, 1987). Social identity theory (SIT) proposes that social identity, defined as "that part of an individual's self-concept which derives from ... knowledge of ... membership of a social group (or groups) together with the value and emotional significance attached to that membership" (Tajfel, 1978, p. 63), is key to collective action. *Collective action* can be defined thus: "a group member engages in collective action strategies anytime that he or she is acting as a representative of the group and the action is directed at improving the conditions of the entire group" (Wright, Taylor, & Moghaddam, 1990, p. 995). SIT suggests that people identify with a low-status (or disadvantaged) group to mobilize for collective action to achieve social change, and predicts that people will do so more strongly when sociostructural factors like the instability and illegitimacy of the intergroup status differential suggest more hope and scope for social change, and when intergroup boundaries are impermeable (Ellemers, 1993; Tajfel, 1978). In line with these ideas, Bettencourt, Charlton, Dorr, and Hume (2001) showed meta-analytic evidence for the influence of these sociostructural factors, and Van Zomeren, Postmes, and Spears (2008) for the effect of group identification on collective action. Indeed, the extent to which individuals identify with their group explains the effect of these sociostructural factors on collective action (Mummendey, Kessler, Klink, & Mielke, 1999; Tajfel, 1978).

However, high and low identifiers with a low-status group differ in more than only their strength of identification and their participation in collective action. For example, stronger group identification relates to stronger group-level self-definition and perception (e.g., perceiving the self and the social world in terms of "we" and "they"; Ellemers et al., 1999), and with stronger emotional experience on the basis of group membership (e.g., experiencing group-based anger and action tendencies to confront the outgroup; Van Zomeren, Spears, Fischer, & Leach, 2004; Van Zomeren, Spears, & Leach, 2008). Furthermore, high identifiers tend to stick with their group in times of trouble or threat because they are strongly committed to achieve social change (Ellemers, Spears, & Doosje, 1997). Low identifiers, on the other hand, only do so when external, instrumental factors suggest that social change also fosters individual change. For example, Doosje, Spears, and Ellemers (2002) observed that low identifiers pragmatically felt more connected to their low-status group when there was hope and scope for the group to achieve higher intergroup status. Similarly, Van Zomeren, Spears, and Leach (2008) found lower identifiers to be more motivated for collective action when their instrumental group efficacy beliefs were stronger.

We therefore propose that low identifiers' motivations for collective action typically differ from those of high identifiers. More specifically, low identifiers should be motivated to achieve individual change (resembling the intuitive economist), whereas high identifiers should be motivated to achieve social change (resembling the intuitive politician or theologian).[3] Below we map existing theory and research on collective action onto this classification of motivations for collective action.

A Classification of Motivations for Collective Action

As noted in the introduction to this issue, early work on collective action emphasized objective status variables as predictors of social protest (e.g., Davies, 1962; Gurr, 1970; McCarthy & Zald, 1977; Olson, 1968). Such frameworks proposed that structural status differences between groups (as measured by various indicators such as wealth and health) explained low-status group members' participation in collective action to achieve social equality. In these approaches, less attention was paid to the role of individuals' subjective perceptions, beliefs, and

---

[3]The use of general metaphors allows for an examination of where collective action researchers have hitherto based their theories on. However, these metaphors can never fully account for the rich and complex ideas about individuals' motivation for collective action, nor are they intended to be. It is not the purpose of this article to reduce theories to one-liner aphorisms that are presented as if they completely reflect these theories. The three metaphors should thus not to be interpreted as advocates of reductionism, but as underlying guiding assumptions of theories of collective action.

emotions in motivating efforts to create social change. However, as can be seen in all contributions to this issue, recent theory and research focuses mainly on these psychological variables, both in relation to the individual (e.g., individual cost–benefit calculations), and to the individual in the context of the larger social structure (e.g., through individuals' social identity).

Within this psychological perspective, there is some consensus that individuals' subjective sense of group-based injustice, efficacy, and identity are important explanations of collective action (Klandermans, 1997; for a meta-analysis, see Van Zomeren, Postmes, 7 Spears, 2008). Some approaches focus on instrumental explanations of collective action that emphasize individuals' calculation of costs and benefits (Klandermans, 1984; Stürmer & Simon, 2004), their sense of efficacy to solve group-related problems such as collective disadvantage (Hornsey et al., 2006; Mummendey et al., 1999; Van Zomeren et al., 2004), or the mobilization of resources that help to bring about social change (McCarthy & Zald, 1977). Alternatively, approaches like relative deprivation theory (Crosby, 1982; Runciman, 1966; Stouffer, Suchman, DeVinney, Start, & Williams, 1949; Walker & Smith, 2002) and SIT (Tajfel, 1978; Tajfel & Turner, 1979) focused on the role of injustice and identity variables in collective action. For example, Smith and Ortiz (2002) showed meta-analytically that defining relative deprivation as group-based motivates collective action more than defining it as individual-based (see also Dubé-Simard & Guimond, 1986; Kawakami & Dion, 1995; Smith & Spears, 1996). Moreover, research has shown that enacting one's social identity through collective action empowers relatively powerless individuals (Drury & Reicher, 1999, 2000; Reicher, 1996). We propose that these subjective predictors of collective action map nicely onto the individual-based and group-based metaphors of protest, and their application to low and high identifiers.

Intuitive Economists

A core assumption about human motivation is that people are individual-based intuitive economists (Edwards, 1962) who make social judgments and decisions by calculating the costs and benefits of a particular action and its anticipated consequences. Individuals choose the type of judgment or action that maximizes their individual gains and minimizes their individual losses (i.e., maximizing subjective utility). This motivation for collective action is reflected in early but influential sociological work on collective action (e.g., Olson, 1968), which heavily influenced later approaches to collective action in terms of its individual rationality assumption (e.g., Klandermans, 1984; McCarthy & Zald, 1977; Simon et al., 1998).

More specifically, early sociological work focused on the "free-rider" problem of collective action (Olson, 1968). Olson framed collective action as a social dilemma, which raised the problem of "free-riding" that arises when rational actors individually decide whether to engage in collective action to maximize subjective utility. The basis of this problem is that *collective* benefits are not fungible in the sense that they are like a public good: Once achieved, everybody profits from it. The possible costs, however, are individual costs because one needs to decide to participate without the guarantee that others will join. The ideal solution for each rational actor is therefore to do nothing (i.e., take a "free ride"), and hope that others do the protesting.

Klandermans (1984) developed this line of thought further by specifying three cost–benefit motives for collective action: The collective motive, and the social and reward motives (for a review see Stürmer & Simon, 2004). The first motive captures the value of the instrumental goal of a collective action for the individual, and the individual's expectation that collective action will achieve this goal. The social motive represents the individual's value of what significant others think about collective action, and his or her expectation that they will approve or disapprove of collective action. The reward motive is characterized by individual costs and benefits of collective action (such as missing an important meeting or having to spend a lot of time and effort). These motives all focus on planned and intentional behavior, which fits with the metaphor of the calculating intuitive economist (Fishbein & Ajzen, 1975).

Olson's work also influenced other approaches in terms of its premise of individual-based rationality (for a similar individual interest theme within analytic Marxism, see Elster, 1989). For example, resource mobilization theory (McCarthy & Zald, 1977) focused on the macrolevel of collective action phenomena like the power politics between social movement organizations and authorities. The theory assumed that social protest constitutes a set of rational collective actions by groups to advance their collective interests, pressuring those in power to submit to the demands of the aggrieved. However, its exclusive focus on the macro-level often left resource mobilization theorists to view people as intuitive economists. Other approaches referred in this respect to individuals' subjective sense of group efficacy as a motivation for collective action (Hornsey et al., 2006; Mummendey et al., 1999; Van Zomeren et al., 2004). This concept refers to expectations that one's group is able to achieve social change through collective action. The more resources one can mobilize, the more people should believe their group to be efficacious.

In sum, our analysis suggests that both individual cost–benefit calculations and group efficacy beliefs represent motivations of the intuitive economist in collective action research (see Table 1). Although Klandermans (1984) was criticized for being too individualistic (see Schrager, 1985), the three cost–benefit motives have been shown to predict collective action among various social movements (e.g., Klandermans, 1984; Stürmer & Simon, 2004). Moreover, group efficacy beliefs also predict collective action (Hornsey et al., 2006; Mummendey et al., 1999; Van Zomeren et al., 2004). However, two developments in social psychology challenge

Table 1. A Classification of Motivations of Collective Action

Low Identifiers	→ **Intuitive Economists** • Maximize subjective utility (Olson, 1968) • Calculation of costs and benefits (Klandermans, 1984; Stürmer & Simon, 2004) • Group efficacy beliefs (Mummendey et al., 1999; Van Zomeren et al., 2004)
High Identifiers	→ **Intuitive Politicians** • Maintain positive identities vis-à-vis social groups to whom one is accountable (Reicher et al., 1995) • Awareness that power struggle is fought out in the public domain (Simon & Klandermans, 2001) → **Intuitive Theologians** • Defend "sacred" norms and values from secular encroachment (Skitka et al., 2005; Tetlock, 2002)

the universality of the traditional *homo economicus* assumptions inherent in the intuitive economist metaphor.

First, the "cognitive revolution" in psychology generally cast doubt on individuals' capability to calculate costs and benefits to assess where maximal utility lies. For example, Tversky and Kahneman (1974) showed that people use specific heuristics for social judgment. Rather than calculating each and every anticipated individual cost and benefit, people use rules of thumb, make errors of judgment, and often show self-serving biases (see Kunda, 1990). Thus, individuals were not always the precise intuitive economists some had suspected them to be. Second, and more relevant to our argument, individuals' motivations for collective action do not form and occur in a social vacuum. Because individuals have social identities that connect them with the larger social structure, being a member of a low-status group motivates social competition for status (Tajfel, 1978). As noted, individuals become more motivated to engage in collective action through their stronger psychological identification with their low-status group under sociostructural conditions of illegitimacy and instability of the intergroup status differential, and the impermeability of intergroup boundaries (Bettencourt et al., 2001; Ellemers, 1993; Mummendey et al., 1999; Simon et al., 1998; for a review see Stürmer & Simon, 2004). This analysis fits nicely with the idea that low identifiers reflect intuitive economists (calculating individual interests as *homo economicus*), whereas high identifiers reflect intuitive politicians and intuitive theologians (where other principles come into play and even take precedence, such as displayed by *homo politicus* and *homo moralis*).[4]

---

[4] We use the *intuitive politician* metaphor with regard to high identifiers, but we acknowledge that low identifiers can be strategic too regarding their personal interests (e.g., Doosje et al., 2002; for a

Intuitive Politicians

Individuals need a social compass that allows them to navigate through their social web of accountabilities to different social groups (e.g., to their fellow group members, but also to the powerful authorities) in order to survive and prosper as group members (Tetlock, 2002). More specifically, the key to the intuitive politician metaphor is individuals' motivation to achieve social change despite intergroup differences in power. Intuitive politicians' motivation lies in "the knowledge that one is under the evaluative scrutiny of important constituencies in one's life who control valuable resources and who have some legitimate right to inquire into the reasons behind one's opinions or decisions. *This knowledge activates the goal of establishing or preserving a desired social identity vis-à-vis these constituencies*" (Tetlock, 2002, p. 454, italics added). In other words, intuitive politicians care deeply about accountability concerns because they are aware that social change can be resisted and even thwarted by those in power. Therefore intuitive politicians anticipate the effects of their behavior on others who have some degree of social control or influence in promoting, or preventing, social change (e.g., fellow group members). Indeed, those in power are typically motivated and capable to resist social change (e.g., Reicher, 1996; Sidanius & Pratto, 1999). The notion of intergroup power differences thus extends the traditional emphasis of SIT on the intergroup status differential between groups (Tajfel, 1978; Tajfel & Turner, 1979; see also Sachdev & Bourhis, 1985).

Two recent developments in the collective action literature speak to this view of people as group-based intuitive politicians. First, the social identity model of deindividuation effects (SIDE for short; Reicher, Spears, & Postmes, 1995; Spears & Lea, 1994; for a review see Klein, Spears, & Reicher, 2007) extends SIT by suggesting that low-status group members strategically communicate their willingness to engage in collective action to different audiences. In another extension of SIT, Simon and Klandermans (2001) proposed that social identity becomes particularly important to collective action when social identity becomes politicized. People with a politicized identity are more self-conscious about the societal power struggle that is fought out in the public arena, and hence their identity has collective action as its raison d'être. In line with these ideas, the Elaborated Social Identity Model (Drury & Reicher, 1999, 2000; Reicher, 1996; Stott & Reicher, 1998)

---

discussion see Spears & Smith, 2001). Although they can use the group as a means to their individual ends and try to hide their individual self-interest in the process, the intuitive politicians we identify are high identifiers who have group interests at heart. Thus, it is their strategic use of their group-based motivation to achieve social change that differentiates high from low identifiers. Moreover, we also acknowledge that high identifiers can be economists to the extent that they calculate collective costs and benefits (e.g., Louis, Taylor, & Neil, 2004). However, this is not how the metaphor is usually applied.

suggests that politicization of an identity helps relatively powerless individuals to have a collective influence.

Firstly, research on the SIDE model (e.g., Reicher & Levine, 1994; Reicher, Levine, & Gordijn, 1998; Scheepers, Spears, Doosje, & Manstead, 2006; Spears, Lea, Corneliussen, Postmes, & Ter Haar, 2002; Van Zomeren, Spears, & Leach, 2009) suggests that an intergroup or intragroup communication context presents different strategic, communicative possibilities for low-status group members. An intergroup channel of communication imposes accountability to the out-group, whereas an intragroup channel of communication imposes accountability to (and provides access and exposure to) the in-group. This is important because powerful out-groups have the power to sanction or punish the in-group for communicating a desire for social change unless the in-group has the power to challenge them, whereas communicating a desire for social change to fellow group members can mobilize the in-group for collective action by providing social support. Indeed, research has shown that when people are anonymous to out-group members and identifiable to fellow group members (such that they are able to coordinate and express mutual support) they are more likely to express those aspects of their social identity punishable by the out-group. This exemplifies the motivation of the intuitive politician to achieve social change while maintaining a positive identity vis-à-vis fellow group members or those in power.

This analysis implies a substantial shift in the interpretation of the lack of collective action. Whereas intuitive economists would not act because of the seduction of free-riding, a perceived lack of group efficacy, or their assessment of stronger costs than benefits, intuitive politicians may remain inactive when facing those in power because they do not want their goal (i.e., social change) to be thwarted by foolish and dangerous provocations (Gramsci's "pessimism of the intellect"). Indeed, recent research has shown that individuals therefore only communicate their anger and willingness to protest when facing those in power when they feel sufficiently powerful to challenge them (Van Zomeren et al., 2009). Moreover, in line with the notion that intuitive politicians' motivation for collective action is group-based, high identifiers were found to be more strategic in these communications than low identifiers (Van Zomeren & Spears, 2009). Thus, intuitive politicians can be seen as "entrepreneurs of identity" (Besson, 1991; Reicher & Hopkins, 2001), who strategically take into account the audiences to which they communicate their desire for achieving social change.

A second theoretical development concerns Simon, Stürmer, and colleagues' argument that identification with a social movement organization is more important to collective action than identification with the disadvantaged group because the former is a politicized form of identity (for a review, see Stürmer & Simon, 2004). As Simon and Klandermans (2001) proposed, people "evince politicized collective identity to the extent that they engage as self-conscious group members in a power struggle on behalf of their group knowing that it is the *more inclusive societal context* in which this struggle has to be fought out" (p. 319, italics added). They argue that people can develop "activist" identities that include a focus on third-party support for their struggle. Politicized identity develops when people perceive shared grievances, make adversarial attributions, and realize the involvement of society at large (i.e., the system). Stronger identification with this more specific and developed social identity indeed predicts collective action better than identification with the less specific social identity (see Stürmer & Simon, 2004, for a review).

The notion of politicized identity is important because it identifies the general public as another important social group (a source of support and power) that intuitive politicians like to impress and use to achieve social change (Herrera & Reicher, 1998; see also Hornsey et al., 2006). This is especially important for low-status or low-power groups because they are most likely to need the support of the general public to pressure those in power to concede to their demands. Indeed, it is through the experience of participation in collective action that people become aware that such support is necessary to achieve social change (e.g., Drury & Reicher, 1999, 2000; Reicher, 1996). Taken together, theory and research on intuitive politicians suggests that they will "tailor" their identity-relevant responses to collective disadvantage to (1) their own group (who can be mobilized through intragroup communication channels), (2) those in power (who can be challenged through intergroup communication channels), (3) third parties (who can be addressed and mobilized to pressure those in power to concede).

Intuitive Theologians

Individuals can also be motivated to believe that the ground rules of the current social structure are not relative, but absolute. This provides a moral benchmark for a group that, once transgressed, results in a motivation among individuals to protect these "sacred" values (Tetlock, 2002). For example, protesters against the legalization of abortion may engage in collective action as intuitive theologians who respond to "perceived threats to sacred values, *values that—by community consensus—are deemed beyond quantification or fungibility*" (Tetlock, 2002, p. 454, italics added). In other words, intuitive theologians are motivated to protect "sacred" group values from "secular" encroachment. This fits nicely with research on social identity that suggests that—unlike low identifiers—high identifiers commit even more strongly to their group's identity when under siege (e.g., Ellemers et al., 1997).

Remarkably little, however, is known about this motivation for collective action. Theory and research have discussed variables like ideology (Van Stekelenburg et al., 2009), and moral connotations of relative deprivation (Folger, 1986). However, the intuitive theologian metaphor refers specifically to moral conviction: Strong attitudes toward an issue that are deemed to be absolute (Skitka et al.,

2005). This key element of absoluteness has not been examined in the literature on collective action. However, there is emerging evidence for the moral dimension as central to the intergroup realm (e.g., Leach, Ellemers, & Barreto, 2007), and there are some indications that intuitive theologians can be important to theory and research on collective action.

According to Tetlock et al.'s (2000) sacred value protection model, when sacred values are transgressed, individuals experience motivated arousal that transforms into moral outrage responses (i.e., a desire to vilify the transgressors), and moral cleansing responses (i.e., a desire to reaffirm the transgressed value). In line with this proposal, Tetlock et al. (2000) showed that strongly religious people responded with moral outrage and moral cleansing when people doubted the moral superiority of Jesus. In addition, Van Zomeren and Lodewijkx (2005) showed that observers' responses to innocent victims of "senseless" violence resulted in similar sacred value protection responses, presumably because their fundamental beliefs in a just world were transgressed. Furthermore, Skitka, Baumann, and Mullen (2004) showed that moral outrage decreased political tolerance after the 9/11 attacks on the World Trade Center in New York. All these findings suggest that individuals may protect their moral conviction from "secular" encroachment. However, moral conviction has not explicitly been related to individuals' group-based motivation for collective action.

Nonetheless, intuitive economist and politicians might be puzzled by responses of moral outrage after transgressions of their moral conviction. These responses do make sense, however, when thinking of people as intuitive theologians who defend their subjective moral boundaries. The lack of research on collective action from an intuitive theologian perspective therefore suggests the undiscovered potential of this group-based metaphor of protest. However, simply noting a gap does not necessarily make clear meaningful ways to fill it, so we will develop new hypotheses about intuitive theologians (as well as intuitive economists and politicians) below. We also apply our analysis to the domains of practice and policy, because our analysis suggests that viewing humans as having different motivation for collective action requires different interventions to move them in action.

Developing New Hypotheses and Practical Recommendations

Our analysis of classifying different motivations for collective action onto individual-based and group-based metaphors of social functionalism resulted in two core insights: First, the individual-based motivations reflect low identifiers' motivations for collective action, whereas the group-based motivations reflect high identifiers' motivations for collective action. Second, although theory and research has examined intuitive economists and politicians' motivation for collective action, it has not examined intuitive theologians' motivation for collective action. Indeed, if we want to understand, for example, the Chinese student taking a stand to force a tank come to a halt, the psychology of the intuitive economist alone would not suffice. Rather, explanations that base individuals' motivations in their awareness and accountability to particular audiences, or in their protection of sacred values, provide different and complementary explanations of why people protest. We discuss the implications of this analysis for each metaphor below.

Intuitive Economists

Note that our analysis does not suggest that intuitive economists are unimportant to collective action. Even those who identify weakly with a disadvantaged group may end up protesting as long as they have individual-based instrumental reasons for doing so. And even when the individual-based intuitive economist motivates people not to engage in collective action (e.g., take a free-ride), group-based motivations may still lead people to do so. This implies, for one, that although the free-rider problem has long been thought to be at the roots of the problem of nonparticipation in collective action (Olson, 1968), this problem seems to be a problem primarily for low identifiers. Moreover, our analysis implies that because low identifiers have different motivations for collective action than high identifiers, their mobilization for collective action should follow different motivational trajectories.

Our analysis leads more specifically to the following three testable hypotheses. First, low identifiers should engage in more calculation of costs and benefits than high identifiers, and engage in more instrumental reasoning when deciding to engage in collective action (e.g., in terms of relying on their group efficacy beliefs). Second, low identifiers should also be in more need of information about such instrumental factors than high identifiers. Third, low identifiers should be more open to social influence targeting these instrumental factors than high identifiers. Especially the latter hypothesis has important practical and socially consequential implications.

Indeed, our analysis implies that intuitive economists are especially important to acknowledge for social movements because focusing on sympathizers' instrumental motivations (e.g., cost–benefit calculations, group efficacy beliefs) may particularly mobilize the low identifiers to engage in collective action. Given that typically only a very low percentage of the mobilization potential of a disadvantaged group is mobilized for collective action (Klandermans, 1997; Klandermans & Oegema, 1987; Oegema & Klandermans, 1994), understanding low identifiers' motivation for collective action is important to both theory and practice of collective action. Therefore, a practical recommendation derived from our analysis is that social movement campaigns should provide low identifiers with information about the benefits of collective action (including the group's efficacy to achieve its goals) to satisfy the intuitive economists within.

Intuitive Politicians

What about high identifiers? Our analysis implies that high identifiers' motivation for collective action depends on which group-based metaphor is relevant for them. On the one hand, the intuitive politicians among them are motivated to maintain positive social identities in the face of other important groups in their social world to whom they are accountable through intergroup power differences. On the other hand, the intuitive theologians among them are more likely to defend the fundamental values of their social group when these are under siege.

Our analysis contributes to the psychology of the intuitive politician in terms of two testable hypotheses. First, if a sense of politicized identity is necessary for intuitive politicians to become motivated for strategic collective action despite intergroup differences in power, then individuals whose identity is not politicized should not be similarly affected by (or simply care less for) third-party support as individuals with a politicized identity. Indeed, only the latter should realize the strategic opportunities provided by the audience of the general public and try to put them to use (as indicated by, e.g., a willingness to persuade them to join their struggle). In contrast, individuals whose identity is not politicized should not care about the general audience at best and may even be more strongly motivated to take a free-ride at worst. Note that this should be true even when individuals have a strong sense of (unpoliticized) identification with the larger social group.

Second, because the social identity tradition emphasizes the importance of the larger social structure in determining whether low-status group members will engage in collective action despite intergroup power differences, there may be an interaction between sociostructural conditions on the one hand, and audience factors on the other hand (e.g., Scheepers et al., 2006). More specifically, we hypothesize that audience considerations should only be relevant when sociostructural factors indicate hope and scope for social change. This means that intuitive politicians require at least some prospects of social change in order to engage in strategic, power-based, identity-relevant behavior.

Alternatively, intuitive politicians may still aim to achieve social change even in the face of a status quo supported by the existing social structure. An interesting question here is how intuitive politicians can manage to prevent fellow group members from accepting the status quo when there is little hope or scope for social change. We hypothesize that one way to prevent collective acceptance of the status quo is strategically to use intragroup channels of communication (and the in-group audience it includes), in which social identities can become politicized "underground," while acting as if accepting the status quo when facing those in power. If true, then those with a politicized identity should perceive and value the possibility of "underground resistance" more than those whose identity is not politicized when chances of social change are limited.

The intuitive politician metaphor also has important implications for practice and policy because of its focus on intergroup power differences. First of all, social movements should aim to develop politicized identities among their sympathizers. In contrast to the individual-based intuitive economists, intuitive politicians should be targeted through their group-based motivations. Social influence attempts (e.g., a mobilization campaign) should therefore focus on the "activist" content of individuals' social identity (and with it group norms that prescribe acting on behalf of the group; see Stürmer & Simon, 2004), on the importance of the power struggle fought out in the public domain, and on the importance of third parties to pressure those in power to concede. Thus, mobilizing intuitive politicians requires a greater focus on intergroup power differences and thus different motivations compared to mobilizing intuitive economists.

Intuitive Theologians

As noted, we believe that the intuitive theologian metaphor offers most scope for theoretical innovation and novel research. We therefore develop three new hypotheses to be explored by future research on collective action.

First, if intuitive theologians are motivated for collective action through defending the moral boundaries of their social group, then the strength of their moral identity (e.g., Aquino & Reed II, 2002) should directly predict their engagement in collective action. Moral identity establishes the boundaries between those who agree and those who disagree on moral values deemed absolute and integral to the self. Interestingly, research has shown that stronger moral identity results in stronger prosocial behavior to out-group members (Reed II & Aquino, 2003). This suggests that intuitive theologians may even take part in collective action on behalf of out-groups (e.g., McGarty, Bliuc, Thomas, & Bongiorno, 2009). However, theory and research on moral conviction (e.g., Skitka et al., 2004; 2005) suggests that intuitive theologians become enraged when individuals' moral identity is threatened, resulting in a strong defense of their moral boundaries. This should be indicated especially by moral outrage responses toward the out-group (i.e., feelings of anger and a desire to vilify those who represent the moral threat; see Skitka et al., 2004; Tetlock et al., 2000). Research should test these competing hypotheses.

Second, if moral identities are developed on the basis of subjective sacred values, then research should examine which values are most commonly perceived as "moral" (i.e., the normative content of such identities). For example, Baumeister and Leary's (1995) proposition of a fundamental need to belong suggests that, at the group level, denying belongingness to those who deserve it would enrage intuitive theologians (because they are highly identified with the group and hence use harsher inclusion and exclusion criteria; Branscombe, Wann, Noel, & Coleman, 1993). A good example of this line of thought may be collective action against the extradition of asylum seekers (i.e., exclusion from one's nation). Moreover, moral conviction may also motivate collective action to support universal human rights (as for instance organized by Amnesty International or Human Rights Watch). Thus, issues of belonging and universal human rights can be likely bases of moral identities (i.e., the normative content of a moral identity) and hence represent a motivation for collective action to protect them.

Third, our analysis suggests that there may be a difference between moral conviction on the individual and the group level. For example, whereas individual moral conviction (which is part of individuals' personal identity) should apply their beliefs to any other individual, collective moral conviction (which is part of individuals' social identity) should apply their beliefs more to in-group than out-group members (i.e., moral in-group bias). This may operate in two different directions: (1) giving the benefit of the doubt to morally transgressing in-group but not out-group members and (2) including out-group members into the in-group when out-group members transgress against the moral beliefs of the out-group (i.e., when they betray their own group). Thus, we hypothesize different implications of individual and collective moral conviction. Future research should test these hypotheses to improve our understanding of the psychology of the intuitive theologian.

In practical terms, it is not hard to think of real-life examples of intuitive theologians collectively rising to meet those who are perceived as a moral threat. For example, when thinking about the U.S. misconduct of Iraqi prisoners, feelings of moral outrage among those identifying with the Iraqi, Arab, or more generally the Muslim world may result in collective action to defend their moral boundaries. Interestingly, however, it may be the case that moral conviction is not restricted to low-status group members' motivation for collective action. Indeed, moral conviction may be a strong motivation for collective action for individuals from low or high status groups, as long as they identify strongly with their moral identity. For practitioners of collective action, raising individuals' sense of moral identity and moral threat should therefore be a potent motivator of collective action to defend "absolute truths."

Conclusion

This article proposed a classification of a variety of motivations for collective action along the lines of three general metaphors of social functionalism (Tetlock, 2002), and the distinction between high and low identifiers with a low-status group (Ellemers et al., 1999; Tajfel & Turner, 1979). This classification is not meant to be exhaustive and aims to inspire scientific discussion. It suggests the general insights that low identifiers are more likely to resemble intuitive economists whereas high identifiers are more likely to resemble intuitive politicians and theologians, and that progress and innovation in theory and research on collective action lies in the group-based metaphors in general, and in the intuitive theologian metaphor in particular. Our analysis resulted in new hypotheses for all three metaphors, with an emphasis on the largely undiscovered country of intuitive theologians' motivations for collective action.

With these insights in mind, let us conclude by returning to the student blocking the way of a Chinese tank at Tiananmen Square on the 1989 World Press Photo. What motivated him to stand still in defiance of tons of steel? We believe we can understand his act of protest better if we assume him to be an intuitive politician or theologian than an intuitive economist: Perhaps he knew that cameras were flashing, making his action a protest statement for the world's audience to witness. Perhaps he was driven by moral outrage over the Chinese intervention that transgressed fundamental, sacred values. Whatever the answer, this article hopes to show that asking questions that go beyond traditional assumptions about human motivation is important for a better understanding and appreciation of the diversity and complexity of individuals' motivations for collective action.

References

Aquino, K., & Reed II, A. (2002). The self-importance of moral identity. *Journal of Personality and Social Psychology, 83*, 1423–1440.
Baumeister, R. F., & Leary, M. F. (1995). The need to belong: Desire for interpersonal attachments as a fundamental human motive. *Psychological Bulletin, 117*, 497–529.
Besson, Y. (1991). *Identities et conflits au Proche-Orient*. Paris: L'Harmattan.
Bettencourt, B. A., Charlton, K., Dorr, N., & Hume, D. L. (2001). Status differences and ingroup bias: A meta-analytic examination of the effects of status stability, status legitimacy, and group permeability. *Psychological Bulletin, 127*, 520–542.
Branscombe, N. R., Wann, D. L., Noel, J. G., & Coleman, J. (1993). In-group or out-group extremity: Importance of the threatened social identity. *Personality and Social Psychology Bulletin, 19*, 381–388.
Crosby, F. J. (1982). *Relative deprivation and working women*. New York: Oxford University Press.
Davies, J. (1962). Toward a theory of revolution. *American Sociological Review, 27*, 5–18.
Doosje, B., Spears, R., & Ellemers, N. (2002). Social identity as both cause and effect: The development of group identification in response to anticipated and actual changes in the intergroup status hierarchy. *British Journal of Social Psychology, 41*, 57–76.
Drury, J., & Reicher, S. D. (1999). The inter-group dynamics of collective empowerment: Substantiating the social identity model of crowd behavior. *Group Processes and Intergroup Relations, 4*, 381–402.
Drury, J., & Reicher, S. D. (2000). Collective action and psychological change: The emergence of new social identities. *British Journal of Social Psychology, 39*, 579–604.
Dubé-Simard, L., & Guimond, S. (1986). Relative deprivation and social protest: The personal-group issue. In J. Olson, C. Herman, & M. Zanna (Eds.), *Relative deprivation and social comparison: The Ontario symposium* (Vol. 4, pp. 201–216). Hillsdale, NJ: Erlbaum.
Edwards, W. (1962). Subjective probabilities inferred from decisions. *Psychological Review, 69*, 109–135.
Ellemers, N. (1993). The influence of socio-structural variables on identity management strategies. In W. Stroebe & M. Hewstone (Eds.), *European review of social psychology* (Vol. 4, pp. 22–57). Oxford: Blackwell.
Ellemers, N., Spears, R., & Doosje, B. (1997). Sticking together or falling apart: In-group identification as a psychological determinant of group commitment versus individual mobility. *Journal of Personality and Social Psychology, 72*, 617–626.

Ellemers, N., Spears, R., & Doosje, B. (1999). *Social identity: Context, commitment, content*. Oxford: Blackwell.
Elster, J. (1989). *Nuts and bolts for the social sciences*. Cambridge: Cambridge University Press.
Fishbein, M., & Ajzen, I. (1975). *Belief, attitude, intention, and behaviour*. Reading, MA: Addison-Wesley.
Folger, R. (1986). A referent cognitions theory of relative deprivation. In J. M. Olson, C. P. Herman, & M. P. Zanna (Eds.), *Relative deprivation and social comparison: The Ontario symposium* (Vol. 4, pp. 217–242). Hillsdale, NJ: Erlbaum.
Gurr, T. R. (1970). *Why men rebel*. Princeton, NJ: Princeton University Press.
Herrera, M., & Reicher, S. D. (1998). Making sides and taking sides: An analysis of salient images and category constructions for pro- and anti-Gulf War respondents. *European Journal of Social Psychology, 28*, 981–993.
Hornsey, M. J., Blackwood, L., Louis, W., Fielding, K., Mavor, K., Morton, T., et al. (2006). Why do people engage in collective action? Revisiting the role of perceived effectiveness. *Journal of Applied Social Psychology, 36*, 1701–1722.
Kawakami, K., & Dion, K. L. (1995). Social identity and affect as determinants of collective action: Toward an integration of relative deprivation and social identity theories. *Theory and Psychology, 5*, 551–577.
Klandermans, B. (1984). Mobilization and participation: Social-psychological expansions of resource mobilization theory. *American Sociological Review, 49*, 583–600.
Klandermans, B. (1997). *The social psychology of protest*. Oxford: Basic Blackwell.
Klandermans, B., & Oegema, D. (1987). Potentials, networks, motivations, and barriers: Steps toward participation in social movements. *American Sociological Review, 52*, 519–531.
Klein, O., Spears, R., & Reicher, S. D. (2007). Social identity performance: Extending the strategic side of SIDE. *Personality and Social Psychology Review, 11*, 28–45.
Kunda, Z. (1990). *Social cognition: Making sense of people*. Cambridge, MA: MIT Press.
Leach, C. W., Ellemers, N., & Barreto, M. (2007). Group virtue: The importance of morality (vs. competence and sociability) in the positive evaluation of in-groups. *Journal of Personality and Social Psychology, 93*, 234–249.
Louis, W. R., Taylor, D. M., & Neil, T. (2004). Cost-benefit analyses for your group and your self: The rationality of decision-making in conflict. *International Journal of Conflict Management, 15*, 110–143.
McCarthy, J. D., & Zald, M. N. (1977). Resource mobilization and social movements: A partial theory. *American Journal of Sociology, 82*, 1212–1241.
McGarty, C., Bliuc, A., Thomas, E., & Bongiorno, R. (2009). Collective action as the material expression of opinion-based group membership. *Journal of Social Issues, 65*, 839–857.
Mummendey, A., Kessler, T., Klink, A., & Mielke, R. (1999). Strategies to cope with negative social identity: Predictions by social identity theory and relative deprivation theory. *Journal of Personality and Social Psychology, 76*, 229–245.
Oberschall, A. (1973). *Social conflict and social movements*. Englewood Cliffs, NJ: Prentice Hall.
Oegema, D., & Klandermans, B. (1994). Why social movement sympathizers don't participate: Erosion and non-conversion of support. *American Sociological Review, 59*, 703–722.
Olson, M. (1968). *The logic of collective action. Public goods and the theory of groups*. Cambridge, MA: Harvard University Press.
Reed II, A., & Aquino, K. (2003). Moral identity and the expanding circle of moral regard toward out-groups. *Journal of Personality and Social Psychology, 84*, 1270–1286.
Reicher, S. D. (1996). Social identity and social change: Rethinking the context of social psychology. In P. Robinson (Ed.), *Social groups and identities: Developing the legacy of Henri Tajfel* (pp. 316–336). Oxford: Butterworth-Heinemann.
Reicher, S. D. (2001). Crowds and social movements. In M. Hogg & S. Tindale (Eds.), *Blackwell Handbook of Social Psychology: Group Processes* (pp. 182–208). Oxford: Blackwell.
Reicher, S. D., & Hopkins, N. (2001). *Self and nation*. London: Sage Publications.
Reicher, S. D., & Levine, M. (1994). Deindividuation, power relations between groups and the expression of social identity: The effects of visibility to the out-group. *British Journal of Social Psychology, 33*, 145–163.

Reicher, S. D., Spears, R., & Postmes, T. (1995). A social identity model of deindividuation phenomena. In W. Stroebe & M. Hewstone (Eds.), *European review of social psychology* (Vol. 6, pp. 161–198). Oxford: Blackwell.

Reicher, S. D., Levine, M., & Gordijn, E. (1998). More on deindividuation, power relations between groups and the expression of social identity: Three studies on the effects of visibility to the in-group. *British Journal of Social Psychology, 37*, 15–40.

Runciman, W. G. (1966). *Relative deprivation and social justice: A study of attitudes to social inequality in twentieth-century England*. Berkeley: University of California Press.

Sachdev, I., & Bourhis, R. Y. (1985). Social categorization and power differential in group relations. *European Journal of Social Psychology, 15*, 415–434.

Scheepers, D., Spears, R., Doosje, B., & Manstead, A. S. R. (2006). Diversity in in-group bias: Structural factors, situational features, and social functions. *Journal of Personality and Social Psychology, 90*, 244–260.

Schrager, L. S. (1985). Private attitudes and collective action. *American Sociological Review, 50*, 858–859.

Sidanius, J., & Pratto, F. (1999). *Social dominance: An inter-group theory of social hierarchy and oppression*. New York: Cambridge University Press.

Simon, B., & Klandermans, B. (2001). Politicized collective identity: A social-psychological analysis. *American Psychologist, 56*, 319–331.

Simon, B., Loewy, M., Stürmer, S., Weber, U., Freytag, P., Habig, C., et al. (1998). Collective identification and social movement participation. *Journal of Personality and Social Psychology, 74*, 646–658.

Skitka, L. J., Baumann, C. W., & Mullen, E. (2004). Political tolerance and coming to psychological closure following the September 11, 2001, terrorist attacks: An integrative approach. *Personality and Social Psychology Bulletin, 30*, 743–756.

Skitka, L. J., Bauman, C. W., & Sargis, E. F. (2005). Moral conviction: Another contributor to attitude strength or something more? *Journal of Personality and Social Psychology, 88*, 895–917.

Smith, H. J., & Ortiz, D. J. (2002). Is it just me? The different consequences of personal and group relative deprivation. In I. Walker & H. J. Smith (Eds.), *Relative deprivation: Specification, development, and integration* (pp. 91–115). Cambridge: Cambridge University Press.

Smith, H. J., & Spears, R. (1996). Ability and outcome evaluations as a function of personal and collective (dis)advantage: A group escape from individual bias. *Personality and Social Psychology Bulletin, 22*, 635–642.

Spears, R., & Lea, M. (1994). Panacea or panopticon? The hidden power in computer-mediated communication. *Communication Research, 21*, 27–459.

Spears, R., & Smith, H. J. (2001). Experiments as politics. *Political Psychology, 22*, 309–330.

Spears, R., Lea, M., Corneliussen, R. A., Postmes, T., & Ter Haar, W. (2002). Computer mediated communication as a channel for social resistance: The strategic side of SIDE. *Small Group Research, 33*, 555–574.

Stott, C. J., & Reicher, S. (1998). Crowd action as intergroup process: Introducing the police perspective. *European Journal of Social Psychology, 26*, 509–529.

Stouffer, S. A., Suchman, E. A., DeVinney, L. C., Star, S. A., & Williams, R. M. (1949). *The American soldier: Vol. 1. Adjustment during army life*. Princeton, NJ: Princeton University Press.

Stürmer, S., & Simon, B. (2004). Collective action: Towards a dual-pathway model. In W. Stroebe & M. Hewstone (Eds.), *European review of social psychology* (Vol. 15, pp. 59–99). Hove, UK: Psychology Press.

Tajfel, H. (1978). The achievement of intergroup differentiation. In H. Tajfel (Ed.), *Differentiation between social groups* (pp. 77–100). London: Academic Press.

Tajfel, H., & Turner, J. C. (1979). An integrative theory of intergroup conflict. In W. G. Austin & S. Worchel (Eds.), *The social psychology of intergroup relations* (pp. 33–47). Monterey, CA: Brooks/Cole.

Tetlock, P. E. (2002). Social functionalist frameworks for judgment and choice: Intuitive politicians, theologians, and prosecutors. *Psychological Review, 109*, 451–471.

Tetlock, P. E., Kirstel, O. V., Elson, S. B., Green, M. C., & Lerner, J. S. (2000). The psychology of the unthinkable: Taboo trade-offs, forbidden base rates, and heretic counterfactuals. *Journal of Personality and Social Psychology, 78*, 853–870.

Turner, J. C., Hogg, M. A., Oakes, P. J., Reicher, S. D., & Wetherell, M. S. (1987). *Rediscovering the social group: A self-categorization perspective*. Oxford: Basil Blackwell.
Tversky, A., & Kahneman, D. (1974). Judgment under uncertainty: Heuristics and biases. *Science, 27*, 1124–1131.
Van Stekelenburg, J., Klandermans, B., & Van Dijk, W. W. (2009). Context matters: Explaining why and how mobilization context influences motivational dynamics. *Journal of Social Issues, 65*, 815–838.
Van Zomeren, M., & Lodewijkx, H. F. M. (2005). Motivated responses to "senseless" violence: Explaining emotional and behavioral responses through person and position identification. *European Journal of Social Psychology, 35*, 755–766.
Van Zomeren, M., & Spears, R. (2009). [SIDE effects for high and low identifiers with collectively disadvantaged groups]. Unpublished raw data.
Van Zomeren, M., Spears, R., Fischer, A. H., & Leach, C. W. (2004). Put your money where your mouth is! Explaining collective action tendencies through group-based anger and group efficacy. *Journal of Personality and Social Psychology, 87*, 649–664.
Van Zomeren, M., Postmes, T., & Spears, R. (2008). Toward an integrative social identity model of collective action: A quantitative research synthesis of three socio-psychological perspectives. *Psychological Bulletin, 134*, 504–535.
Van Zomeren, M., Spears, R., & Leach, C. W. (2008). Exploring psychological mechanisms of collective action: Does the relevance of group identity influence how people cope with collective disadvantage? *British Journal of Social Psychology, 47*, 353–372.
Van Zomeren, M., Spears, R., & Leach, C. W. (2009). [Challenging the powerful: Explaining the strategic expression of group-based anger]. Unpublished raw data.
Walker, I., & Smith, H. J. (2002). *Relative deprivation: Specification, development, and integration*. Cambridge: Cambridge University Press.
Wright, S. C., Taylor, D. M., & Moghaddam, F. M. (1990). Responding to membership in a disadvantaged group: From acceptance to collective protest. *Journal of Personality and Social Psychology, 58*, 994–1003.

MARTIJN VAN ZOMEREN received his PhD in Social Psychology from the University of Amsterdam (2006). His main research interests concern the emotional processes involved in intra- and intergroup behavior such as collective action (Van Zomeren, Spears, Fischer, & Leach, 2004; Van Zomeren, Spears, & Leach, 2008; Van Zomeren, Postmes, & Spears, 2008). His doctoral dissertation, which examined social-psychological paths to protest as different ways of coping with collective disadvantage, received the APA Division 49 2007 Dissertation Award, and second prize in the 2007 competition for SPSSI's Dissertation Award. He is currently an assistant professor at the Department of Social and Organizational Psychology of the University of Groningen.

RUSSELL SPEARS is Professor of Social Psychology at Cardiff University. His research interests are in social identity and intergroup relations, including work on group-based emotions. He has published numerous papers and co-authored/co-edited *The social psychology of stereotyping and group life* (Blackwell, 1997), *Social identity: Context, commitment, content* (Blackwell, 1999), and *Stereotypes as explanations* (CUP, 2002).

Pathways to Collective Protest: Calculation, Identification, or Emotion? A Critical Analysis of the Role of Group-Based Anger in Social Movement Participation

Stefan Stürmer[*]
FernUniversität in Hagen

Bernd Simon
Christian-Albrechts-Universität zu Kiel

The dual-pathway model of collective action proposes two motivational pathways to collective protest, one is based on cost–benefit calculations and another is based on collective identification. The present research examined the role of feelings of group-based anger as an additional path. Study 1, a field study in the context of students' protest in Germany (N = 201), provided evidence for a unique effect of anger. Study 2, a laboratory experiment (N = 182), examined the desire to release aggressive tension as a psychological process underlying this effect. As hypothesized, analyses confirmed that anger affected participants' willingness to protest only to the extent that this behavior provided the opportunity of cathartic reduction in aggressive tensions. Moreover, an experimental manipulation providing an alternative means to release tension reduced the relationship between anger and willingness to protest to nonsignificance. The implications of these findings for reconceptualizing the role of anger in collective protest are discussed.

Although typically many members of disadvantaged groups sympathize with the goals of social movements fighting injustice against their in-group often only a small percentage of them actually participate in collective activities staged to realize these goals. In social movement research, the social psychological processes that determine group members' motivation for participating in social movement

---

[*]Correspondence concerning this article should be addressed to Stefan Stürmer, Institut für Psychologie, FernUniversität in Hagen, 58084 Hagen, Germany. Tel: +49 (0) 2331 987 2776, Fax: +49 (0) 2331 987 4730 [e-mail: stefan.stuermer@FernUni-Hagen.de].

activities have therefore become a key issue (e.g., Klandermans, 1997). In the following section, we will briefly outline two influential social-psychological approaches addressing this question. We will then introduce a dual-pathway model of social movement participation which integrates the key motivational processes identified by these approaches—cost–benefit calculation processes and (politicized) collective identification—into a single motivational approach (e.g., Stürmer & Simon, 2004a). In the remainder of this article we will address the role of possible additional (or even alternative) motivational pathways. We focus our analyses on the role of emotional processes, specifically group members' feelings of group-based anger about collective injustice.

Calculating the Costs and Benefits of Participation

A prominent approach to the question when people will actively participate in social movement activities is the four-step model of social movement participation developed by Klandermans and colleagues (e.g., Klandermans, 1984, 1997; Klandermans & Oegema, 1987). According to this model, becoming an active participant is an effortful process involving four different steps: First, people must sympathize with a movement and thus become part of the potential for mobilization; second, they must be targeted by mobilization attempts; third, they must develop the motivation to participate in particular collective actions; fourth and finally, they must overcome possible barriers to participation. In the present research we focus on the determinants of people's motivation to participate in social movement activities. Accordingly, it is the third step of this model which is of particular relevance for the present analysis.

Klandermans (1984, 1997) distinguishes three different motives for social movement participation; each motive originates from different types of expected costs and benefits. First, the collective motive derives from the movement's collective goals. In line with expectancy-value approaches, this motive is conceptualized as the multiplicative function of the subjective value of the goals of the social movement and the subjective expectation that these goals will be reached. Second, the normative (or social) motive derives from the expected reactions of significant others to one's participation in collective action (e.g., ridicule or admiration by friends or family). It is conceptualized as the multiplicative function of the subjective (positive or negative) quality of others' expected reactions and the personal importance of these reactions. Finally, the reward motive results from selective incentives pertaining to more personal costs and benefits such as losing money or time, or having a good time with friends. Like the collective motive, the reward motive is conceptualized as a multiplicative function of value and expectancy components. The relevance of these three motives for participation in social movements has been shown in a variety of empirical studies conducted in several different social movement contexts (e.g., Klandermans, 1997).

Collective Identification Processes

The conceptualization of the social and political actor as someone who maximizes his or her individual benefits has been challenged as atomistic and overindividualistic (e.g., Kelly & Breinlinger, 1996; Simon et al., 1998). This criticism is in accord with the social identity approach which is a more general and more formalized account of how collective behavior is regulated by collective identity processes (Tajfel & Turner, 1986; Turner, Hogg, Oakes, Reicher, & Wetherell, 1987). According to the social identity approach, social movement participation represents collective behavior in terms of one's group membership. Therefore, a strong sense of collective identity is necessary for group members to engage in collective behaviors aimed at improving their ingroup's situation (e.g., Tajfel & Turner, 1986; see introduction to this issue for a more detailed coverage of this approach). In line with this general notion, a large body of empirical work demonstrates that group members' identification with the ingroup (i.e., the extent to which the group is enduringly valued and self-involving) is a significant predictor of group members' motivation to actively participate in social movements fighting for collective goals (e.g., Kelly & Breinlinger, 1996; Simon et al., 1998; Stürmer & Simon, 2004b; Stürmer, Simon, Loewy, & Jörger, 2003). Further, this research also significantly advanced our understanding of when collective identification will actually translate into active participation. For instance, in our own research program on this issue (see Simon, 2004; Stürmer & Simon, 2004a, for reviews) we (together with our colleagues) investigated the role of two different forms of identification in a series of field studies in different social movement contexts. Specifically, we measured identification with the disadvantaged group from which the social movement under study typically recruited its members (e.g., old people, gay men, fat people) as well as their identification with the movement or social movement organization (e.g., the Gray Panthers, the gay movement, the National Association to Advance Fat Acceptance). The movement or the social movement organization provides more politicized forms of collective identity because they are situated explicitly in a context of power struggle and social change (Simon & Klandermans, 2001). Through the process of identification with the social movement the movement's norms, interests and goals become self-defining, resulting in an "inner obligation" to become actively involved (Kelly & Breinlinger, 1996; Stürmer et al., 2003). We thus hypothesized that identification with the movement should be particularly conducive to active participation. In line with this analysis, results converged in showing that identification with the disadvantaged group increased people's willingness to participate in social movements (or their actual participation) only to the extent that it was transformed into a more politicized form of identification. Moreover, findings provided evidence for the hypothesized mediating role of feelings of an inner obligation in the identification-participation link (for reviews see Simon, 2004; Stürmer & Simon, 2004a).

The Dual-Pathway Model of Collective Action

To articulate the Klandermans model and the social identity approach, we also considered indicators of cost–benefit calculation as predictors of participation in our research program. Although the studies focused on different political, social, organizational, and even national contexts (e.g., the older people's movement vs. the gay movement; formal social movement organization vs. activist networks; Germany vs. United States) they yielded very similar findings. Most importantly, collective identification, specifically identification with the movement, contributed uniquely to the prediction of intended or actual social movement participation even when the effects of the cost–benefit calculations suggested by the Klandermans model were controlled. Integrating these results with findings from studies on sociopolitical participation in other domains (e.g., volunteerism), we proposed a dual-pathway model of collective action with one pathway based on cost–benefit calculations and another one based on collective identification (Simon et al., 1998; Stürmer & Simon, 2004a). Whereas the calculation pathway can be interpreted in terms of group members' instrumental involvement motivated primarily by specific extrinsic rewards, the identification pathway represents intrinsic involvement based on group members' inner obligation to act upon internalized movement-specific norms and goals (e.g., Stürmer et al., 2003).

Additional Pathways: Anger about Collective Injustice

In the recent years, following a more general trend in psychological research, the role of emotional processes has regained increasing attention in the intergroup literature. Several researchers have proposed to reconsider group-based feelings of anger about collective injustices as an important motivational force in collective protest participation (e.g., Leach, Iyer, & Pedersen, 2006; van Zomeren, Spears, Fischer, & Leach, 2004). A key argument of this proposition revolves around the idea that anger is characterized by an agitated phenomenological experience (e.g., high physiological arousal) which should energize group members' motivation to fight back if treated unfairly (see Leach et al., 2006, p. 1234).

The idea that anger spurs protest has its predecessors. It figured prominently in several (early) approaches to collective behavior (Le Bon, 1947; see also Zimbardo, 1969). In essence, these theories suggest that participants in crowds, due to a loss of individuality in the crowd and a related deinhibition of primitive emotional impulses, are prone to acts of senseless violence, and irrational destruction.[1] Modern social psychological approaches have unmasked this conception as distorted, theoretically ill premised, and last but not least, class-inflicted (e.g., Turner et al., 1987, especially pp. 171–202; also Klandermans, 1997; Simon & Klandermans, 2001). It is important to note that these latter approaches do not posit that feelings of anger are unimportant in social movement participation; by contrast, several approaches suggests that collectively shared feelings of anger play an important part in creating a potential for mobilization or politicization (see, for instance, Simon & Klandermans, 2001, p. 325). Still, they are premised on the assumption that the behavior that people display in the context of collective protest typically results from rather mindful, conscious, and deliberate decision processes (e.g., weighing costs and benefits of participation, acting upon an inner obligation to enact politicized collective identity).

In our view, in contemporary research on the role of anger in collective action specifically two issues have remained relatively underresearched. First, and surprisingly, recent research designed to test the role of group-based anger in collective protest has either completely ignored the processes underlying deliberate decision making (e.g., cost–benefit calculation or identification processes) in the analyses (e.g., Leach et al., 2006), or these processes were considered rather selectively in the investigations (e.g., van Zomeren et al., 2004). In fact, in a series of studies of our own research program outlined above, we did not observe a unique effect of feelings of group-based resentment (a conceptual "relative" of group-based anger) on group members' willingness to participate in social movement activities (or their actual participation), when the contributions of cost–benefit calculation or identification processes were controlled (reported in Stürmer & Simon, 2004a). The question whether and to what extent feelings of anger provide actually a unique motivating process in social movement participation thus needs further investigation. The first study presented here was designed to address this issue.

A second underresearched phenomenon concerns the psychological mechanisms underlying the hypothesized effect of group-based anger. Drawing on the literature on stress, coping, and emotion regulation (e.g., Lazarus, 1991), van Zomeren et al. (2004, p. 650) suggest that the effect of group-based anger on collective action participation reflects emotion-focused coping (i.e., attempts to regulate aversive emotions tied to the negative situation). However, theses authors do not present any empirical data testing this contention. The notion of participation as emotion-focused coping raises important questions concerning the relationship between individual and collective interests. One lesson to learn from the stress and coping literature is that strategies of emotion-focused coping

---

[1] Of course, we are also aware of important differences between the intergroup emotion approach and work in the LeBonian tradition such as that emotion is seen as functional from the former perspective and not as irrational.

may be dysfunctional in the sense that they interfere with problem-focused coping strategies (i.e., attempts to effectively change the negative situation). If group members are motivated by a desire to reduce their negative tensions involved in the experience of anger one should expect a preference to engage in behaviors that are perceived as functional at the individual level (e.g., forms of protest that allow the individual a "cathartic" reduction of anger-related negative tensions). Does this imply, then, that anger may prompt participation in such forms of protest even if they are, from the perspective of the collective, dysfunctional with regard to the achievement of the movement's goals (e.g., violent protest)? Moreover, should not one expect that if people may strive to reduce their feelings of anger, anger may be rather unreliable as a motivator of social movement participation because people may opt to achieve this goal by alternative (and behaviorally less costly) means? Our second study was designed to explore these issues.

Study 1

As already indicated the main objective of this first study was to examine whether feelings of group-based anger about perceived injustice influence people's willingness to participate in social movement activities above and beyond the processes specified by the dual-pathway model (cost–benefit calculation and collective identification processes). For this purpose, we conducted a questionnaire field study in the context of a recent protest movement in Germany, namely the students' protest to prevent tuition fees. In Germany, public universities traditionally charged no tuition fees, and plans to introduce fees of up to €500 per semester per student have sparked fierce protest all over the country (http://www.bildung-am-abgrund.de). We felt that this context would provide a particularly good opportunity to examine the role of group-based anger in social movement participation because the political circumstances (shared grievances, escalating conflict with authorities) created a potential for high emotional involvement.

Method

Participants and Procedure

The sample included 201 students from various faculties at the University of Kiel (M age $= 22.95$ years, $SD = 3.88$ years, range 18–47 years). One hundred fifty-two participants were female; one participant did not provide information regarding his or her gender. Thirty-three percent reported to have a monthly income above €500. Questionnaires were distributed at the end of lectures and seminars on campus. The study was introduced as part of a research project on students' attitudes towards the students' protest movement to prevent tuition fees. On the average, it took participants about 10 minutes to complete the questionnaire. Care was taken that none of the participants completed more than one questionnaire and that questionnaires were completed individually and anonymously.

Measures

Group-based anger. Following van Zomeren et al. (2004) we measured this variable by asking participants to indicate how angry, how irritated and how furious they felt due to the planned implementation of tuition fees. Participants rated each item on 7-point scales ranging from 1 (*do not agree*) to 7 (*totally agree*). For each participant we calculated a composite score for this variable by averaging over the three items (Cronbach's $\alpha = .89$).

Identification with students. To measure this variable we used the following four items: "I feel strong ties with other students," "I identify with other students," "I am glad to be a student," and "Being a student is an important part of my personality." Participants rated each item on 7-point scales ranging from 1 (*do not agree*) to 7 (*totally agree*). For each participant we calculated a composite score for identification with students by averaging over the four items (Cronbach's $\alpha = .77$).

Identification with the students' movement. To measure this variable, the four items used to measure identification with students were reworded so that they referred to identification with the students' movement to prevent tuition fees instead of the social category of students (e.g., "I feel strong ties with the students' movement."). Participants rated each item on 7-point scales ranging from 1 (*do not agree*) to 7 (*totally agree*). For each participant we calculated a composite score for identification with the students' movement by averaging over the four items (Cronbach's $\alpha = .87$).

Inner obligation. Building on our previous research (Stürmer et al., 2003) we also included an item in the questionnaire tapping participants' feelings of inner obligation to actively promote the movements' goals: "I feel a sense of inner obligation to actively promote the goals of the students' movement." Participants rated this item on a 7-point rating scale ranging from 1 (*do not agree*) to 7 (*totally agree*).

Collective motive. In line with Klandermans's (1984) expectancy-value approach, we measured the value and expectancy components of the collective motive separately and then combined them multiplicatively. For the value component, participants indicated how important it is to them to prevent the planned implementation of tuition fees. Participants rated the importance of this goal on a 7-point rating scale ranging from 1 (*unimportant*) to 7 (*important*). For the expectancy component, participants indicated the extent to which they expected that the implementation of tuition fees could be prevented through students' protest. Participants rated this item on a 7-point scale ranging from 1 (*under no circumstances*) to 7 (*certainly*). For each participant we created a score for the collective motive by multiplying the ratings for the value and expectancy components. Scores for this motive can thus vary between +1 and +49.

Normative motive. Again, we measured two components separately. First, participants rated others' expected reaction to their participation in students' protest activities for four groups of significant others: (1) other students, (2) academic advisors/staff, (3) family members, and (4) nonstudent friends. Participants rated these items on 7-point scales ranging from −3 (*rather negative*) to +3 (*rather positive*). Second, respondents rated the personal importance of the reactions of the four groups of people on 7-point scales ranging from 1 (*unimportant*) to 7 (*very important*). A single score for the normative motive was calculated as follows. For each group of significant others, we first multiplied the rating of the expected (positive or negative) reaction by the corresponding personal-importance rating. We then averaged these product terms. Scores for this motive can thus vary between −21 and +21.

Reward motive. We measured value and expectancy components separately. For the value component, participants evaluated two possible individual benefits (having a good time, getting to know nice people) and two possible individual costs (loosing time for one's studies, getting associated with unpleasant people) resulting from their participation in students' protest activities. Participants rated the subjective value of each outcome on 7-point scales ranging from −3 (*rather negative*) to +3 (*rather positive*). For the expectancy component, respondents rated the likelihood of each of the two benefits and the two costs on 7-point scales ranging from 1 (*under no circumstances*) to 7 (*certainly*). To create a score for the reward motive we first multiplied for each benefit and each cost the corresponding value and expectancy components. We then averaged these product terms across the two benefits and the two costs. Finally, the mean product term for the two benefits was added to the (negative) mean product term for the two costs. Scores for this motive can thus vary between −21 to +21.

Willingness to participate in future protest of the students' movement. For each of the following seven activities, participants indicated the strength of their willingness to participate: "public marches," "public manifestations," "sit-ins or occupations," "university strikes," "initiating a petition," "protest letters to members of parliament and politicians," and "protest letters to academic advisors and staff." Participants rated their willingness to participate in these activities on 7-point rating scales ranging from 1 (*very low*) to 7 (*very high*). For each participant we calculated a composite score for their willingness to participate in protest by averaging over the seven items (Cronbach's $\alpha = .87$).

Results and Discussion

Preliminary Analyses

Using participants' sociodemographic characteristics (age, gender, reported monthly net income) as statistical control variables in preliminary multiple regression analysis with anger, collective identifications, the three motives as predictors and willingness to participate in collective protest as criterion showed that controlling for participants' sociodemographics did not affect the predictive values the psychological predictors. Moreover, in these analyses, none of the sociodemographic variables had a significant unique predictive value, all $ps \geq .363$. We thus did not consider these variables in the main analyses reported below.

Main Analyses

Correlational analyses revealed that the three motives and the two identification measures were all significantly and positively correlated with willingness to participate, all $rs \geq .16$, $ps \leq .026$. Moreover, we also observed a significant and positive correlation between group-based anger and willingness to participate, $r = .40$, $p < .001$. To examine whether feelings of anger about the planned imposition of tuition fees influenced students' willingness to participate in protest activities above and beyond the processes specified by the dual-pathway model (cost–benefit calculation and collective identification processes), we performed a multiple regression analysis in which the three motives, the two identification measures and anger were considered simultaneously as predictors of willingness to participate, $R^2 = .48$, $F(6, 194) = 29.73$, $p < .001$. The findings of this analysis can be summarized as follows. First, they provide clear support for the dual-pathway model. Specifically, representing respectively the model's calculation and collective identification pathways, the collective, normative and reward motives and identification with the students' movement each made unique and positive contributions to the prediction of willingness to participate, all $\beta s \geq .13$, $t(194)s \geq 2.27$, $ps \leq .024$. Second, the data also confirm the importance of the politicization of collective identification. Of the two identification variables only identification with the students' movement—representing a more politicized form of identification—made a significant and positive contribution to the prediction of willingness to participate. In fact, despite a significant and positive zero-order correlation between identification with students and willingness to participate ($r = .16, p = .026$), when the contributions of the additional predictors were controlled, identification with students had a significant negative predictive value, $\beta = -.16$,

$t(194) = -2.61, p = .010.$[2] Third and finally, results also provide tentative evidence for the idea that feelings of group-based anger may influence people's willingness to participate in social movement activities above and beyond the processes specified by the dual-pathway model. Specifically, when the contributions of the three motives and the two identification variables were controlled anger retained a marginally significant predictive value, $\beta = .10$, $t(194) = 1.72$, $p = .088$.[3]

Further Analyses: The Identification Inner-Obligation Hypothesis

Our theoretical analysis suggests that the effect of identification with the social movement on willingness to participate in social movement activities is mediated by an inner obligation to actively promote the movement's goals (e.g., Stürmer et al., 2003). To secure further evidence for this identification-inner obligation hypothesis we conducted a meditational analysis (Baron & Kenny, 1986, p. 1177) employing the item tapping participants' feelings of an inner obligation to actively promote the movement's goals as the critical mediator variable. In line with this hypothesis, when we included the measure of inner obligation as additional predictor in the multiple regression analysis reported above, $R^2 = .54$, $F(7, 193) = 31.88$, $p < .001$, the inner-obligation measure had a significant predictive value, $\beta = .35$, $t(193) = 4.88$, $p < .001$, while, at the same time, the unique predictive value of identification with the students' movement dropped to nonsignificance, $\beta = .06$, $t(193) = 0.71$, $p = .480$. A Sobel test confirmed that the indirect effect of identification with the students' movement by way of inner obligation was indeed significant, standardized indirect effect = .24, $z = 4.44$, $p < .001$. The size of the regression coefficients of the three motives, identification with students and group-based anger in this analysis were virtually identical to those reported above. In fact, presumably due to a reduction of error variance in the criterion through including another predictor, in the multiple regression analysis with inner obligation the *p*-value for the anger coefficient was now below the conventional level of statistical significance, $\beta = .11$, $t(193) = 2.04, p = .043$.

---

[2]The negative predictive value for identification with students in the multiple regression analysis reported in Study 1 was not replicated in Study 2; we thus refrain from further speculations about this finding. Importantly, and replicating previous research (Simon et al., 1998; Stürmer & Simon, 2004a), mediational analysis (Baron & Kenny, 1986) confirmed that identification with students had a significant and positive indirect effect on willingness to participate in protest activities that was mediated by identification with the students' movement, standardized indirect effect = .09, $z = 3.31$, $p < .001$.

[3]Additional moderated regression analysis (Aiken & West, 1991) exploring potential interactive effects among anger, the three motives, and collective identifications provided no evidence that the role of anger was moderated by calculation or identification processes or vice versa, all *p*s for the critical interaction (or moderation) terms $\geq .249$. To summarize, these analyses suggest that the unique effect of anger on willingness to protest operated independent of the processes specified by the dual-pathway model (i.e., calculation and identification).

Study 2

Study 1 provided some evidence for the idea that anger may provide a unique motivational pathway to social movement participation above and beyond the cost–benefit calculation and collective identification processes specified by the dual-pathway model (e.g., Stürmer & Simon, 2004a). The main objective of Study 2 was thus to advance our understanding of the psychological mechanism underlying the effectiveness of this variable. Specifically, building on van Zomeren et al.'s (2004, p. 650) speculation that collective action participation based on group-based anger reflects emotion-focused coping, we examined whether and to what extent the effect of anger on willingness to protest is driven by a desire to reduce this negative emotional state. To test this mechanism, we designed a laboratory experiment in which we first evoked feelings of group-based anger among our research participants (university students) through presenting them a (bogus) proposal by the university's rectorate for raising administration and library fees for students in the very near future. Participants randomly assigned to a catharsis condition later experienced an event designed to reduce their negative feelings, while participants randomly assigned to a control condition did not have a similar experience. The design of the manipulation employed in this study was informed by Freud's (1905/1960) ingenious analysis of the cathartic function of hostile jokes (including political jokes, satires, and caricatures). Freud suggests that hostile jokes (e.g., jokes that challenge the superior status of an authority) present a symbolic form of attack or aggression and thus provide a low-cost opportunity of cathartic reduction in aggressive impulse (see Singer, 1968, for an empirical demonstration of this mechanism). Following this analysis, in order to provide an opportunity of cathartic reduction, we let participants in the experimental condition read jokes challenging professors' superior status and exposing their flaws. If the effect of group-based anger on protest participation is indeed driven by people's desire to reduce negative tensions, one should expect that the relationship between research participants' feelings of anger about the proposal (measured before the catharsis manipulation) and their willingness to participate in protest (measured after the catharsis manipulation) is weaker among participants who experienced the cathartic event than among participants in the control condition who did not have such an experience. Technically speaking, we thus tested in the present experiment whether the experimental manipulation effectively attenuated the strength of the relationship between participants' feelings of anger (the main predictor) and their willingness to participate in protest activities (the main criterion).

Because the present study is the first systematic empirical test of this mechanism in the context of collective protest participation that we know of, we incorporated several features into the design of Study 2 to strengthen the validity of our interpretation. First, we tested our main hypothesis with regard to two conceptually distinct criteria of willingness to participate, namely (1) willingness to participate in protest activities suited to release negative tensions (e.g., activities involving acts of verbal aggression toward the outgroup, hereafter—borrowing from the distinction between hostile and instrumental aggression—labeled "hostile protest"), and (2) willingness to participate in activities focusing on the achievement of the collective goals (e.g., activities involving the presentation of political arguments— hereafter labeled "instrumental protest"). We expected that the moderating effect of our experimental manipulation would be particularly pronounced in analyses using willingness to participate in hostile protest as the criterion variable, because this behavior provides a more immediate opportunity for emotion-focused coping and thus also for cathartic reduction in negative feelings. Second, we also included a measure tapping directly on participants' desire to release tension. Demonstrating that our catharsis manipulation would not only reduce the strength of the relationship between anger and willingness to participate in protest, but also the strength of the relationship between anger and their desire to release tension would provide more convincing support for the hypothesized cathartic mechanism. Third and finally, to conceptually isolate the effect of group-based anger, and in keeping with the procedure in Study 1, we also included measures of the cost–benefit calculation and identification processes in the design and used these measures as statistical control variables in our analyses.

Method

Design and Participants

One hundred eighty-two students from various faculties at the Christian-Albrechts-University (111 women and 71 men, M age $= 22.78$ years, $SD = 3.40$ years, range 19–44 years) participated in this experiment, which contrasted a control condition with a catharsis condition. One hundred eleven participants were female. Forty-three percent reported to have a monthly income above €500. Two additional participants were not included in the sample because of missing data on key psychological measures. Participants were randomly assigned to conditions. They received €5 for their participation.

Procedure

Participants were recruited on campus and asked whether they were willing to participate in a survey on students' attitudes toward the reforms of the German university system allegedly conducted by an independent research institute. Between five and eight participants were invited for each experimental session. Upon arrival at the laboratory, participants were seated in individual cubicles where they were presented a first questionnaire including items gathering sociodemographic information (e.g., participant's gender, age, monthly net income). After completion of the first questionnaire all participants were told that they would next receive a questionnaire containing one of four specific reform proposals allegedly being discussed at their university and that their task was to evaluate this proposal. Participants in both conditions then received a (bogus) text in which the university's rectorate proposed to increase administration and library fees for students in order to improve the university's financial situation. It was stated that, in total, these fees would lead to an additional financial expenditure of €300 for the average student per semester. In addition, participants learned that the rectorate preferred to implement this proposition without the formal approval of students because it felt "most students were not capable to truly understand the complex situation of the university." After reading the proposal, all participants were asked to complete a series of questions including measures of anger, collective identification, and expected costs and benefits of participation in protest activities.

Catharsis manipulation. Before we assessed participants' willingness to participate in activities to protest against the proposal, participants worked through a section containing the catharsis manipulation. To embed this manipulation into the cover story, participants in both conditions read a brief introductory statement stating that the purpose of the following questions was to learn more about the students' culture at their university. In the catharsis condition participants were then asked to indicate whether it was rather common or rather uncommon among students at their university to make fun of their professors. Subsequently, they were presented four professor jokes allegedly circulating among students at other universities which were derived from real Internet web pages. For each joke, participants were asked to rate how funny they felt it was. The jokes read as follows: (1) A professor is eating in the cafeteria. Without hesitation a student takes a seat at his table. The professor asks somewhat irritated: "Since when then do eagles and pigs sit at the same table?" Student: "Ok. I am gonna fly then." (2) Half an hour past a professor has collected all exams, a student wants to hand his in. The professor refuses to accept it. The student puffing his chest up: "Do you know to whom you are talking to?" "No...," answers the professor. "Great" says the student and pushes his exam in the pile of the others. (3) A philosophical exam contained the following sentence: "If this is a question, respond to it." One of the answers: "If this is an answer, grade it!" (4) Topic of the lecture: "Sarcasm as a rhetorical means." At the beginning of the lecture the professor asks for an example. One student answers: "I cannot tell you how much I appreciate your lectures."

In the control condition, participants completed a filler task. Specifically, they were asked to indicate how dissatisfied they felt with the cultural and recreational program in their university town. Then, they were asked to rate their dissatisfaction with cultural and recreational programs in each of the following domains: (1) music and movies (e.g., theatres, concerts), (2) sports (e.g., clubs, university sports), (3) culture (e.g., museums, exhibitions), (4) gastronomy (e.g., pubs, restaurants).

After having provided their ratings, participants in both conditions were asked to complete some items tapping on their current mood. On the subsequent pages of the questionnaire participants were asked to complete a series of questions including measures of willingness to participate in protest activities to stop the implementation of the proposal and a measure of their general desire to release tension. They were then fully debriefed and thanked.

Measures

We presented all theoretically relevant measures intermixed with filler items related to the cover story (e.g., items measuring participants' approval of the alleged proposal). The order of items presented below corresponds to the appearance of the items in the questionnaires.

Group-based anger. To measure their feelings of anger participants indicated how irritated, how furious, and how angry they felt due to the rectorate's proposal. Each item was rated on 7-point scales ranging from 1 (*do not agree*) to 7 (*totally agree*). For each participant we calculated a composite score by averaging over the three items (Cronbach's $\alpha = .88$).

Identification with students. To measure this variable we used the same four items as in Study 1. Participants rated each item on 7-point scales ranging from 1 (*do not agree*) to 7 (*totally agree*). For each participant we calculated a composite score for identification with students by averaging over the four items (Cronbach's $\alpha = .76$).

Identification with the students' movement. To measure this variable we used the same four items as in Study 1. Participants rated each item on 7-point scales ranging from 1 (*do not agree*) to 7 (*totally agree*). For each participant we calculated a composite score for this variable by averaging over the four items (Cronbach's $\alpha = .90$).

Collective motive. We measured the value and expectancy components of the collective motive separately and then combined them multiplicatively. For the value component, participants indicated how important it is to them to prevent the realization of the proposal (raising administration and library fees for students). Participants rated the importance of this goal on a 7-point rating scale ranging from 1 (*unimportant*) to 7 (*important*). For the expectancy component, participants indicated the extent to which they expected that the implementation of the proposition could be prevented through students' protest. Participants rated this item on a 7-point scale ranging from 1 (*under no circumstances*) to 7 (*certainly*). For each participant we created a score for the collective motive by multiplying the rating for the value component by the expectancy rating. Scores for this motive can thus vary between +1 and +49.

Normative motive. In order not to inflate the numbers of items in the questionnaire, we focused the measurement of this motive on one specific group of significant others, namely friends. Specifically, participants were asked to indicate on a 7-point scale ranging from 1 (*rather negative*) to 7 (*rather positive*) how their friends would react if they participated in protest activities to prevent the implementation of the university's proposal. Participants then rated the personal importance of the reactions of their friends on a 7-point scale ranging from 1 (*unimportant*) to 7 (*very important*). A single score for the normative motive was calculated by multiplying the rating of the expected (negative or positive) reactions by the personal-importance rating. Scores for this motive can thus vary between +1 to +49.

Reward motive. We used an "overall" item to assess participants' expectations regarding the personal costs and benefits resulting from their participation in protest activities. On a 7-point scale ranging from 1 (*rather negative consequences*) to 7 (*rather positive consequences*), participants indicated whether their participation would entail more positive or negative consequences for them.

Check of catharsis manipulation. Immediately after participants had completed the experimental or the filler tasks, participants were asked to indicate their current mood. Inserted among some filler questions was the manipulation check item measuring how irritated participants felt at the moment. Participants rated this item on a 7-point rating scale ranging from 1 (*do not agree*) to 7 (*totally agree*).

Willingness to participate in collective protest. In the final section of the questionnaire, participants rated a series of items referring to various different protest activities. For each activity, participants indicated, on 7-point rating scales ranging from 1 (*very low*) to 7 (*very high*), their willingness to participate. Four items referred to hostile protest activities: "Going personally into the rector's office to take the members of the rectorate to task," "Sending an email to the rector's office to vent my anger about the proposition," "Joining a public demonstration with other students to vent our anger regarding how the rectorate treats us," and "Writing a letter with other students to the rectorate in which we express our frustration and outrage about the proposition." Four activities referred to instrumental protest activities: "Participating in a public demonstration in which we present our arguments against the implementation of the proposition," "Sending an email to the rectorate in which I present my arguments against the proposition," "Writing a personal letter to the rectorate in which I present my arguments against the proposition," and "Organizing a public discussion about the proposition including all parties involved in the dispute." For each participant, we calculated separate composite scores for willingness to participate in hostile protest (Cronbach's $\alpha =$ .76) and instrumental protest (Cronbach's $\alpha = .68$) by averaging over the corresponding ratings.

Desire to release tension. At the very end of the questionnaire participants indicated for a series of activities whether they would like to engage in this activity right now. Inserted among a series of filler activities was one item asking participants to indicate the strength of their desire to release inner tension. Participants rated this item on a 7-point rating scale ranging from 1 (*do not agree*) to 7 (*totally agree*).

Result and Discussion

Preliminary Analyses

Sociodemographic characteristics. Using participants' sociodemographic characteristics (age, gender, reported monthly net income) as statistical control variables in preliminary multiple regression analyses with anger, collective identifications, and the three motives as predictors and willingness to participate in hostile protest or willingness to participate in instrumental protest as criterion confirmed that including participants' sociodemographics did not affect the predictive values of the psychological predictors. Moreover, in these analyses, none of the sociodemographic variables had a significant unique predictive value, all $ps \geq .740$. We thus did not consider these variables in the main analyses reported below.[4]

Manipulation check. To check the effectiveness of the catharsis manipulation, we examined whether participants in the catharsis condition, after reading the hostile jokes about professors, felt less irritated than participants in the control condition. This analysis yielded a significant difference between conditions suggesting that reading the jokes had, in fact, attenuated participants' negative tensions; control condition: $M = 2.41$, $SD = 1.63$, catharsis condition: $M = 1.78$, $SD = 1.23$, $t(165.33) = 2.95$, $p = .004$ (degrees of freedom for t test with unequal variances).

---

[4]Finding across studies that the sociodemographics did not exert direct effects on willingness to participate when psychological predictors were considered at the same time parallels results obtained in previous studies on social movement participation in other contexts (e.g., Stürmer et al., 2003).

Main Analyses

Grand means and standard deviations for all relevant variables and their intercorrelations for the total sample of participants are presented in Table 1. Importantly, the experimental variable was not significantly correlated with feelings of anger ($r = .00, p = .98$), confirming that before we administered the manipulation in both conditions there was the same potential for group-based anger to become a motivator of willingness to participate. Our theoretical perspective suggests that the catharsis manipulation should attenuate the strength of the relationship between participants' feelings of anger (measured before the manipulation) and their willingness to participate in protest activities, especially in hostile protest (measured after this manipulation). To test this prediction, we used the procedure recommended by Aiken and West (1991) for examining interaction or moderation effects with correlational data. We conducted separate two-step hierarchical regression analyses in which our main criterion measures (willingness to participate in hostile or instrumental protest) were regressed on the predictor variables (anger, identifications, motives) and the experimental manipulation (coded 1 for control condition and −1 for catharsis condition) in a first step, with six Predictor × Experimental Manipulation interaction terms in the second step. The interaction terms were calculated by multiplying each of the six predictor variables (separately) with the coded experimental variable. Evidence for a significant impact of the experimental manipulation on the link between anger and willingness to participate would be obtained when the Anger × Experimental Manipulation interaction term entered in the second step has a significant and positive predictive value. (Including the interaction terms involving the remaining predictor variables served as control of whether our experimental manipulation produced any other than the predicted interaction effects.)

Willingness to Participate in Hostile Protest

When entered in the first step, anger was a significant and positive predictor, $\beta = .19, t(174) = 2.61, p = .010$. Furthermore, of the additional variables, the collective motive, $\beta = .32, t(174) = 4.52, p < .001$, was a significant predictor, while the normative motive, $\beta = .13, t(174) = 1.90, p = .059$, and the reward motive emerged as marginally significant predictors, $\beta = .11, t(174) = 1.68, p = .094$. The unique predictive values of identification with students, identification with the students' movement, and the experimental variable were nonsignificant, all $ps \geq .168$; overall $R^2 = .36, F(7, 174) = 13.74, p < .001$. Importantly, confirming a significant impact of the experimental manipulation on the effectiveness of anger, when entered in the second step, the Anger × Experimental Manipulation interaction term had a significant and positive predictive value, $\beta = .39, t(168) = 2.10, ps = .038$, for the remaining interaction terms all $ps \geq .432$.

Table 1. Means, Standard Deviations and Intercorrelations for Predictor and Criterion Variables (Study 2)

Variables	M	SD	1	2	3	4	5	6	7	8	9	10
1 Experimental manipulation	n.a.	n.a.		.00	.02	−.03	−.01	−.07	−.04	−.04	−.06	.11
2 Group-based anger	4.07	1.77			.20**	.47***	.43***	.26**	.20**	.43***	.37**	.33***
3 Identification with students	4.66	1.19				.47***	.13	.32***	.04	.15*	.23**	.12
4 Identification with movement	3.28	1.44					.42***	.37***	.23**	.40***	.52***	.23**
5 Collective motive	16.92	10.47						.15*	.28***	.50***	.49***	.28***
6 Normative motive	13.79	8.78							.23**	.29***	.25**	.21**
7 Reward motive	4.38	1.31								.29***	.26***	.17*
8 Hostile protest	2.45	1.28									.65***	.43***
9 Instrumental protest	3.61	1.39										.30***
10 Desire to release tension	1.73	1.33										

Note. $N = 182$. The experimental manipulation was coded 1 for control condition and −1 for catharsis condition. Scores for anger, identifications, willingness to protest, and desire to release tension can vary between 1 and 7. Scores for the collective and normative motives can vary between 1 and 49 and for the reward motive between 1 and 7.
*$p < .05$. **$p < .01$. ***$p < .001$ (two-tailed).

To further decompose this interaction, we conducted separate multiple regression analyses for the control and catharsis conditions. The results of the multiple regression analyses for the two conditions are presented in Table 2. In line with our expectation, in the control condition, group-based anger was a significant and positive predictor of willingness to participate in hostile protest, $\beta = .36$, $t(84) = 3.65$, $p < .001$, whereas in the catharsis condition this relationship was reduced to nonsignificance, $\beta = .04$, $t(84) = 0.39$, $p = .695$. (Note that the variances of group-based anger and hostile protest did not significantly differ between the control and the catharsis condition, Levene's $Fs \leq 2.04$, $ps \geq .155$. Hence, it is unlikely that the observed differences resulted from differing variances for these variables.)

Willingness to Participate in Instrumental Protest

We expected that group-based anger should be more influential in predicting willingness to participate in hostile protest than in predicting willingness to participate in instrumental protest. The hierarchical regression analysis on willingness to participate in instrumental protest provided clear support for this assumption. In contrast to the analysis on willingness to participate in hostile protest, group-based anger did not have a unique predictive value, $\beta = .06$, $t(174) = 0.84$, $p = .405$, when entered in the first step in the analysis. Only identification with the students' movement, $\beta = .34$, $t(174) = 4.23$, $p < .001$, and the collective motive, $\beta = .29$, $t(174) = 4.04$, $p < .001$, emerged as significant predictors; the regression weights of the remaining variables were all nonsignificant, all $ps \geq .205$; overall $R^2 = .37$, $F(7, 174) = 14.78$, $p < .001$. Moreover, entering the Anger × Experimental Manipulation interaction term in the second step provided no evidence for a significant impact of the experimental manipulation on the relationship between anger and willingness to participate in instrumental protest activities, for all interaction terms in this analysis $ps \geq .265$. Separate multiple regression analyses for the control and catharsis conditions corroborate these results (Table 2).

Desire to Release Tension

To further substantiate the validity of our interpretation we ran an analogous two-step hierarchical regression analysis as reported above but used the measure of the desire to release tension as the criterion. Importantly, with regard to the role of group-based anger, results of this analysis paralleled all relevant findings of the analysis with willingness to participate in hostile protest as criterion. When entered in the first step, anger was a significant and positive predictor, $\beta = .22$, $t(174) = 2.71$, $p = .007$; the remaining determinants were all nonsignificant; all $ps \geq .076$, overall $R^2 = .17$, $F(7, 174) = 4.90$, $p < .001$. Moreover, when entered in the second step, the Anger × Experimental Manipulation interaction

Table 2. Separate Multiple Regression Analyses With Willingness to Participate in Hostile Protest, Willingness to Participate in Instrumental Protest or Desire to Release Tension as Criteria (Study 2)

	Control condition				Catharsis condition			
	β	t(84)	R^2	F(6, 84)	β	t(84)	R^2	F(6, 84)
Hostile protest			.50	13.76***			.26	4.80***
Group-based anger	.36	3.65***			.04	0.39		
Identification with students	.04	0.43			−.07	−0.60		
Identification with movement	.10	0.90			.11	0.93		
Collective motive	.26	2.68**			.37	3.49*		
Normative motive	.17	1.73			.10	0.99		
Reward motive	.06	0.65			.10	1.02		
Instrumental protest			.51	14.67***			.24	4.47**
Anger	.11	1.10			.00	0.04		
Identification with students	.08	0.85			−.08	−0.74		
Identification with movement	.36	3.35**			.32	2.65*		
Collective motive	.30	3.20**			.27	2.45*		
Normative motive	.04	0.39			.04	0.41		
Reward motive	.08	0.87			.03	0.28		
Desire to release tension			.25	4.68***			.10	1.56
Anger	.35	2.87**			.05	0.45		
Identification with students	−.06	−0.51			.17	1.37		
Identification with movement	.02	0.16			−.04	−0.27		
Collective motive	.14	1.15			.17	1.48		
Normative motive	.21	1.89			.03	0.26		
Reward motive	−.06	−0.53			.15	1.37		

*$p < .05$. **$p < .01$. ***$p < .001$ (two-tailed).

term received a significant regression weight, $\beta = .43$, $t(168) = 2.06$, $p = .041$, for the remaining interaction terms all ps $\geq .149$. Separate multiple regression analyses for the two experimental conditions further confirmed that group-based anger was a significant and positive predictor of participants' desire to release tension in the control condition, $\beta = .35$, $t(174) = 2.87$, $p = .005$, but not in the catharsis condition, $\beta = .05$, $t(174) = 0.45$, $p = .652$ (see also Table 2).

Taken together, the results of this laboratory experiment provide sound support for the proposition that the unique effect of group-based anger on willingness to protest is based on a desire to reduce negative tensions. In line with this perspective, we observed that anger about collective injustice was a significant and positive predictor of participants' willingness to participate in protest activities suited to reduce their negative emotional state (hostile protest), but it did not predict participants' willingness to engage in more task-oriented protest activities (instrumental protest) providing a lower chance of cathartic reduction. Moreover, and particularly indicative, the relationship between group-based anger and hostile protest was reduced to nonsignificance when participants, before indicating their willingness to participate, encountered an event providing a cathartic reduction in aggressive tensions. Using participants' general desire to release tension as an additional criterion replicated these results.[5]

To create an opportunity of cathartic reduction of aggressive impulse in the present experiment we let participants read jokes challenging professors' superior status and exposing their flaws. Even though this manipulation captures Freud's (1905/1960) original reasoning, one might argue that the nature of the jokes may have instigated an additional (or even alternative) social psychological process—positive self-affirmation in terms of reassuring positive collective identity (a process that is, by the way, also implicated in Freud's analysis). Still, if reading the jokes served indeed as positive self-affirmation, rather than catharsis, one should expect that this manipulation affected the role of the identification variables in the criterion's prediction rather than the role of anger (e.g., Jetten, Spears, & Postmes, 2004). This was not the case, however. As depicted in Table 2 (and reported in detail above), the manipulation did only affect the strength of the relationship between anger and willingness to engage in hostile protest (or the desire to release tensions), while the relationships of all other predictors with the criterion measures (including those involving collective identifications) remained unaffected.

---

[5]One may wonder why our experiment—which demonstrated significant differences between the control and catharsis conditions in the role of anger—did not also show significant differences between conditions in the levels of participants' willingness to participate in hostile protest or their desire to release tension. With regard to this issue it should be noted, however, that in the control (or baseline) condition willingness to engage in hostile protest or desire to release tension was rather low already; both grand means were significantly below the scale midpoint "4," $t(90)$s ≤ -11.56, $p < .001$ (see also Table 1). Accordingly, it seems likely that our "failure" to observe a further decrease in the levels of the dependent variables in the experimental condition was due to floor effects.

Positive collective self-affirmation can thus be deemed unlikely as an alternative explanation for any of the obtained results.

Additional Analysis for Study 1 and Study 2

So far we have focused in our analyses on the unique (direct) effect of group-based anger on willingness to participate in protest. Still, it seems also plausible that anger may exert indirect effects on willingness to participate. Simon and Klandermans (2001, p. 325) argue that blaming an external opponent for the in-group's predicament, and becoming angry at "them" for what they do to "us" is an important antecedent of politicized collective identity. Applying this analysis to the present context, one could argue that, with increasing (outgroup-directed) anger about collective injustice, students' identification with the movement should intensify; this, in turn, should strengthen their willingness to participate in collective protest. To explore this anger-identification-participation hypothesis we ran a series of path analyses in Study 1 and Study 2 testing whether group-based anger, in addition to its direct effect on willingness to participate in protest, also had a significant indirect effect that was mediated by identification with the students' movement. Analyses confirmed that this was indeed the case. In both studies group-based anger was a significant unique predictor of identification with the movement, $\beta s \geq .25$, $ts \geq 3.84$, $ps < .001$ (standardized regression coefficients from multiple regression analyses with identification with students' movement, and motives as controls). Moreover, the indirect effect of anger on willingness to protest via identification with the students' movement was in both studies significant, both indirect effects $\geq .09$, $zs \geq 2.85$, $ps \leq .004$. (Note that in Study 2 this result refers to willingness to participate in instrumental protest as identification with the students' movement had no unique effect on willingness to participate in hostile protest.)

General Discussion

Following a more general trend in psychological research, researchers have suggested to reconsider feelings of group-based anger as an important motivational force in collective protest participation (e.g., Leach et al., 2006; van Zomeren et al., 2004). In the present article, we presented two studies designed to subject the role of this variable to a critical theoretical and empirical examination. Study 1, a questionnaire field study, examined whether feelings of anger about perceived collective injustice exerts a unique or direct effect on group members' willingness to participate even when the effects of cost–benefit calculation and collective identification processes were controlled. Study 2, a laboratory experiment, examined the psychological underpinnings of the effect of group-based anger and willingness to participate in social movement activities. Finally, we also explored in both studies whether anger exerts an indirect effect on group members' willingness to participate in social movement activities.

The results of our analyses can be integrated as follows. First, our research suggests in line with van Zomeren et al.'s (2004) assumption, that group-based anger may indeed exert a unique or direct effect on group members' willingness to participate in social movement activities. However, our research also suggests that, in comparison to cost–benefit calculation and identification processes, this emotional route to protest is rather fragile. Our analysis suggests that feelings of anger create a desire to reduce it. Sometimes this desire may prompt people to participate in protest because they have learned that this behavior provides an effective means to achieve this end. More often, however, as protest participation is typically costly and effortful, they may use less costly, and eventually even nonpolitical, means to vent their anger. Our experiment in which the mere reading of hostile jokes undermined the link between anger and willingness to protest provides a clear empirical demonstration of the fragility of the anger effect. Our failure to detect a significant direct link between feelings of anger in a series of previous studies (see Stürmer & Simon, 2004a) suggests that the limited role of anger observed in the present research is not restricted to the specific social movement context in which we conducted our research (students' protest), but that it is a rather general phenomenon.

Another important implication of our research, we believe, is that anger may prompt people to engage in behaviors that are, from a strategic perspective, rather counterproductive—an implication that, like the fragility of the anger effect, directly follows from the assumed individualistic motivational principle underlying the effectiveness of anger (i.e., the desire to reduce negative tensions). In this respect the effects of anger and collective identification processes stand in marked contrast to each other. Our experimental data show that anger only predicted participants' willingness to participate in protest activities suited to reduce their individual negative state (hostile protest), but it did not predict participants' willingness to engage in activities that were suited to achieve the collective goal (instrumental protest). For identification with the social movement, on the other hand, the exact opposite pattern was observed. We do not want to imply here that forms of hostile protest or the public expression of anger are always counterproductive; yet, in the context in which we tested our hypotheses (students' protest), from a strategic perspective, behaviors such as "running personally into the rector's office and taking people to charge" clearly have a counterproductive, if not irrational, overtone.

Even though our analysis highlights critical limits of anger as a motivator in collective protest, it also offers a "new look" on this process in the context of collective politicization. In line with Simon and Klandermans' (2001) conceptual treatment of this issue, our additional analyses confirmed that anger had a significant indirect effect on group members' willingness to participate via increased identification with the students' movement (i.e., their politicized collective identity). We believe that the true potential of anger in social movement participation lies precisely in this connection, the link between individual emotional experiences and the politicization of collective identity. To the extent that feelings of anger strengthen individuals' identification with the social movement (or more generally, their group-oriented political consciousness) individual emotional experiences become relinked to the group and its goals. This process ensures that anger unfolds its energizing potential in mindful and purposeful actions in the service of the collective. From a more applied perspective, it is thus certainly an important task for entrepreneurs of social movements to direct the translation of feelings of anger about collective injustice into politicized collective identity—an issue that seems also of utmost importance to political artists seeking to stimulate collective action through political satire, cabaret, and the like (instead of undermining it through creating an opportunity for cathartic anger reduction). Future investigation on the rhetoric of successful political leaders, especially on how they define ways and means to express shared feelings of anger in order to achieve common goals, may not only prove to be a promising venue to advance our theoretical understanding of this process. It has also the potential, we believe, to produce practical knowledge about how to increase active participation.

References

Aiken, L. S., & West, S. G. (1991). *Multiple regression: Testing and interpreting interactions.* Newbury Park, CA: Sage.
Baron, R. M., & Kenny, D. A. (1986). The moderator-mediator variable distinction in social psychological research: Conceptual, strategic, and statistical considerations. *Journal of Personality and Social Psychology, 51,* 1173–1182.
Freud, S. (1960). *Jokes and their relation to the unconscious.* New York: Norton., (Original work published 1905).
Jetten, J., Spears, R., & Postmes, T. (2004). Intergroup distinctiveness and differentiation: A meta-analytic integration. *Journal of Personality and Social Psychology, 86,* 862–879.
Kelly, C., & Breinlinger, S. (1996). *The social psychology of collective action: Identity, injustice and gender.* London: Taylor & Francis.
Klandermans, B. (1984). Mobilization and participation: Social psychological expansions of resource mobilization theory. *American Sociological Review, 49,* 583–600.
Klandermans, B. (1997). *The social psychology of protest.* Oxford, UK: Blackwell.
Klandermans, B., & Oegema, D. (1987). Potentials, networks, motivations, and barriers: Steps towards participation in social movements. *American Sociological Review, 52,* 519–531.
Lazarus, R. S. (1991). *Emotion and adaption.* New York: Oxford University Press.
Leach, C. W., Iyer, A., & Pedersen, A. (2006). Anger and guilt about in-group advantage explain the willingness for political action. *Personality and Social Psychology Bulletin, 32,* 1232–1245.
Le Bon, G. (1947). *The crowd: A study of the popular mind.* London: Ernest Benn (Original work published 1895).
Simon, B. (2004). *Identity in modern society: A social psychological perspective.* Oxford: Blackwell.
Simon, B., & Klandermans, B. (2001). Politicized collective identity. A social psychological analysis. *American Psychologist, 56,* 319–331.

Simon, B., Loewy, M., Stürmer, S., Weber, U., Freytag, P., Habig, C., et al. (1998). Collective identification and social movement participation. *Journal of Personality and Social Psychology, 74*, 646–658.
Singer, D. L. (1968). Aggression arousal, hostile humor, catharsis. *Journal of Personality and Social Psychology* (Monograph Supplement), *8*, 1–14.
Stürmer, S., & Simon, B. (2004a). Collective action: Towards a dual-pathway model. In W. Stroebe, & M. Hewstone (Eds.), *European Review of Social Psychology* (Vol. 15, pp. 59–99). Hove, UK: Psychology Press.
Stürmer, S., & Simon, B. (2004b). The role of collective identification in social movement participation: A panel study in the context of the German gay movement. *Personality and Social Psychology Bulletin, 30*, 263–277.
Stürmer, S., Simon, B., Loewy, M., & Jörger, H. (2003). The dual-pathway model of social movement participation: The case of the fat acceptance movement. *Social Psychology Quarterly, 66*, 71–82.
Tajfel, H., & Turner, J. C. (1986). The social identity theory of intergroup behavior. In S. Worchel & W. G. Austin (Eds.), *The social psychology of intergroup relations* (pp. 7–24). Monterey, CA: Brooks/Cole.
Turner, J. C., Hogg, M. A., Oakes, P. J., Reicher, S. D., & Wetherell, M. S. (1987). *Rediscovering the social group. A self-categorization theory.* Oxford, UK: Blackwell.
van Zomeren, M., Spears, R., Fischer, A., & Leach, C. W. (2004). Put your money where your mouth is! Explaining collective action tendencies through group-based anger and group efficacy. *Journal of Personality and Social Psychology, 87*, 649–664.
Zimbardo, P. (1969). The human choice: Individuation, reason and order versus deindividuation, impulse and chaos. In W. J. Arnold & D. Levine (Eds.), *Nebraska Symposium on Motivation* (Vol. 17, pp. 237–307). Lincoln: University of Nebraska Press.

STEFAN STÜRMER is Professor and Chair of Social Psychology at the FernUniversität in Hagen (Germany). He received his PhD in Social Psychology from the Christian-Albrechts-Universität zu Kiel, Germany (2000). His research focuses on the role of intergroup processes in social movement participation, cooperation, helping, and altruism.

BERND SIMON received his PhD in Social Psychology from the Westfälische-Wilhelms-Universität in Münster, Germany (1989). He is Professor and Chair of Social Psychology and Evaluation Research at the Christian-Albrechts-University in Kiel (Germany). In his research, he investigates inter- and intragroup processes, with particular emphasis on issues of identity, power, politicization, and respect.

Collective Psychological Empowerment as a Model of Social Change: Researching Crowds and Power

John Drury*
University of Sussex

Steve Reicher
University of St Andrews

The issue of psychological empowerment in crowd events has important implications for both theory and practice. Theoretically, the issue throws light on both intergroup conflict and the nature and functions of social identity. Practically, empowerment in collective events can feed into societal change. The study of empowerment therefore tells us something about how the forces pressing for such change might succeed or fail. The present article first outlines some limitations in the conceptualization of both identity and empowerment in previous research on crowd events, before delineating the elaborated social identity model of crowds and power. We then describe recent empirical contributions to the field. These divide into two areas of research: (1) empowerment variables and (2) the dynamics of such empowerment. We finally suggest how psychological empowerment and social change are connected through crowd action. We conclude with some recommendations for practice following from the research described.

Conceptualizing Crowds and Power

The reference in this article's title to Canetti's (1962) *Crowds and Power* is an acknowledgement of his astute linkage of these two concepts. Historically, crowds are formed by those without institutional power. Crowds resisting the institutional order are all expressions of the powerless (Rudé, 1981; Thompson, 1971). Elements of the ruling class tend not to band together in crowds because they simply do not need to! Crowd psychology emerged as a science in 19th century Europe precisely to combat the newly emergent working-class crowds (Nye, 1975).

While the power of the reactionary crowd (Reicher, 1996c; Reicher & Haslam, 2006a,b) and the necessity for a discourse adequate to both liberatory

---

*Correspondence concerning this article should be addressed to John Drury, School of Psychology, University of Sussex, Falmer, Brighton BN1 9QH, UK [e-mail: J.Drury@sussex.ac.uk].

and reactionary collectives (Drury, 2002) must be recognized, the concern here is in the power of the crowd to contribute to positive social change. The psychological interest in this process is in the collective empowerment of those who participate in such change. We define such empowerment as that positive social-psychological transformation, related to a sense of being able to (re)shape the social world, that takes place for members of subordinated groups who overturn (or at least challenge) existing relations of dominance. We will argue that this kind of phenomenon is social-psychologically important, for two reasons. First, empowerment is subjectively a life-changing experience; and second, empowerment links crowd events to social movements and hence possible social change. Indeed we will argue that social identity is the fulcrum of social change precisely because it is through the collective empowerment of those with otherwise subordinated identities that broader social relations can change.

The article focuses first on some research we have been involved in which delineates the factors—particularly invisibility—that contribute toward subjective empowerment among crowd members faced with powerful out-groups. We then suggest how collective empowerment is not simply due to external variables but is also a dynamic process at least partly explicable in terms of collective actors' own practices in intergroup contexts. We conclude theoretically with a model of empowerment in social change. Stressing the importance of empowerment in the social-psychological explanation of social change, we argue, restores emotions to the core of the discipline. Finally, we draw out some practical implications of this body of research.

Before describing our recent research, however, we need to provide some context by briefly tracing how empowerment has been examined (and ignored) in research on collective action in general and crowd behavior in particular.

The topic of subjective power in crowd events was raised at the very outset of the discipline of social psychology, in Le Bon's (1895/1968) influential text *The Crowd*. For all the objections subsequently amassed against Le Bon's distorted and partial perspective (McPhail, 1991; Reicher, 1987; Reicher & Potter, 1985), at least he acknowledged the importance of power in crowd phenomenology. However, Le Bon also argued that the subjective sense of power among crowd members was in fact illusory. The achievements of the crowd were simply those of atavistic destruction rather than progress. The crowd, he argued, was essentially a conservative force. Hence for Le Bon power in crowds was raised as a psychological issue only to be ultimately dismissed as a nonissue at a social level.

Research on collective action[1] took a number of directions following Le Bon's populist text. But his key ideas always remained a touchstone for those

---

[1] The term *collective action* will be used here interchangeably with *crowd behavior* to reinforce the notion that such "behavior" is meaningful. Our argument is that there is no radical break from "rational" individual conduct to "irrational" collective conduct (Reicher, 1987).

who followed, whether they supported him or attacked him. Hence, starting in the 1950s, one strand of experimental social psychology borrowed Le Bon's suggestion that the self and hence self-control was lost in the crowd. However, these various "deindividuation" theories (Diener, 1980; Prentice-Dunn & Rogers, 1989; Zimbardo, 1970) had nothing to say about the transformation of subjective power. Crowd members did not display barbaric behavior through a sense of illusory empowerment, but simply out of behavioral disinhibition. In this sense, the whole tradition of deindividuation research can be considered a backward step from the pronouncements of Le Bon on the relation between crowds and power.

At around the same time, however, evidence from protests in U.S. college campuses against the Vietnam war, and the outbreak of urban "race" riots in many U.S. cities, prompted other social scientists to question the notion of crowd irrationality. Based on both their own experiences and detailed studies of these crowd events, social scientists suggested that even the most violent crowd behavior was meaningful (e.g., Turner & Killian, 1972.)

The emphasis on the "rationality" of crowd behavior was taken to a logical conclusion in game theory (Berk, 1974; Brown, 1965) and resource mobilization theory (RMT; e.g., Gamson, 1975). The latter sought to exorcise Le Bon by eliminating altogether the psychological element (such as grievances or strains) from the explanation of collective action. RMT explained the actions of collectives in resistance simply by reference to the objective resources available to them. In jettisoning psychology, however, these approaches also jettisoned the whole issue of psychological empowerment. Power became reduced to a matter of the balance of forces in the eye of the analyst.

More recent versions of RMT have attempted to reinsert a psychological dimension by acknowledging the importance of the self (e.g., Gamson, 1992). This is in line with developments in sociological social movement theory generally toward a greater emphasis on the subjective and the socially constructed (e.g., Melucci, 1989). Without such a shift in emphasis, theories of collective action could not begin to conceptualize let alone explain experiential phenomena such as those encapsulated in the following extract taken from the events of May 1968 in France:

> The occupants of Censier suddenly cease to be unconscious, passive objects shaped by particular combinations of social forces; they become conscious, active subjects who begin to shape their own social activity... people who have never expressed ideas before, who have never spoken in front of professors and students, become confident in their ability. (Gregoire & Perlman, 1969, pp. 37–41)

The challenge for theory is to explain the emergence of these feelings of exhilarating power without slipping back into Le Bonian irrationalism, and to make sense of any social and psychological consequences deriving from empowered collective action. If this can be achieved, we can go some way toward showing how empowerment in crowd events is part of meaningful social change. The argument of this chapter is that the elaborated social identity model (ESIM; Drury

& Reicher, 2000; Reicher, 1996a,b, 2001; Stott & Reicher, 1998a), a model of crowd dynamics based on the tenets of self-categorization theory, can provide such an explanation.

Social Identity Conditions: Empowerment Variables

The several variants of deindividuation theory share the assumption that anonymity in groups and crowds leads to a loss of self and a loss of control over behavior (see Reicher, Spears, & Postmes, 1995). By contrast, studies in the social identity tradition have shown that anonymity in the group typically leads to a shift from individual to group identity and hence increased conformity to the norms associated with the situationally relevant group (Reicher, 1982, 1984; Spears, Lea, & Lee, 1990). Moreover, a meta-analysis of all studies involving within-group anonymity showed that behavior becomes more normative rather than more uncontrolled (Postmes & Spears, 1998).

Social identity researchers make the further point that, in traditional deindividuation research, anonymity is often treated as a state of group membership rather than a social relationship (Reicher, 2001; Reicher et al., 1995). Hence there is insufficient precision over who precisely group members are anonymous to. This matters: the behavioral effects of invisibility to powerful out-groups (such as the police) or else to fellow group members will each be very different. In the former case, anonymity will undermine the ability of others to impose sanctions on us and hence empower the in-group. In the latter case anonymity will isolate us from our peers and disempower the in-group. Reicher and Levine (1994a,b) showed that increased visibility to a powerful out-group reduces the expression of behaviors punishable by the out-group but normative for the in-group. By contrast, Reicher, Levine, and Gordijn (1998) showed that increased visibility within an in-group specifically increases the expression of in-group normative behavior that are out-group punishable.

These studies move us away from an understanding of anonymity as an antecedent of behavioral disinhibition. Instead, they return us to issues of power, since in various ways they demonstrate constraints on and conditions for the effective expression of group identity in contexts of unequal power relations between groups. The experimental study of power and resistance was consolidated in Reicher and Haslam's (2006a) BBC prison study, a conceptual replication of Zimbardo's Stanford Prison Experiment (Haney, Banks, & Zimbardo, 1973), which itself represents the apogee of traditional "deindividuation" reasoning. This study traced the pathway from rebellion to tyranny in two groups of participants. It gave rise to two key conclusions. First, people did not automatically slip into roles with which they then thoughtlessly complied. Rather, only when they actively identified with a group did they then (creatively) act in terms of group norms. Moreover, shared identification led to effective coordination of action and thereby empowered in-group members in relation to the out-group (and conversely, lack of identification impeded coordination and disempowered the group). Second, where group members were unwilling or unable to use group power to reshape social reality according to their own beliefs, they became more willing to accept the tyrannical domination of others. Overall, then, the study demonstrated the links between identification, power, and the positives of collectivity (mutual aid, empowerment, positive social change) and its potential negatives and failures, while equal providing a vivid illustration of the dangers of group failure.

One of the strengths of the BBC study, and the reason why it provided such insights into the dynamics of identity and power, was the fact that it extended over 10 days and hence it was possible the investigate interactive dynamics which produced collective action. On the one hand it was possible to see how participants sought to define the meaning of events, the nature of groups and relations between groups, and how this affected what they did. On the other hand, one could analyze the way in which the actions of one group framed the responses of the other which in turn impacted back on the first group. This is in stark contrast to the increasing tendency of laboratory experiments to neglect both the ways in which categories are constructed and contested and also to neglect interaction (Haslam & McGarty, 2001; Reicher & Hopkins, 2001; Reicher, Haslam, & Platow, 2007).

We do not in any way wish to underplay the importance of experimentation in clarifying the precise relations between variables. Indeed, from the review above it should be clear that experimentation has been a key tool in the development of our ideas. However the lesson we draw is that a rounded understanding of empowerment as a process of psychological change occurring between people over time requires the additional use of more open and extended methodologies. The lab excels where control is needed, but the dynamics of empowerment in crowd events are by definition uncontrolled and open-ended, where what is of interest is the way participants struggle over definitions (of self, other, and context) rather than how they responds to the experimenter's given definitions. Hence, ethnographies of the unfolding dynamics of collective events—ethnographies which focus on how people feel, how they represent their situation, and what they do[2]—are of particular value. They allow us to see empowerment as an emergent process and not simply a variable which is either present or absent.

Social Identity Consequences: ESIM and the Dynamics of Empowerment

The recognition of the role of empowerment as cause and consequence of collective action came from studies which originally set out to examine the origin

---

[2]In most of the studies described below, ethnography or participant observation was used as a framework to collect observations, interviews, movement documents, and soundtrack recordings. These were then subjected to a thematic analysis. For more details see Drury and Reicher (2000).

of crowd conflict. Reicher and colleagues identified a common pattern across a variety of crowd events, including a student protest (Reicher, 1996b), a mass demonstration against local taxation which became a riot (Stott & Reicher, 1998a), and cases of football crowd "disorder" (Stott & Reicher, 1998b). In essence, the pattern was as follows. Events would start with a heterogenous crowd, the majority of which identified themselves as moderates who simply wanted to express their view to the authorities, and a minority of whom were radical and saw the authorities as an antagonist. However, crowd members were perceived as homogenously dangerous by the authorities (notably the police) and treated as such—that is denied the ability to express themselves as they wished. This then led to a radicalization among moderate crowd members who then joined with the radicals in challenging the police. Not only that, but they came to change their views about the authorities and hence about their own identity in relation to the authorities. In terms of conflict, then, the critical issue became explaining the process of escalation. However, insofar as escalation involved a change of social relations between crowd and authorities and a change of identity among crowd members, this raised a broader question about psychological and social change: how is it that people who enter a crowd event with one sense of identity emerge from it with a different identity? The social identity model of crowd behavior was elaborated into ESIM in order to address this issue.

ESIM involves three elements: concepts, conditions, and dynamics. First, then, ESIM involves, indeed requires, a reconceptualization of "context" and "social identity" and, crucially, of the relationship between them. In general, theorists in the social identity tradition tend to treat context (more accurately, "comparative context" which is to say the organization of social reality in categorical terms) as an objective determinant of social identity. However, if context is prior and separate to identity, it is hard to see how identity can change through action in context. For ESIM, then, the two are interdependent moments in a single historical process. That is, social identity should be seen as the way in which people understand how they are positioned relative to others, along with the forms of action which flow from that position. Context should be understood as those forces external to actors which enable or constrain their action. The key point is that, in crowds, the understandings of one group forms the actions which constrain the actions of the other. That is, identity constitutes context and vice versa.

This point is illustrated in studies of the 1990 London "poll tax" riot (Stott & Drury, 1999, 2000; Stott & Reicher, 1998a). Here, the context for protesters was the actions of the police—who formed cordons, initiated baton charges, and so on. But such actions were at the same time the expression of the police's understanding of their relationship to the protesters—as a threatening, dangerous, hostile crowd.

Second, ESIM suggests that the conditions necessary for the emergence and development of crowd conflict are twofold: (1) There is an asymmetry of categorical representations between crowd participants and an out-group such as the police. For example, during the poll tax riot, where crowd members understood their behavior in sitting down in the road as "legal and legitimate protest," police defined it as a "threat to public order"; where police understood their own action as a defensive response to a situation of growing threat from the crowd, the crowd understood the police action as unprovoked and "heavy handed." (2) There is also an asymmetry of power-relations such that the (police) out-group is able to impose its definition of legitimate practice on the in-group of crowd participants—for example, by having the technology, organization, and strength in numbers initially to form cordons, coordinate baton charges, and thereby determine the physical movement of the crowd.

Third, there is a dynamic whereby police assumptions concerning the homogeneity of the crowd, and police practices which impose a common fate on all crowd members (cf. Dovidio, Piliavin, Gaertner, Schroeder, & Clark, 1991) lead to a self-fulfilling prophecy on a collective scale. That is, the initially heterogeneous crowd becomes homogenous. Moreover, to the extent that police action is seen as not only indiscriminate but also illegitimate (e.g., denying the right to protest and using offensive tactics to disperse the crowd) then the entire crowd will unite around a sense of opposition to the police and the authorities they are protecting. This will be reflected in behavioral changes—notably, a willingness to enter into conflict with the police. It will also be reflected in psychological changes. That is, those who initially saw themselves as moderates change their understanding of their relationship with the authorities and hence their own identity. Being treated as radicals, they came to see themselves as radical. In addition, the emergence of a common radical self-categorization within the crowd leads to feelings of consensus and to expectations of mutual support which empowers crowd members to express their radicalism and to take on the police.

Putting all three elements together, ESIM can be summarized as follows: people's sense of their social position (social identity) changes to the extent that, in acting on their identity (participating in a crowd event), they are repositioned as a consequence of the understandings and reactions of an out-group (treated as oppositionalists by the police), and this repositioning leads both to a new sense of identity and new forms of action (oppositional violence).

In due course, we shall deal in more detail with the various consequences brought about in the dynamic described in ESIM. For now, however, our focus is on psychological empowerment which, as the various studies we have referenced suggest, is central to understanding escalation. It is both an input and an output of the interactive dynamic between crowd and police: Police action created a strong unified crowd out of an initially fragmented collectivity, then crowd members' sense of their strength led them to challenge the police, thus explaining how events developed from sporadic skirmishing into generalized conflict.

However, insofar as the issue of empowerment was an emergent finding from these studies rather than a focus of attention, evidence pertaining to the precise processes involved was limited. Follow-up analyses therefore sought to gather data on group boundaries and subjective empowerment, to substantiate their suggested dynamic role in crowd events (Drury & Reicher, 1999; Drury, Reicher, & Stott, 2003).

Thus for example, Drury and Reicher (1999) showed that participants at a demonstration against the poll tax at a local council meeting began the event in small, exclusive groups of friends, but came together as a united force on the basis of their shared experience of illegitimate exclusion from the council meeting. The sense of crowd unity was evident in participants' behavior, as they oriented together, focusing on the same targets, sang and chanted together, and pushed in unison, rather than remaining in their small subgroups. But participants also explicitly report feeling more psychological empowerment—they felt increased support from others once there was this new sense of shared identity in relation to the council/police out-group. The enhanced sense of empowerment was also evident in both the observed and the self-reported increase in the boldness of their actions aimed at disrupting the meeting.

One of the unexpected outcomes of this study was the finding that for many interviewees the sense of empowerment and euphoria stayed with people after the event. Even though participants were not explicitly asked about such enduring effects, many mentioned them spontaneously. Indeed, some explained this as the reason why they felt confident enough to resist the poll tax in the months after the event itself. Indeed, the poll tax collapsed when the riots and town hall protests were followed up long term by a successful campaign of mass nonpayment (Burns, 1992).

Thus if feelings of empowerment endure beyond the collective event itself, they can explain much more than escalation and psychological change within a single episode. Such feelings can have enduring consequences on two levels. First, they can affect people's personal lives outside the protest event. Thus we found evidence of changes in participants' relationships with the police, their partners, their future career plans and so on:

> I think now when I do see the police sometimes, you know, usually you might nod to them but now I'm very dismissive and I think if I got burgled again I don't know whether I would want to phone the police; I think I'd probably just deal with my burglary in my own way, I wouldn't call upon their help.
> (Antiroads protester, cited in Drury & Reicher, 2000, p. 592)

Second, feelings of empowerment can affect participants' motivation for involvement in subsequent collective action. Having more confidence in the movement and themselves as movement actors can lead to more action in the future:

> I've progressed in that now I would, given time permitting and everything else, I would actually go and help in another campaign somewhere else even if it's only for a day if there's a rally [] that's what I'm saying when I said become more radical; I would actually take time out to help somebody else rather than just sort of being at the end of my road

and then once that's gone forget it, that–actually determined to keep on with the whole roads programme, fighting it wherever, (Antiroads protester, cited in Drury et al., 2003, p. 204)

The wider significance of this is that, to the extent that people feel increasingly able to participate in collective actions such as protests, demonstrations, and other social movement events, then social change becomes possible.

But what is it about the experience of collective action which leads to such an enduring feeling of empowerment which may inspire people to get more involved subsequently? In order to answer this question, we carried out a comparative study of two protest actions which formed part of an extended antiroads campaign (Drury & Reicher, 2005). The first, dubbed by participants a "tree-dressing ceremony" involved the occupation of common land which, along with the ancient tree at its centre, was about to be demolished for road construction. The second involved the mass eviction of protestors from this site a month later.

The two events were chosen for comparison because, prima facie, they each met the conditions of the ESIM, yet their psychological outcomes were different. In both cases there was an asymmetry of representations between police and protesters ("peaceful protest" vs. "disorder"; "illegitimate road" vs. "lawful construction site") and a difference in power between the two groups such that the police and other authorities were in the first instance able to put their perceptions into practice (i.e., excluding and removing the protesters from the "common land"). In both cases also the action of the authorities was seen to be against the whole crowd, both "activists" and "locals" alike, irrespective of people's different levels of involvement in the protest.

However, while the occupation led to joy and empowerment, the eviction was followed by anger and enhanced sense of the legitimacy of the collective cause. The united crowd were able to overpower the police and security in the act of occupation but were themselves overpowered at the eviction. There was something about these material outcomes that not only made people feel empowered (in the first case) or outraged (in the other) within the events, but stayed with them afterward and fed into their future actions.

The obvious answer is that the one was a success and the other was a failure, and in a sense we would agree with that. However, such an answer begs the question of what constitutes success and failure for participants. Some accounts (e.g., Bandura, 2000) root a sense of "collective self-efficacy" in terms of achieving personal goals in the mass.[3] By contrast, just as we argue that crowd action

---

[3] Bandura's distinction between self-efficacy and collective efficacy is itself revealing: for Bandura, the self is just the personal self. By contrast, the social identity approach suggests that the self or identity can be collective as well as personal (Turner, Oakes, Haslam, & McGarty, 1994), each representing a psychologically valid level of self-categorization. As a corollary, the social identity approach also suggests that there are multiple selves or identities corresponding to the multiplicity of our social relations; by contrast, Bandura posits a single unitary self.

in general is underpinned by social identity, so we argue that the definition of success in particular relates to benefits to the collective self. That is, success is a function of actions that serve, even against the power of the out-group, to create a world which is organized on the basis of group beliefs, values, and understandings. Failure is a function of actions which do not achieve this. Thus one can only determine what is a success or a failure—and hence what does or does not lead to enduring empowerment—by understanding the significance of outcomes in relation to the specific understandings associated with a given social identity. Indeed, what might look very much like failure to outsiders may constitute a success as refracted through an in-group lens. Thus, in one of our studies (Drury, Cocking, Beale, Hanson, & Rapley, 2005), animal rights protestors were stopped in their ostensible aim of closing an animal testing laboratory. However, they nevertheless experienced the protest as a notable success, because they had challenged the power of the police over an extended period and, as they saw it, revealed the collusion of the state in animal experimentation.

In the case of the "tree-dressing ceremony" we have been discussing, the protesters collectively flattened fences round the construction site, physically enacting a collective identity defined in terms of concern for the green space of the local area—since it rendered the physical space into a "common," rather than the construction site for the road (the out-group's definition of the space). This is evidenced in comments in which participants celebrated their action as successful enactment of the principles that motivated them—as an assertion of what they were about.

At the eviction, however, the crowd failed to enact the collective self-definition they brought to the event—that is, saving the "common." Instead, the actions of the police and bailiffs imposed an official conception of "public order" and the "rightful" and legal construction of the road. They obliterated the collective vision of campaigners as embodied in the tree-dressing ceremony and the occupation of the tree. And because campaigners described how closely their sense of self was bound up with the notion of common land, so they also described how "crushed" they felt when the tree was seized and destroyed.

This argument can now be stated as a hypothesis about one process by which empowerment emerges as an (enduring) outcome of collective action. Empowerment is an outcome of collective action if and when such action is successful in the specific sense that it serves to realize (or objectify) participants' social identity (and hence their definition of legitimate practice) in the world, over against the power of dominant out-groups. Following Marx (1844/1975), we refer to this process as collective self-objectification (CSO).[4] In other words, empowerment

---

[4] We also denote this same concept in some places as "collective self-realization" (e.g., Reicher & Haslam, 2006b).

as an experiential outcome of action is a function of that action being (for the participants) an imposition of self or identity in the world (and the word *imposition* seems appropriate here since the context is one of intergroup struggle).

While the comparative study was consistent with this hypothesis, CSO was simply "read off" from behaviors and reports of empowerment. In a follow-up study to assess the subjective importance of "identity imposition," 37 activists were asked to describe and explain two or more empowering experiences, as well as two or more disempowering experiences (Drury et al., 2005). Responses were coded using ESIM categories (i.e., unity, support, and CSO) as well as from the "bottom-up" to take into account any subjective factors we had not considered a priori (e.g., "organization," "atmosphere," "others' determination").

CSO, unity, and support were the three most frequently cited types of explanation for feelings of empowerment. Unity and CSO were both significant predictors of increased participation. By the same token, the obverse of each of the three key factors implied by the ESIM—disunity, lack of support, failure of CSO (as well as "police control")—featured prominently in participants' accounts of disempowering experiences. Failure of CSO and the related notion of police control predicted reduced participation.[5] This interview study therefore provides support for the posited role of CSO in processes of disempowerment and hence, along with other aspects of the ESIM, a link from empowering experiences within a particular event to ongoing participation in further events.

Our most recent studies (Drury & Cocking, 2007) have taken us back into the laboratory in order to tease out the different effects of success as a generic positive outcome and CSO as the successful imposition of social identity on social reality. To be more precise, we addressed a key prediction which flows from the argument that it is specifically CSO that leads to enduring empowerment: that is, the same positive achievement may be differentially empowering to different groups as a function of its relevance to their differing social identities. Thus we induced different identities in participants for which intellectual achievement was more or less central. They were then asked to complete a number of activities which were described as "intelligence/ability" tasks, and bogus feedback was given as to their success or failure. Finally, participants completed a number of analogue empowerment measures: "subjective success," future expectations of success, desire for participation, and positive feelings. While there was evidence that positive feedback increased the sense of success for all participants, the key findings were that the effect of such feedback on feelings of empowerment was greater when the tasks were identity relevant, and the effects of failure feedback

---

[5]The close statistical relation between some of these variables, and the obvious conceptual connection between some of them (e.g., police control and failure of CSO) suggests that, while analytically separable, for participants themselves these factors may be experienced as aspects of a single "gestalt" of perceptions.

on feelings of disempowerment was also greater for those to whom the tasks were identity relevant. Thus it was not simply objective "success" per se that mattered in empowerment and motivation for future participation, but also whether that success was identity relevant.

Having reviewed the current research, we can now explicate four key conceptual aspects of CSO as a model of empowerment (Drury et al., 2005).

(a) Context Change as Self-Change

CSO is derivable from the tenets of self-categorization theory (Turner, Hogg, Oakes, Reicher, & Wetherell, 1987): identity is a function of, and varies with, social relational context. CSO is simply the application of this principle to the particular case of change in power relations. Thus, just as an oppositional self-concept is a function of involvement in relations with the authorities which become defined as antagonistic to the collective self (Drury & Reicher, 2000), so an empowered self-concept is a function of participation in social relations defined in terms of power-transformation—from the out-group to the in-group.

(b) Novelty

It is not mundane actions that are experienced as empowering and inspiring but rather ones which are perceived to turn the existing world "upside-down." The preconditions for CSO are therefore ongoing relations of unequal power between social groups. CSO entails the overturning, disrupting or at least disturbing these relations (even if only temporarily). CSO refers to the actions of groups in resistance who challenge the status quo, rather than those of dominant groups whose actions serve to reproduce the status quo.

(c) Action as Realization of Legitimate Practice

But why should identity-based action upon the world lead to feelings of empowerment? Because action which expresses the collective definition of legitimacy over against that of dominant forces, which realizes the collective's (hitherto suppressed) identity, turns an subjective imperative on how the world should be into an objective feature of the world. When one's action serves to change the world to reflect one's identity in this way, such an action–outcome thereby evidences, through the perceived changed context (point A, above), that one's group is indeed an active and powerful subject. The self-changed context reflects back to the world-changing self. In short, being a subject rather than an object of others' actions is a definition of empowerment or agency.

(d) Provisionality/Contingency

The endurance of feelings of empowerment reflects the extent to which these changed relations themselves can endure. Subsequent to any in-group CSO, sooner or later, the dominant out-group may be able to reassert itself. Such reassertion would entail the realization of the identity of the out-group and the suppression once again of that of the in-group. In such a case, the context reverts to one in which the in-group is defined as relatively powerless (cf. point (a), above). By the same token that successful in-group action provides evidence that one is a powerful agent (point (c), above), successful out-group action provides counterevidence to this self-perception. Therefore defeat, and hence the reimposition of out-group definitions of legitimate practice, is experienced as disempowering.

A Model of Collective Empowerment and Social Change

Simon and Klandermans (2001) recently proposed an integrative model of social and psychological factors behind mobilization, according to which empowerment or, in their terms, agency, is a function of politicized collective identity. Simon and Klandermans point out that, despite its importance, this agency or empowerment function has largely neglected in social psychology (though see Kelly & Breinlinger, 1995). We have sought to address this neglect through delineating a particular account of the emergence of collective empowerment. We now bring the different strands of this review together, complementing Simon and Klandermans's model of politicized collective identity, by outlining the place of empowerment within a broader ESIM account of collective action and social change.

The first point we wish to make is that, in laying renewed stress on the importance of empowerment, we reintroduce emotions to the core of crowd psychology. The sense of being able to shape one's world is necessarily a passionate and exhilarating affair. This might seem like a return to the classic crowd psychology tradition mainly associated with Le Bon and later "irrationalist" accounts of collective behavior (e.g., Berkowitz's, 1972, frustration-aggression model). However, LeBonian theorizing equates emotionality with negativity in at least two senses. One, the emotions that it highlights are predominantly aversive (frustration, anger fear, etc.). Two, it contrasts emotion to reason and hence takes collective passions as an indication of collective irrationality. By contrast, as should be clear from the foregoing discussion of CSO, we point to the role of positive emotions (joy, euphoria, exhilaration) as being linked to immediate empowerment, enduring meaningful psychological change and positive social change (Drury et al., 2005). In short, our model unlike classic accounts is a positive collective psychology (Drury, 2008). As should be equally clear, we see these feelings as integrally linked to a changed understanding of ourselves in the social world. In other words, collective emotions and reason are interdependent rather than counterposed.

We can take this argument one step further. When we talk of "reason," a distinction can be made between what we have termed "cognitive" and "strategic" aspects of group behavior (Klein, Spears, & Reicher, 2007; Reicher, Spears, & Postmes, 1995). The former refers to the way in which we represent the world—both how things are and how they should be. The second refers to our practical ability to act in the world. When it comes to acts of resistance, both are implicated and both are related to emotion. Thus, on the one hand collective action depends upon a perception that the status quo is unfair and illegitimate (Tajfel, 1978) along with the accompanying sense of shared grievance or outrage (Simon & Klandermans, 2001). On the other hand, such action depends upon a calculation that one is able to overcome the forces that protect the status quo. The factors going into such a calculation include the size and level of unity among the ingroup compared to the out-group (Drury & Reicher, 1999; Reicher, 1996a), the resources available to the in-group, the level of social movement organization that can sustain an extended mobilization (this is the critical insight provided by RMT—see McCarthy & Zald, 1977), and the personal resources available to group members—including time and energy—which allow them to sustain extended participation without "burnout" (Drury et al., 2005). All these will be related to the positive feelings associated with a sense of empowerment.

Our analysis of differential outcomes of collective action (Drury & Reicher, 2005) suggests that there are multiple determinants of collective action (and inaction) for social change. Some who may feel a greater sense of outrage feel able to take action in the form of expressing their voice (rather than in the expectation of directly overturning existing social relations); others take further action on the basis of an enhanced sense of what is possible, yet their sense of legitimacy in what they do remains constant. We therefore reject the traditional dualism of symbolic versus instrumental determinants of collective action. Rather, we suggest that there are different sorts of goals. Emotion and "reason" are always interwoven as causes of collective action, not separate pathways.

On the one hand, resistance may reflect enhanced definitions of legitimacy of own action and illegitimacy of out-group action, rather than enhanced empowerment. On the other hand, lack of resistance may reflect disempowerment (disunity, lack of support, lack of numbers relative to police power and control) rather than the acceptance of given social relations as legitimate (cf. Jost & Banaji, 1994). It is not failure of CSO per se, however, that enhances feelings of self-legitimacy—indeed, one can imagine circumstances where the sense of outrage and "victory" co-exist. However, we would suggest that outrage associated with failure of collective action can act as a spur to further action only to the extent that there are still practical arrangements (e.g., a social movement organization) to make such future action possible.

Empowerment, then, is but one element—albeit a necessary one—that feeds into the process of social change. We have stressed that empowerment is an output from as well as an input into this process (as described in ESIM). Indeed change occurs as a cycle of interactions between groups in which subordinated groups emerge from each round at a higher level of empowerment which then sets the ground for the next cycle. But here again, empowerment is but one of several such outputs which go together in producing this positive cycle of radicalization. We earlier promised to return to these various psychological changes that take place as a consequence of the dynamic described by ESIM. They can be divided into three broad categories.

First, as crowd members are repositioned as a function of the reactions of out-groups (notably, the police) so their sense of identity changes along with the boundaries of collective selfhood and the sense that particular others are in-group or out-group to them. In the roads protests we have described, "respectable" local protestors found themselves positioned as radicals, came to see themselves as radicals, and therefore came to see other radical environmentalists (from whom they had previously distanced themselves) as part of the same overall group (Drury & Reicher, 2000).

Second, as protestors came to see the police as defenders of powerful interests in society rather than neutral arbiters among different interests, so their perception of the legitimacy of police actions changed. Policing as a whole came to be seen as illegitimate and particular actions came to be construed as instances of this illegitimacy: protestors complained of police colluding with private contractors, failing to protect the protestors from the actions of these contractors, indiscriminate arrests of protestors, and excessive violence (Drury et al., 2003).

Third, as their understanding of the nature of the social world changed, so the aims of the protest and even what counted as success (and hence led to a sense of empowerment) also changed. Thus, if the police come to be seen as "agents of the state" rather than "guardians of the peace," so the very act of standing up to them and getting them to reveal their "true" nature became a goal of protest. Thus, we have described how, relatively early in the antiroads campaign, the eviction of protestors from common land was counted a failure in terms of stopping construction taking place. However, by the time of the later eviction of protestors from houses along the route of the road, protestors counted the event a great success due to the widespread publicity of police dragging protestors from precarious perches on the roofs of the condemned buildings (Drury & Reicher, 2000; Drury et al., 2003).

In sum, we can see an unfolding dynamic which operates simultaneously on all the constructs that we have identified as critical: how we represent ourselves in the world and how the world should be; what we count as success and the resources we have to achieve that success; the emotions that accompany a sense of living in an unjust world but being able to change it. Through the reactions of the authorities, a progressive process of delegitimation and radicalization can take place as the mounting challenge of the mass leads to more intense measures by the authorities which in turn broadens and intensifies the radical beliefs and feelings of the crowd. That is, in combination, the various psychological changes we have outlined mobilize people to act in ways that produce social change. The development of the U.K. antiroads movement into the wider "anticapitalist" movement in the 1990s is a classic case in point (Drury, 2007; Drury et al., 2003).

Practical Implications

The practical implications of this body of research are threefold for those involved in collective action who seek to change the existing order. First, since collective empowerment is argued to be at the heart of social change, its preconditions clearly need to be established. The first of these is achieving shared identity. Thus, for example, with reference to some of the findings described here, those seeking social change will attempt to enhance identity salience and visibility within the in-group and to facilitate identity-normative conduct. In short, all practices which contribute toward enhancing shared identification should be employed.

Second, those seeking to mobilize masses for or against the existing order need to be able to define goals and hence CSO such that the actions of the group are understood as possible, successful, and identity relevant. Those seeking to change the existing order will recognize the role that even limited shared actions can play in building a powerful movement. No matter how small, if the action is understood as instantiating one's collective identity over against one's oppressors, then empowerment can develop into a virtuous cycle of broader, deeper, and more advanced resistance. If, as we have argued, identity and context are of the same order, the cycle needs to escalate to that level where the routines of the existing order are revealed as the (contingent) practices of other people rather than as inevitable, natural features of the world.

Third and finally, while no social movement can, from its start, transform the wider social world, it can at least structure its own internal reality so as to objectify its social identity. By so doing they increase the sense that a new world is possible. This is a version of the argument that ends and means should be consistent. Here, however, it is not a moral issue, but a matter of practicalities. To realize in the here and now aspects of a world that does not yet exist (e.g., freedom, authenticity, equality) is to bring that world closer—through empowering its agents with the belief that they can create it. In a very concrete sense, then, social movement activists need to be architects of the imagination.

References

Bandura, A. (2000). Exercise of human agency through collective efficacy. *Current Directions in Psychological Science, 9*, 75–78.

Berk, R. (1974). A gaming approach to crowd behaviour. *American Sociological Review, 39*, 355–373.
Berkowitz, L. (1972). Frustrations, comparisons and other sources of emotional arousal as contributors to social unrest. *Journal of Social Issues, 28*, 77–91.
Brown, R. (1965). *Social psychology*. New York: The Free Press.
Burns, D. (1992). *Poll tax rebellion*. Stirling: AK Press.
Canetti, E. (1962). *Crowds and power*. Harmondsworth: Penguin.
Diener, E. (1980). Deindividuation: The absence of self-awareness and self-regulation in group members. In P. B. Paulus (Ed.), *Psychology of group influence* (pp. 209–242). Hillsdale, NJ: Lawrence Erlbaum.
Dovidio, J. F, Piliavin, J. A., Gaertner, S., Schroeder, D. A., & Clark, R. D., III. (1991). The arousal: Cost-reward model and the process of intervention: A review of the evidence. In M. Clark (Ed.), *Prosocial behaviour: Review of personality and social psychology* (Vol. 12, pp. 86–118). Newbury Park, CA: Sage.
Drury, J. (2002). "When the mobs are looking for witches to burn, nobody's safe": Talking about the reactionary crowd. *Discourse & Society, 13*, 41–73.
Drury, J. (2007). *Dynamics of (dis)empowerment in recent social movement participation: Collective identity and social change*. Invited paper, Workshop on 'Collective Identities, Mobilization, and Political Participation', Free University of Brussels, Belgium, July.
Drury, J. (2008, June). Dynamics of empowerment in collective action participation: Elaborating social identity and social change. Paper presented at *15th General Meeting of the European Association of Experimental Social Psychology*. Opatija, Croatia.
Drury, J., & Cocking, C. (2007). *Identity and success definition: An experimental study*. Unpublished manuscript. University of Sussex.
Drury, J., & Reicher, S. (1999). The intergroup dynamics of collective empowerment: Substantiating the social identity model. *Group Processes and Intergroup Relations, 2*, 381–402.
Drury, J., & Reicher, S. (2000). Collective action and psychological change: The emergence of new social identities. *British Journal of Social Psychology, 39*, 579–604.
Drury, J., & Reicher, S. (2005). Explaining enduring empowerment: A comparative study of collective action and psychological outcomes. *European Journal of Social Psychology, 35*, 35–58.
Drury, J., Reicher, S., & Stott, C. (2003). Transforming the boundaries of collective identity: From the "local" anti-road campaign to "global" resistance? *Social Movement Studies, 2*, 191–212.
Drury, J., Cocking, C., Beale, J., Hanson, C., & Rapley, F. (2005). The phenomenology of empowerment in collective action. *British Journal of Social Psychology, 44*, 309–328.
Gamson, W. A. (1975). *The strategy of social protest*. Homewood, IL: Dorsey.
Gamson, W. A. (1992). The social psychology of collective action. In A. D. Morris & C. M. Mueller (Eds.), *Frontiers in social movement theory* (pp. 53–76). New Haven: Yale University Press.
Gregoire, R., & Perlman, F. (1969). *Worker-student action committees: France May '68*. Detroit: Black and Red.
Haney, C., Banks, C., & Zimbardo, P. (1973). A study of prisoners and guards in a simulated prison. *Naval Research Review, 9*, 1–17.
Haslam, S. A., & McGarty, C. (2001). A 100 years of certitude? Social psychology, the experimental method and the management of scientific uncertainty. *British Journal of Social Psychology, 40*, 1–21.
Jost, J. T., & Banaji, M. R. (1994). The role of stereotyping in system-justification and the production of false consciousness. *British Journal of Social Psychology, 33*, 1–27.
Kelly, C., & Breinlinger, S. (1995). Identity and injustice: Exploring women's participation in collective action. *Journal of Community and Applied Social Psychology, 5*, 41–57.
Klein, O., Spears, R., & Reicher, S. (2007). Social identity performance: Extending the strategic side of SIDE. *Personality and Social Psychology Review, 11*, 28–45.
Le Bon, G. (1968). *The crowd: A study of the popular mind*. Dunwoody, GA: Norman S. Berg. (Original work published 1895)
Marx, K. (1975). Economic and philosophical manuscripts (G. Benton, Trans.). In *Early writings*. Harmondsworth: Penguin. (Original work written 1844)
McPhail, C. (1991). *The myth of the madding crowd*. New York: Aldine de Gruyter.

Melucci, A. (1989). *Nomads of the present: Social movements and individual needs in contemporary society*. London: Hutchinson Radius.

Nye, R. A. (1975). *The origin of crowd psychology: Gustave Le Bon and the crisis of mass democracy in the third republic*. London: Sage.

Postmes, T., & Spears, R. (1998). De-individuation and anti-normative behaviour: A meta-analysis. *Psychological Bulletin, 123*, 238–259.

Prentice-Dunn, S., & Rogers, R. W. (1989). Deindividuation and the self-regulation of behavior. In P. B. Paulus (Ed.), *Psychology of group influence* (2nd ed., pp. 87–109). Hillsdale, NJ: Lawrence Erlbaum.

Reicher, S. D. (1982). The determination of collective behaviour In H. Tajfel (Ed.), *Social identity and intergroup relations* (pp. 41–84). Cambridge: Cambridge University Press.

Reicher, S. D. (1984). Social influence in the crowd: Attitudinal and behavioural effects of de-individuation in conditions of high and low group salience. *British Journal of Social Psychology, 23*, 341–350.

Reicher, S. D. (1987). Crowd behaviour as social action. In J. C. Turner, M. A. Hogg, P. J. Oakes, S. D. Reicher, & M. S. Wetherell (Eds.), *Rediscovering the social group: A self-categorization theory* (pp. 171–202). Oxford: Blackwell.

Reicher, S. (1996a). Social identity and social change: Rethinking the context of social psychology. In W. P. Robinson (Ed.), *Social groups and identities: Developing the legacy of Henri Tajfel* (pp. 317–336). London: Butterworth.

Reicher, S. (1996b). "The Battle of Westminster": Developing the social identity model of crowd behaviour in order to explain the initiation and development of collective conflict. *European Journal of Social Psychology, 26*, 115–134.

Reicher, S. (1996c). *The Crowd* century: Reconciling practical success with theoretical failure. *British Journal of Social Psychology, 35*, 535–553.

Reicher, S. (2001). The psychology of crowd dynamics. In M. A. Hogg and R. S. Tindale (Eds.), *Blackwell handbook of social psychology: Group processes* (pp. 182–208). Oxford: Blackwell.

Reicher, S., & Haslam, S. A. (2006a). Rethinking the psychology of tyranny: The BBC prison study. *British Journal of Social Psychology, 45*, 1–40.

Reicher, S. D., & Haslam, S. A. (2006b). Tyranny revisited: Groups, psychological well-being and the health of societies. *The Psychologist, 19*, 46–50.

Reicher, S., Haslam, S. A., & Platow, M. (2007). The new psychology of leadership. *Scientific American Mind*, August/September, 22–29.

Reicher, S., & Hopkins, N. (2001). *Self & nation*. London: Sage.

Reicher, S., & Levine, M. (1994a). Deindividuation, power relations between groups and the expression of social identity: The effects of visibility to the outgroup. *British Journal of Social Psychology, 33*, 145–163.

Reicher, S., & Levine, M. (1994b). On the consequences of deindividuation manipulations for the strategic communication of self: Identifiability and the presentation of social identity. *European Journal of Social Psychology, 24*, 511–524.

Reicher, S., Levine, M., & Gordijn, E. (1998). More on de-individuation, power relations between groups and the expression of social identity: Three studies on the effects of visibility to the ingroup. *British Journal of Social Psychology, 37*, 15–40.

Reicher, S., & Potter, J. (1985). Psychological theory as intergroup perspective: A comparative analysis of "scientific" and "lay" accounts of crowd events. *Human Relations, 38*, 167–189.

Reicher, S., Spears, R., & Postmes, T. (1995). A social identity model of deindividuation phenomena. *European Review of Social Psychology, 6*, 161–198.

Rudé, G. (1981). *The crowd in history: A study of popular disturbances in France and England, 1730–1848*. London: Lawrence & Wishart.

Simon, B., & Klandermans, B. (2001). Politicized collective identity: A social psychological analysis. *American Psychologist, 56*, 319–331.

Spears, R., Lea, M., & Lee, S. (1990). De-individuation and group polarization in computer-mediated communication. *British Journal of Social Psychology, 29*, 121–134.

Stott, C., & Drury, J. (1999). The intergroup dynamics of empowerment: A social identity model. In P. Bagguley & J. Hearn (Eds.), *Transforming politics: Power and resistance* (pp. 32–45). London: Macmillan.
Stott, C., & Drury, J. (2000). Crowds, context and identity: Dynamic categorization processes in the "poll tax riot". *Human Relations, 53*, 247–273.
Stott, C., & Reicher, S. (1998a). Crowd action as inter-group process: Introducing the police perspective. *European Journal of Social Psychology, 28*, 509–529.
Stott, C., & Reicher, S. (1998b). How conflict escalates: The inter-group dynamics of collective football crowd "violence". *Sociology, 32*, 353–377.
Tajfel, H. (Ed.) (1978). Interindividual and intergroup behaviour. In H. Tajfel (Ed.), *Differentiation between social groups: Studies in the social psychology of intergroup relations* (pp. 27–60). London: Academic Press.
Thompson, E. P. (1971). The moral economy of the English crowd in the eighteenth century. *Past & Present, 50*, 76–136.
Turner, R. H., & Killian, L. M. (1972). *Collective behavior* (2nd ed.). Englewood Cliffs, NJ: Prentice-Hall.
Turner, J. C., Hogg, M. A., Oakes, P. J., Reicher, S. D., & Wetherell, M. S. (1987). *Rediscovering the social group: A self-categorization theory.* Oxford: Blackwell.
Turner, J. C., Oakes, P. J., Haslam, S. J., & McGarty, C. (1994). Self and collective: Cognition and social context. *Personality and Social Psychology Bulletin, 20*, 454–463.
Zimbardo, P. G. (1970). The human choice: Individuation, reason and order versus de-individuation, impulse and chaos. In W. J. Arnold & D. Levine (Eds.), *Nebraska symposium on motivation 1969* (pp. 237–307). Lincoln: University of Nebraska.

JOHN DRURY is Senior Lecturer in Social Psychology at the University of Sussex, UK. His research interests include psychological change in crowd events, mass emergency behavior, and variability in the experience of crowded events. He also teaches and writes in the area of critical discourse analysis. He has just completed work on a three-year project, funded by the Economic and Social Research Council, into the relationship between social identity and mass evacuation behavior. He is a consulting editor for the *British Journal of Social Psychology*.

STEVE REICHER is Professor of Psychology at St Andrews University, UK. His research interests can be grouped into three areas. The first is an attempt to develop a model of crowd action that accounts for both social determination and social change. The second concerns the construction of social categories through language and action. The third concerns political rhetoric and mass mobilization— especially around the issue of national identity. He is the author of dozens of scholarly papers and book chapters on crowd behavior and leadership. He is a former editor of the *British Journal of Social Psychology,* and Fellow of the Royal Society of Scotland.

Collective Action—and Then What?

Winnifred R. Louis*

University of Queensland, School of Psychology

Two aspects of the social psychology of collective action are of particular interest to social movement organizers and activists: how to motivate people to engage in collective action, and how to use collective action to create social change. The second question remains almost untouched within social psychology. The present article delineates research from political science and sociology concerning variables that moderate the effectiveness of collective action and maps these variables against intergroup research. Within intergroup social psychology, there is a theoretical literature on what needs to be done to achieve change (e.g., changing identification, social norms, or perceptions of legitimacy, stability, permeability). The article considers possible testable hypotheses concerning the outcomes of collective action which can be derived from intergroup research and from the synthesis of the three disciplines. For theoreticians and practitioners alike, a program of research which addresses the social-psychological outcomes of collective action and links these to identities, norms, intentions, and support for social change in bystanders, protagonists, and opponents has a great deal of interest.

Two aspects of the social psychology of collective action are of particular interest to social movement organizers and activists: how to motivate people to engage in collective action, and how to use collective action to create social change.[1] The first has received a great deal of research attention. Empirical data suggest that people can be motivated to engage in collective action by individual instrumental

---

*Correspondence concerning this article should be addressed to Winnifred Louis, School of Psychology, McElwain Bldg, The University of Queensland, St. Lucia, QLD, Australia 4072 [e-mail: w.louis@psy.uq.edu.au].

[1] Many of the terms used in this article are defined differently across disciplines or theoretical approaches. In this article *collective action* is defined as the intentional action of individuals sharing a common group membership to benefit a group. It does not require physical and temporal proximity of members acting (e.g., I include voting and signing petitions), explicit political aims (although I focus on the political domain in this article), or prior planning (e.g., I include rioting). By *social change* I denote both formal policy change to benefit a group, and informal changes in their social value, status or power. *Outcomes of collective action* include social change but also variables such as identities, norms, sociostructural beliefs, and intergroup attitudes.

incentives and social rewards (e.g., Klandermans, 1997); social identities, or one's sense of oneself as part of a group (Tajfel & Turner, 1979; also, Deaux, Reid, Martin, & Bikmen, 2006; Simon & Klandermans, 2001; van Zomeren, Spears, Fischer, & Leach, 2004); collective effectiveness, or success in achieving group goals (e.g., Klandermans, 1997; Tajfel & Turner, 1979; Turner, Hogg, Oakes, Reicher, & Wetherell, 1987); and collective emotions such as anger (e.g., Iyer, Shmader, & Lickel, 2007; van Zomeren et al., 2004).

The second question, how to use collective action to create social change, remains almost untouched within social psychology. In fact, the outcomes of collective action have rarely been addressed—in producing policy change or provoking a backlash, at the social level; at the individual level, in consolidating or eroding identification, the sense of oneself as part of the group. The present article attempts to delineate research from political science and sociology concerning variables that moderate the effectiveness of collective action and to map these variables against intergroup research. Within intergroup social psychology, there is a theoretical literature on what needs to be done to achieve change (e.g., changing identification, social norms, or perceptions of legitimacy, stability, permeability). Little research has addressed the effectiveness of collective action in achieving these ends, the factors that moderate that effectiveness, or indeed the psychological effects of any kind of collective action on protagonists, opponents or third parties. For activists and organizers, in short, there is a gap in the literature.

The goal of this article is to describe the hypotheses that social psychologists adopting a social identity approach could make concerning the effectiveness of collective action in motivating political opponents, bystanders, and participants in collective action to change. The contributions of a model of agentic normative influence are outlined, in drawing attention to the role of out-group norms and strategic responses to achieve group goals (Louis & Taylor, 2002; Louis, Taylor, & Neil, 2004; Louis, Taylor, & Douglas, 2005). In this section of the article, a broad scope is adopted, with the aim of sketching out some of the studies needed to fill the gap in the study of collective action and social change from a social-psychological perspective. The empirical literature from sociology and political science concerning the effectiveness of collective action is then reviewed, and its implications for social psychology are addressed. Finally, I reconsider in depth a subset of untested, theoretically interesting hypotheses for intergroup psychology and the sociology/political science of collective action research which can be derived from an integration of these research streams.

An Analysis of Intergroup Approaches to Effective Collective Action

This first section of the article discusses the implications of an important theoretical framework in intergroup psychology, social identity theory, in understanding the outcomes of collective action. The model is described elsewhere in the special issue (van Zomeren & Iyer, 2009) and the literature (e.g., Bettencourt, Dorr, Charlton, & Hume, 2001; Tajfel & Turner, 1979; Turner et al., 1987). In the present article, accordingly, readers' understanding of what social identities are will be taken for granted. I will also assume readers' familiarity with the propositions that salient identities motivate conformity to group norms, and that sociostructural beliefs about permeability, instability, and illegitimacy define threat for social identities and motivate status competition.

For the purposes of this article I stress that, in the social identity approach, individuals will engage in collective action to increase the status of the group under threat, but the model also proposes that collective action will emerge naturally at other times. Activism frequently persists in the face of pessimism regarding the action's ostensible goals (e.g., Cocking & Drury, 2004; Oegema & Klandermans, 1994). As noted above, collective action can be psychologically motivating when it expresses group emotions such as anger, moral outrage, or guilt (e.g., Iyer et al., 2007; van Zomeren et al., 2004), affirms the group's distinctiveness (e.g., Jetten, Spears, & Postmes, 2004), directly expresses the group identity (e.g., Simon & Klandermans, 2001; Stürmer & Simon, 2005), or affirms the illegitimacy of an intergroup relationship (e.g., Wright & Tropp, 2002). From the point of view of social psychology more broadly, research regarding the antecedents of collective action is associated with testable hypotheses concerning the outcomes of collective action, yet few if any studies have examined the hypotheses which naturally flow from the research.[2] Does engaging in collective action assuage the degree or the aversiveness of anger, moral outrage, or guilt? Does collective action convey to bystanders, protagonists, or opponents the distinctiveness of a group, or the illegitimacy, impermeability, and instability of an intergroup relationship? From a theoretical perspective, the hypotheses are interesting because they address the feedback from behavior to cognitions and emotion, which is rarely studied in intergroup psychology.

Under a learning model, for example, collective action would be reinforced if the action reduced aversive outcomes (such as guilt), and enhanced subjectively positive outcomes (emotions such as pride, or tangible successes such as effectiveness in creating social change). Yet both at the individual and the group level, research exists to support the hypothesis that individuals' emotions and beliefs might be changed by collective action to rationalize the behavior in the absence of positive outcomes. At the individual level, self-perception theory suggests that action can lead to identification as an actor, facilitating future action in the absence of any external rewards (e.g., Libby, Shaeffer, Eibach, & Slemmer, 2007). Research on commitment processes suggests that collective action could reinforce

---

[2] Many of these hypotheses are revisited in the discussion below—the reader may find it helpful to flip ahead and review Tables 1 and 2, which list a sampling of the untested hypotheses concerning outcomes of collective action which can be derived from social-psychological research.

and polarize identification and group norms (e.g., Freedman & Fraser, 1966), while dissonance research suggests that polarization could occur not despite but because of negative outcomes of the action (e.g., Cooper, 2007). Both theory and research exist to extend these processes to the group level (e.g., Bliuc, McGarty, Reynolds, & Muntele, 2007; Festinger, Riecken, & Schachter, 1956; Haslam et al., 2006). Drury and colleagues, who have initiated the social-psychological study of the outcomes of collective action (Drury & Reicher, 2009; see also, Drury & Reicher, 2000, 2005; Drury, Cocking, Beale, Hanson, & Rapley, 2005), have specifically documented increases in identification, collective empowerment, and collective self-objectification as a result of collective action, suggesting a virtuous circle of action and motivation reinforcement even in the absence of movement "success."

There are thus competing hypotheses concerning the psychological outcomes of collective action. Simple learning theory suggests that the motivating beliefs, identities, and norms will persist and strengthen if they are reinforced by the desired outcomes of the behavior. However, self-perception research suggests that behavior itself can reinforce its motivation, independent of outcomes. Dissonance research suggests that aversive outcomes can be most likely to reinforce the underlying motivational (or rationalizing) cluster of beliefs, emotions, and identities. All of these models imply a growing spiral of committed action—yet social movements rise and fall, and wax and wane. Identifying the underlying processes, moderators, and contingencies which govern when these relationships apply is an exciting theoretical challenge.

Concerning the specific outcome of social change, little or no research has addressed the means by which group collective action might successfully change a status system, yet a number of key variables are clearly identified in intergroup theory and in many cases have been identified as triggers for collective action. A useful starting point from a social identity perspective is the proposition that collective action will create a change in the status system only to the extent it changes socio-structural beliefs or group identities.

What ought to work: Collective action to achieve social change. To start, four practices of effective social change may be derived from social identity theory. First, members of disadvantaged groups may create or increase the salience of an inclusive superordinate identity, so that advantaged group members perceive disadvantaged group members as part of a larger social identity, or "we" (e.g., Hornsey, Blackwood, & O'Brien, 2005; Wohl & Branscombe, 2005; Wohl, Branscombe, & Klar, 2006). By creating a salient superordinate identity, the collective action could change advantaged group members' legitimacy perceptions concerning intergroup inequalities, and foster emotions such as moral outrage that could induce reparatory action (e.g., Iyer et al., 2007; Nickerson & Louis, 2008). For example, in the "I have a dream" rally, Martin Luther King electrified White and Black Americans by presenting thousands of cheering rally participants united in support of a vision of a common national (American) identity. In the model advocated here, identification with a multiracial American identity would be associated with lowered perceptions of the status quo as legitimate and increased moral outrage and support for reparatory action.

Second, disruptive social action could create a sense of instability for advantaged group members, which would motivate change away from the status quo. Instability is threatening, as mentioned above, and should motivate defensive or conciliatory action to reduce the perceived threat (Louis et al., 2004, 2005; see also, e.g., Ng, 1982). Thus, for example, a wave of riots by members of disadvantaged groups could increase support for conciliatory action because they increase the perception that the status quo is unstable and threatened.

Third, challenging the permeability beliefs of advantaged group members could have the dual benefit of attenuating their sense of threat (reducing collective support for discrimination) and presenting a possible conflict between group values of egalitarianism and discriminatory practices (e.g., Wright & Taylor, 1998). If demonstrations occur to publicize examples of discriminatory behavior that hinders social mobility for disadvantaged group members, advantaged group members' intentions to discriminate further could be reduced both because of perceived security and because the discriminatory behavior itself is seen as contrary to the values of the group.

Fourth, if the challenge evokes an injunctive norm where discrimination is seen as inappropriate and widely disapproved of, the action could lead advantaged group members to change (Smith & Louis, 2008). Along similar lines as above, if demonstrations occur to publicize examples of discriminatory behavior that is seen as contrary to the values of the advantaged group itself, and particularly if advantaged group members are seen as participating in the demonstrations and condemning the behavior, the discrimination of nonparticipating advantaged group members could be reduced because they conform to the visible members of their group who have rejected the behavior.

What might backfire: Collective action that fails to achieve social change.
One interesting prediction which can be derived from social influence research is that if the collective action highlights a descriptive norm that discrimination is common and widely practiced, the action could create a backlash of increased discrimination! An example would be an antiracist campaign with a slogan such as "Ours is the most racist country in the world!" While designed to alert people to a problem, the slogan also provides a normative message that racism is common which could actually increase willingness to endorse racist action (Smith & Louis, 2008). Similarly, discrimination could be increased if collective action increases identification with the advantaged group. This rebound could occur by heightening the salience of differences between the groups, increasing cognitions of rejection (Barlow, Louis, & Hewstone, 2009), or perceived discrimination (Branscombe,

Schmitt, & Harvey, 1999), or by creating defensive resistance to an attempted imposition of a superordinate identity (e.g., Hornsey & Hogg, 2000).

An interesting trade-off is also created by the fact that action designed to highlight the commonalities among advantaged groups and disadvantaged groups and create a new superordinate "we" may achieve more positive intergroup attitudes (Wohl & Branscombe, 2005; Wohl et al., 2006). At the same time, however, it may lower disadvantaged groups' identification and collective action intentions (Greenaway, Quinn, & Louis, 2008, 2009) and further lower the salience of intergroup inequalities, and advantaged groups' intentions to take remedial action (Greenaway et al., 2009). That is, an action that is effective in mobilizing other disadvantaged group members would be one which emphasized the similarity among disadvantaged group members and their difference from the advantaged group, yet this depiction of the threatening intergroup context could fuel advantaged group identification, hostility, and discrimination.

It is certainly within the purview of social psychologists to study the effects of in-group and out-groups' collective action in changing perceptions of the intergroup relationship, identification, and norms and via these mediating factors changing willingness to redress or confront a status inequality. As well as being theoretically interesting, in elaborating the reciprocal role of behavior to identity and threat perceptions, the research would have important implications for social movement organizers.

The Role of Group Norms: An Agentic Normative Influence Model

To consider conscious decision making about options in response to intergroup conflict, I have proposed a model of agentic normative influence which focuses on norms concerning how to take action to benefit the group—the appropriateness of demonstrating versus grumbling versus rioting, for example (Louis et al., 2004, 2005). I propose that group norms shape which costs and benefits people pay attention to, how likely the consequences are seen to be, and how much they are seen to be worth. When people identify with a group in conflict, they link the costs and benefits for themselves to the group level of analysis, so that a self-sacrificing action may be seen as subjectively beneficial because it benefits the group, even though the action leads to objectively harmful consequences on an individual level. The perception of suicide bombing as personally valued martyrdom is an extreme but obvious example of willingness to consider progroup action personally beneficial despite severe personal costs of the behavior. In addition, those who identify strongly with a group may be directly motivated by perceptions of the benefits of action for the group, as when someone who does not believe in heaven is nevertheless willing to die for a cause (Louis et al., 2004). These beliefs about the benefit or cost to the group of actions such as voting or soldiering are learned, in the agentic normative influence model, from group norms (Louis et al., 2005).

An important consequence of this approach is to draw attention to exposure to group norms as an outcome of collective action, and to collective action as a vehicle for the contestation of norms and identities (see also, e.g., Drury & Reicher, 2000, 2005, 2009; Simon & Klandermans, 2001). When participants engage in collective action, they are psychologically as well as physically positioned so that others' views of the social reality are communicated and reflected to them. Through participation in collective action, actors may learn to value the dimensions of success which advantage their group. Put differently, participating in collective action teaches group members, through social creativity, not only whether the group is effective on one dimension (such as policy change) but how the group is effective: which dimensions of the social world do change in response to action. By learning to value the achievements of the group's collective action and to evaluate the effectiveness of collective action along dimensions of success, motivation for future collective action is sustained and enhanced.

An alternative model can be derived from many theories of action, however, in which identification operates in parallel to rational-choice decision making (e.g., Simon & Klandermans, 2001; Stürmer & Simon, 2005), for example through self-stereotyping processes. Again, the social as well as the theoretical implications of the competing models are worth exploring, and the nature of the effect—the impact of collective action upon beliefs, norm perceptions, and identities—are appropriate to social-psychological research.

Empirical Studies: Does Collective Action Create Social Change?

Ineffectiveness research. We take a step back now from the social psychology of perception, intention, action, and identity and turn to the sociology and political science of policy change. Dispiritingly, some sociological research suggests that democratic collective action is globally ineffective. For example, Giugni (2004) analyzed social movement organizing in three areas (environmental, antinuclear, and peace) in three countries (the United States, Switzerland, and Italy) in the late 20th century, concluding that social movements had no impact on national policy (see also, e.g., McAdam & Su, 2002; Soule & Olzak, 2004). This research is associated with the contention that public policy is linked virtually isomorphically to public opinion polls, particularly on the "salient" issues that are seen as important by at least 1% of the public (see Manza, Cook, & Page, 2002, for a review).

In the most structured line of this research, Burstein (Burstein, 2006; Burstein, Bauldry, & Froese, 2005) sampled 60 bills proposed in an American sitting of congress. Overall, 66% failed and 33% passed (a strong bias against change, which would of course be orders of magnitude larger if failed proposals for social change were broadened to include issues that never made it to the stage of proposed legislation). For bills about "off-the-radar" nonsalient issues, 77% failed versus

23% succeeding, so that inertia was stronger unless the spotlight of public opinion was fixed on the target. Where the public opposed change the success rate was lower still (86% failed and 14% succeeded). In contrast, on issues where the public supported change, the success rate was higher (41% succeeded). Where an issue remained salient over time, policy change in the direction of public opinion occurred 79% of the time. Burstein's own conclusion is thus that social movement action generally has little causal role in policy change, as both are shaped by the third factor of public opinion.

Research asserting the responsiveness of government to public opinion is starkly at odds with public perceptions of how government works. Pharr, Putnam, and Dalton (2000, pp. 9–10) note that from the 1960s to 1998, the proportion of Americans agreeing that "Most elected officials don't care what people like me think" rose from a third to nearly two thirds. In Europe and Japan, according to the authors, more variability is apparent up until the 1980s, but a general downward trend in perceived responsiveness of politicians to public opinions may be discerned over the last 20 years.

Effectiveness research: Opportunity structures. Other researchers present a more intuitive analysis of the value of collective action. Focusing on Southern businesses' responses to civil rights activism, Luders (2006) notes several instances of rapid capitulation to collective action. Luders' theoretical model can be simplified as relating effectiveness to three factors. The first two are higher vulnerability of the target to disruption costs (e.g., lost profits from disruptive collective action, or from the effects of negative publicity upon social movement supporters' consumer decisions) and lower vulnerability to concession costs (e.g., lost profits from countermobilization by opponents). Both of these relationships in turn are moderated by the target's ability to take unilateral action and/or to mobilize a like-minded coalition of businesses to meet the social movement's demands. If the target cannot meet the movement's demands, the collective action is doomed to be ineffective. Relative success in persuading businesses to desegregate is attributed by Luders to civil rights actors' targeting vulnerable sectors, for example with consumer-oriented and local/immobile sectors offering more success than businesses which did not deal directly with consumers and/or were more mobile and able to escape disruption costs.

Similar analyses of successful collective action campaigns through economic leverage on businesses have been identified in environmental areas (e.g., Seel & Plows, 2000) and labor rights activism (e.g., Spar, 1998). Within political research, collective action has been associated with increases in government welfare spending (e.g., Fording, 1997), as well as policy change (e.g., Skocpol, Abend-Wein, Howard, & Lehmann, 1993). More broadly, researchers such as Foley (2003) have argued that campaign effectiveness varies significantly as a function of favorable political opportunity structures. In these models, mobilized interest groups are necessary for policy change, but not sufficient (see also, Tarrow, 1994). Effective social change is achieved when collective actors pick a target that can change and that is responsive to the costs or benefits offered by the collective action and less responsive to the costs or benefits of countermobilization by political opponents.

Moderators: Type of movement, resources, and relationships with authority. Collective action by social movement organizations, interest groups, and political parties are not theoretically distinguished in social psychology, but important differences in outcomes can be observed and await social-psychological theorizing. For example, Burstein and Linton's (2002) review of existing research suggests that substantive effects on policy change were found 15% of the time for party organizations, and 31% of the time for nonparty organizations. Because the effects of collective action are nonsignificant or of little substantive impact in most published studies, Burstein and Linton argue that the impact of both types of organization is weak. Even a 15% success rate in inducing policy change might be welcome news to most social movement organizers, however!

Many political scientists would explain the lower success of parties relative to other groups by focusing on the proportion of swing voters mobilized as a key determinant of the effectiveness of collective action. Organizations' routine activities are thought to have less effect than novel, disruptive attention-getting techniques, since the former are already "factored in" to public opinion and thus to policy. Party organizations' collective action rarely impacts on policy, in this model, because the action does not change electoral alignment. Effectiveness may also increase in times of change, when the social movement organizations can deliver new information about trends in public opinion to politicians (e.g., Lohman, 1993).

Expanding on this point, Burstein and Linton (2002) note that measures of organizational resources, such as frequency of collective action, or membership, or budget (as proposed by resource mobilization theory), are the wrong organizational independent variables to relate to policy. To the extent that creating swing voters is the key process by which collective action creates policy change, novel collective action needs to be distinguished from routine collective action. New issues, newly formed organizations, new increases in the frequency or magnitude of collective action events: all these are expected to lead to policy change by changing electoral alignment, whereas "routine" actions maintain the status quo. Somewhat consistent with this argument, collective actions were linked by Burstein and Linton to policy outcomes 20% of the time for activities not directed at electoral politics (e.g., strikes), 60% for "routine" electoral activities, and 100% of the time (!) for "novel" electorally oriented activities.

Piven and Cloward (e.g., 1977, pp. 28–32; 1991) have elaborated the argument that routine collective action ("normative") should be distinguished from disruptive ("nonnormative") collective action in many papers.[3] That is, "protest" collective action (rule-breaking) is seen as distinct from collective action that is legitimized within a system (rule-conforming). The argument is that models which neglect this distinction fail to see the extent to which ritualized, normative conflict acknowledges and procedurally reinforces the power of advantaged groups, whereas nonnormative conflict challenges and undermines it (see also, e.g., Fording, 1997). As such, quite different predictors and outcomes may be associated with the two types of collective action. For example, normative collective action is thought to be facilitated, and nonnormative action constrained, by the presence of "vertical bonds" which link powerful and disadvantaged groups. Social psychologists might think of "bonds" in terms of shared goals and/or crosscutting or superordinate identities; in other words, superordinate goals or identities promote normative collective action and inhibit antinormative disruptive collective action. Piven and Cloward note that aggregate measures of collective action in political science and sociology are dominated by normative actions, which are more common, and thus the distinct predictors and outcomes of antinormative action are obscured. Moreover, the normative/nonnormative distinction should not be made categorically but depends on the historical and social context: "Norms change over time, in part as the result of successive challenges which produce new balances of power, reflected in new structures of rules," (Piven & Cloward, 1991, p. 440).

In terms of the outcomes of social change, an additional argument is that disruptive protest is generally more effective for disadvantaged group members because normative actions require disadvantaged groups to organize bureaucratically, and to overcome the influence of powerful groups who are likely to have more skills, money and time. In this sense, disadvantaged groups are better positioned to exert leverage with disruptive tactics. According to this theoretical framework, disruption is ineffective if the elite remains coherent and represses the protest, whereas action is effective if it contributes to fragmentation and (in democracies) electoral realignment. Piven and Cloward and other "dissensus" theorists argue that effective disruptive collective action first breaks the existing advantaged group alignment by polarizing the advantaged group on their responses to the action. A "moderate" advantaged group faction is first disempowered by protest because of defections to more conservative factions. The weakened remaining moderates are then lured/coerced to fall back on alliance with the disadvantaged group, with

---

[3] It is an important proposition of the agentic normative influence that any discussion of normative and antinormative collective action needs to consider the advantaged group's norms in interaction with the norms of the disadvantaged group, although space does not permit a full elaboration of this theoretical debate in the present article. Here, Piven and Cloward implicitly refer to *collective action* in relation to the norms of the advantaged group only, and this is the usage which I continue in the article below.

moderates motivated by their need for the alliance to make concessions to the disadvantaged group.

In this theoretical model, it is emphasized that the relationship between normative and nonnormative collective actors is not necessarily one of cooperation. The two movements are potential competitors for the same constituency. Disruptive protestors can be targeted by normative social movements who fear the alienation of their moderate allies, and/or fear extremists gaining legitimacy as representatives of the disadvantaged group and control over its resources. Similarly, disruptive protestors may attempt to wean normative social movements' supporters away to them via vigorous accusations of insufficient distinctiveness from the political opponents. This line of theorizing is associated with the contention that collective action can become less effective when it is institutionalized, because institutionalization decreases the likelihood of disruptive protest.

Implications for Social Psychology

Social psychologists have repeatedly grappled with the distinction between normative and nonnormative collective action (e.g., Wright, Taylor, & Moghaddam, 1990). Because past research focuses on collective action as an outcome, however, the focus has been on the difference in baselines (normative collective actions are more common) and the different antecedents (antinormative action is a function of more threatening sociostructural beliefs). Very little research has addressed the outcomes of antinormative versus normative collective action in changing the perceptions or political beliefs of members of activist, bystander, and targeted groups.

Institutionalization is also a moderator unaddressed by social psychology, and the subtleties of organizational resources do not clearly map onto to our research on status and power, although variables such as distinctiveness threat and sociostructural beliefs seem implicated. Whether it is novelty per se that leads to effectiveness, versus triggered perceptions of instability, impermeability, or illegitimacy; violation of social norms versus of advantaged group norms versus in-group norms; degree of inconvenience to the advantaged group versus demonstrated commitment and risk taking—all of these could be explored in relation to social-psychological variables such as subsequent salience of the issue, acceptance of the actors' position, and group identities and norms. In addition to the theoretical benefits, moreover, the research would be informative for social movement organizers, who could tailor new actions to achieve targeted psychological outcomes, rather than pursuing change purely to break "routines."

Concerning the bigger question of whether collective action is effective in creating social change, the data from which Burstein and Linton (2002) conclude that the effects of collective action are weak may be interpreted as showing the opposite: this review of top sociological and political science research finds that nonparty organizations impact significantly on policy change in 44% of studies and exerted a substantive impact 31% of the time. While the effects may be small (effect sizes are not reported), the frequently observed significant effects are both surprising and heartening, to a long-time activist. Moreover, in the political science/sociology of effectiveness, indices of social movement action are entered alongside public opinion in regression analyses predicting policy change, and public opinion typically emerges as the strongest unique predictor. The distal role of collective action in shaping public opinion, and the secondary role of public opinion as a mediator of these effects, is not typically examined.

This point bears repeating. The typical analysis in the sociological studies enters variables such as frequency or novelty of collective action in standard multiple regression alongside variables such as public opinion and considers each variable's unique effect in predicting policy change. Typically, the beta for public opinion is the largest and the others are weaker or nonsignificant. This approach is seen as supporting the argument that when a majority of public opinion supports or opposes a policy, policy makers conform to public opinion independent of social movement action. Nevertheless the failure to test a model in which public opinion mediates an indirect effect of collective action on policy change seems unwarranted. To many behavioral science statisticians, modest degree of intercorrelation among independent variables in multiple regression can be dismissed as the product of common method variance (e.g., if $r < .3$; Tabachnick & Fidell, 2007). However, replicated intercorrelations among independent variables violate the assumptions of multiple regression and invite a discussion of either mediation or third-factor causality. Within research on collective action and social conflict, I have argued that the neglect of mediation will result in systematic exaggeration of the role of proximal variables relative to the distal variables that may have shaped them (Louis, Mavor, & Terry, 2003). For example, frequency and novelty of collective action could change public opinion, which in turn changes public policy. This indirect effect would not be apparent from a standard multiple regression, which would only show the unique (direct) effect of public opinion. The indirect effect would be revealed in hierarchical multiple regression and mediation analyses, however.

Similarly, the salience of an issue in the public eye has been shown in much political science research to moderate the role of public opinion in policy change, with governments more responsive to public opinion for issues of high salience (e.g., Burstein, 2006). The distal role of social movements in shaping issue salience and thus public opinion via mediated moderation has not been addressed quantitatively, perhaps because studies of public opinion typically neglect social movement action, and vice versa. Nevertheless, if the impact of public opinion is stronger in data sets where social movement organization activities are also entered as predictors (and vice versa, as reported by Burstein & Linton, 2002), this finding is consistent with a mediated moderation model in which collective action improves the responsiveness of governments to public opinion by heightening the salience of the issue.[4]

From these considerations, I argue that an analysis of the predictors of policy change could benefit the wider collective action literature by including hitherto neglected analyses of mediation, suppression, and moderation. By integrating the salience of particular issues and the acceptance of policy as additional dependent measures linked to collective action, however, social psychologists in particular could both extend their own models of identification, norms, emotions, and sociostructural beliefs, and possibly elaborate some of the underlying processes alluded to in the sociology and political science of policy change. Although longitudinal data collection with activists is difficult and time consuming, most of the social-psychological hypotheses outlined above and discussed below could be tested with longitudinal or panel studies during an ongoing campaign, or indeed with experimental scenario studies. If, as political scientists assert, it is change in swing voters which is the more valuable driver of policy change in the longer term, studies of undergraduate students and other bystanders' reactions to collective action reports may be more socially important, as well as theoretically justifiable and of course methodologically convenient. For example, participants' identities, norms, beliefs, and willingness to redress or perpetuate conflict could be assessed after reading "news" accounts of collective action. Experimental research would also allow for more systematic manipulation of "routine" and "normative" collective action compared to "disruptive" and "antinormative" actions, in order to identify the attributes and processes that trigger or mediate the relationship between particular forms of collective action and outcomes from social change to identity and norm change.

Addressing the Social-Psychological Outcomes of Collective Action

Tables 1 and 2 summarize a subset of the theoretically interesting, largely untested, hypotheses for social-psychological and sociological/political variables. As elaborated below, a great deal of relevant social-psychological theory with clear, testable hypotheses concerning the outcomes of collective action remains to be addressed.

An analysis of intergroup approaches to effective collective action. As a starting point, I argue that the social identity approach justifies the hypothesis that a critical mediator of the effects of collective action would be changing

---

[4]"Stronger" rests on interpretation of discrete codes for the significant and magnitude of effects: Burstein and Linton (2002) assert in footnote 4 that the studies are too disparate and the methodologies too diverse for quantatitive meta-analysis to make much sense.

Table 1. A Research Agenda Testing the Outcomes of Collective Action

Plausible Outcomes	Theoretically Plausible but Untested Hypotheses
Action might directly increase identification with collective actors among onlookers	More likely with normative collective action (H1) More likely if shared superordinate identity asserted (H2)
Action that increases identification with actors among onlookers indirectly may cause:	More acceptance of actors' views (H3). More individualized perceptions of the disadvantaged group (H4) and reduced group identification for members of advantaged groups (H5). Via these further two mediators, action may reduce discrimination (H6) but also motives for reparation and compensation (H7).
Action that increases superordinate identification indirectly may cause:	Reduced group identification for disadvantaged groups (H8), and via this further mediation reduced disadvantaged group collective action intentions (H9).
Action may directly decrease the perceived legitimacy of the status quo.	More likely with identification with actors (H10). More likely with perceived instability (H11) and impermeability (H12); with more salient superordinate identity (H13) and with injunctive and descriptive norms which do not support the status quo (H14).
Action may increase instability	More likely with action that violates out-group norms (H15).
Action may increase impermeability/perceived discrimination	Less likely with superordinate identity claim (H16) Could reduce advantaged group identification (H17), reducing motivation for discrimination (H18) and also for reparation (H19).

Table 2. Implications of Critique Regarding the Effects of Collective Action for Sociological Research

Existing Finding	Five Theoretically Plausible but Untested Hypotheses
Public opinion is the strongest proximal predictor of policy change	The unique effect of public opinion is the product of significant indirect effects of collective action (H1; public opinion is a mediator). The indirect effect of collective action via public opinion is stronger for normative collective action (H2); Antinormative action can lead to a backlash in public opinion (H3a) mediated via decreased identification with the collective actors (H3b)
Public opinion is a stronger predictor of policy change for high salience issues	Collective action increases the salience of an issue (H4a) and therefore the effect of salience in strengthening the impact of public opinion upon policy change is the product of significant indirect effects of collective action (H4b; collective action indirectly moderates the public opinion—policy link via its indirect effects on salience) Antinormative collective action has a stronger effect on salience (H5a) and therefore a stronger moderated mediation effect on policy change (H5b)

identification in participants (e.g., Bliuc et al., 2007), as well as bystanders and advantaged group members. Onlookers may be more likely to accept collective actors' criticisms of the status quo if the onlookers come to identify with the actors, which could be encouraged by collective actors' rhetorical claims to a common identity, as in the antiracist group Australians for Native Title and Reconciliation, which positions itself by its name as representing the larger national superordinate group (see also, e.g., Hornsey et al., 2005). Superordinate identity claims might also be invoked through behavioral conformity to superordinate group norms, as when human rights campaigners wave national flags or sign the national anthem at a rally which seeks to improve minority group rights (see also, Louis & Taylor, 2002).

As noted above, if advantaged group members identify with the collective actors, however, they may disidentify with their own advantaged group, which would have the positive effect of creating positive intergroup attitudes (Wohl & Branscombe, 2005; Wohl et al., 2006), but also may reduce motives to acknowledge status inequalities and to offer reparation (Greenaway et al., 2009). Bystanders from a disadvantaged group could also be motivated by assertions of a shared superordinate identity to disidentify and to reduce their collective action intentions (Greenaway et al., 2009). Finally, if advantaged group members reject the claims posed by a collective action such as a rally with flag waving to a superordinate identity such as a nation (Hornsey & Hogg, 2000), or if advantaged group members position the disadvantaged group as inferior, deviant members of the shared identity (Mummendey & Wenzel, 1999), increased advantaged group identification could ensue with consequent increases in discrimination or rejection of the collective actors' position.

If the identity dynamics were not shaped directly by the behavior and rhetoric of the collective actors, they might be indirectly driven by changes to sociostructural beliefs that shape actions and attitudes (e.g., Louis, Duck, Terry, Schuller, & Lalonde, 2007; Wright & Tropp, 2002). Challenging the legitimacy of the status quo is a common goal of collective action; for example, the "fair trade" movement directly calls into question the fairness of existing trade relations between developed and developing countries. Changes in perceived legitimacy should be more likely to the extent that bystanders identify with the collective actors. If bystanders are not members of the collective actors' constituency (e.g., a disadvantaged group), illegitimacy perceptions could also be facilitated by the assertion of a shared superordinate identity, particularly if that higher group has norms that do not support discrimination or subgroup inequality. Moreover, to the extent that the three dimensions of threat mutually reinforce each other, impermeability and instability perceptions should facilitate the acceptance of claimed illegitimacy (and vice versa).

Perceived instability, or perceptions of change in intergroup relations, promotes identification and action in both groups, as noted above. Arguably, perceived instability would be increased by antinormative action, with its disruptive and unexpected challenge to the status quo (Piven & Cloward, 1991; Wright et al., 1990). Impermeability beliefs are also vital targets of collective action, as Wright's research shows that perceived permeability reduces disadvantaged militance almost entirely. Demonstrating the existence of enduring inequalities between groups, or situations in which disadvantaged group members were denied the opportunity for social mobility solely because of their group membership, could itself increase disadvantaged group members' mobilization for challenging discrimination and reduce advantaged group members' motivation for discrimination by changes to permeability and legitimacy beliefs. However, impermeability beliefs may be more difficult to assert in the context of a claimed superordinate identity as this latter would direct attention away from subgroup differences, potentially reducing both advantaged and disadvantaged group members' identification. All of these theoretically derived predictions await empirical testing in relation to collective action.

I want to note, however, that in outlining a research plan described in terms of quantitative analyses and experimentation, in which variables at the individual and group levels form feedback loops of mutual influence, I do not dismiss the valuable work of Reicher, Drury and colleagues in intergroup psychology or others (particularly those working in positioning theory; Louis, 2008) who have used discursive methods to analyze the psychology of political action and political aspects of psychology. In my own model, group-level variables are seen as influencing action directly (as in Drury's approach), but also indirectly via individual-level variables (mediation) and by cueing the relevance of individual-level variables for collective action (moderation). In turn, interacting individual-level variables such as level of identification and intentions to act predict group-level variables, such as frequency and efficacy of collective action—and neither direction of relationship should be assumed to be linear or well modeled by multiple regression (see Louis, 2008; Louis et al., 2003). However, the fundamentals of any intergroup social-psychological approach, I argue, emphasize the role of group identity, the importance of the group level of analysis, and the value of looking at collective action participation as an independent variable with interesting flow on effects, rather than solely as a dependent measure.

Implications for Activists and Organizers

The present article argues is that there is a wide gap in the literature around the effectiveness of collective action in achieving social change which means that there is no definitive advice allowing practitioners to choose among the many contradictory theoretical models. Burstein and colleagues' work suggests that collective action is globally ineffective in triggering policy change, though it might magnify the impact of sympathetic public opinion by increasing the salience of an issue. Many other theorists have argued that effectiveness depends on a favorable opportunity structure, which can be crudely summarized as a target with the power to change, vulnerability to collective actors' rewards/punishments, and relatively less vulnerability to countermobilization from opponents. Identifying these targets is easier retrospectively than prospectively, however!

Some researchers, particularly dissensus researchers such as Piven and Cloward, would emphasize the value of novel or disruptive or nonnormative collective action over routine, institutionalized action. This point is contested, and the mechanism for effective versus marginalizing disruptive action is not well known. Social-psychological theories could be used to hypothesize that collective action that increases disadvantaged group members' identification by focusing on threatening sociostructural beliefs would create a virtuous cycle of growing protest and action. At the same time, such models would suggest that more salient threat perceptions could also strengthen advantaged group members' identification and motivation to discriminate and countermobilize.

Other social-psychological models would emphasize trying to focus on superordinate shared identities (e.g., "American" instead of Black vs. White, or North vs. South). The logic is that this salient shared identity would erode advantaged group identification and promote perceptions of a shared "we" that would lead advantaged group members to be nice to those from disadvantaged groups since they are all in the superordinate group together. But then again, such models would predict that salient superordinate identities would lower the salience of intergroup inequality, which would lower advantaged group motivation to take responsibility for their past action and make amends, as well as disadvantaged group motivation for militance.

My own intuition is for the dissensus model proposed by Piven and Cloward and others, although I emphasize the mediating role of identities and norm perceptions. I also believe that many of the contradictions above concerning strategy and theoretical predictions reflect real suppression effects, in which triggers such as antinormative action or superordinate "we" claims have both inhibitory and facilitatory effects on social change (they increase it and decrease it at the same time). Suppression effects mean real dilemmas for organizers. For example, disruptive collective action which most strongly boosts the identification and commitment of a disadvantaged group also creates a backlash of increased identification from advantaged group opponents. Similarly, collective action which successfully creates a shared superordinate identity with opponents and fosters a norm of cooperation will *also*, I believe, foster advantaged group members' motivation for denial of past wrongs and inhibit disadvantaged group members' militance (Greenaway et al., 2009).

It is because collective action triggers opposing forces at the same time, I believe, that social movements with moderate and militant wings are advantaged in creating leverage for social change. The militant wing is needed to create salience for the issue through disruptive/antinormative action which also increases the salience of threatening sociostructural perceptions for the constituency and thus increases identification. The moderate wing capitalizes on the mobilized constituency members but complies with the target group's rules or norms and offers the possibility of compromise by emphasizing shared goals or fate. In that sense, the implications of the approach for organizers would be to do what is not being done already. Organizers could focus on disruptive, militant action if the other actors for the goal are moderate, or if existing militant groups are not coordinating their actions strategically with moderates. Militant factions which primarily attack the moderates are quite likely counterproductive in achieving social change; this too awaits empirical testing in social psychology, but activist experience would certainly provide anecdotal evidence! Strategic militants might profitably attack their political opponents through assertions of illegitimacy and impermeability, as well as behaviors that create perceived instability and raise the salience of these normative and identity claims. Their assertion of extreme demands offers the opportunity for moderates to capitalize on disadvantaged group mobilization and advantaged group insecurity with an offer of a less extreme concession.

In contrast, organizers could work to develop moderate "mainstream" approaches if the other collective actors on the issue are militant. Moderates' reward of advantaged groups' concessions creates the possibility for incremental change towards the disadvantaged group's goals; without this validation and reward, the possibility for polarization and increased discrimination is arguably enhanced. As an extension of this point, a context of public sympathy with the cause but little policy action would call for two separate groups, with strategic disruptive/novel/nonnormative action by one faction while a group of more mainstream activists deplores the militants' behavior and uses the spotlight for leverage.

This general approach is not necessarily novel in activist circles, and it must also be acknowledged that both ethical and pragmatic concerns constrain the use of disruption and antinormative action in some contexts. Moreover, the same social-psychological models that may inform and guide the tactical choices of activists and organizers will equally profitably be applied by advantaged group countermobilization; indeed I have discussed these theoretical models at length in the context of recommendations for counter- or antiterrorism policy (Louis, 2009; Louis & Taylor, 2002). A major purpose of this article, however, is to propose that the effects of these forms of collective action should be studied empirically. Through research and field experimentation, the questions of which strategies work when, if at all, and by which means, could be addressed.

Conclusions

Concerning the specific outcome of social change, little or no research has addressed the means by which group collective action might successfully change a status system. A number of key variables are clearly identified in intergroup theory, however, and in many cases have been identified as triggers for collective action. As noted above, a useful starting point from a social-psychological perspective is the proposition that collective action will create a change in the status system only to the extent it changes sociostructural beliefs and group identities and norms. But without being required to engage the social psychology of decision making, sociological and political science research on policy change could benefit from considering the indirect roles of collective action to policy change via changing public opinion (mediation) and via increased salience (mediated moderation).

While no one study can address the research questions described above, a program of research that would address the social-psychological outcomes of collective action and link these to identities, norms, and future action intentions, has a great deal of interest for theoreticians and practitioners alike. With the help of data concerning the impact of collective action on protagonists, opponents, and bystanders, the theory of collective action and conflict and the effectiveness of social movement organizing may both benefit.

References

Barlow, F. K., Louis, W. R., & Hewstone, M. (2009). Rejected! Cognitions of rejection and intergroup anxiety as mediators of the impact of crossgroup friendships on prejudice. *British Journal of Social Psychology, 48*(3), 389–405.

Bettencourt, B. A., Dorr, N., Charlton, K., & Hume, D. L. (2001). Status differences and in-group bias: A meta-analytic examination of the effects of status stability, status legitimacy, and group permeability. *Psychological Bulletin, 127*, 520–542.

Bliuc, A.-M., McGarty, C., Reynolds, K. J., & Muntele, O. (2007). Opinion-based group membership as a predictor of commitment to political action. *European Journal of Social Psychology, 37*, 19–32.

Branscombe, N. R., Schmitt, M. T., & Harvey, R. D. (1999). Perceiving pervasive discrimination among African Americans: Implications for group identification and well-being. *Journal of Personality and Social Psychology, 77*, 135–149.

Burstein, P. (2006). Why estimates of the impact of public opinion on public policy are too high: Empirical and theoretical implications. *Social Forces, 84*, 2273–2290.

Burstein, P., & Linton, A. (2002). The impact of political parties, interest groups, and social movement organizations on public policy: Some recent evidence and theoretical concerns. *Social Forces, 81*, 380–408.

Burstein, P., Bauldry, S., & Froese, P. (2005). Bill sponsorship and congressional support for policy proposals. *Political Research Quarterly, 58*, 295–302.

Cocking, C., & Drury, J. (2004). Generalization of efficacy as a function of collective action and intergroup relations: Involvement in an anti-roads struggle. *Journal of Applied Social Psychology, 34*, 417–444.

Cooper, J. (2007). *Cognitive dissonance: Fifty years of a classic theory*. Thousand Oaks, CA: Sage Publications.

Deaux, K., Reid, A., Martin, D., & Bikmen, N. (2006). Ideologies of diversity and inequality: Predicting collective action in groups varying in ethnicity and immigrant status. *Political Psychology, 27*, 123–146.

Drury, J., & Reicher, S. (2000). Collective action and psychological change: The emergence of new social identities. *British Journal of Social Psychology, 39*, 579–604.

Drury, J., & Reicher, S. (2005). Explaining enduring empowerment: A comparative study of collective action and psychological outcomes. *European Journal of Social Psychology, 35*, 35–58.

Drury, J., & Reicher, S. (2009). Collective psychological empowerment as a model of social change: Researching crowds and power. *Journal of Social Issues, 65*, 707–725.

Drury, J., Cocking, C., Beale, J., Hanson, C., & Rapley, F. (2005). The phenomenology of empowerment in collective action. *British Journal of Social Psychology, 44*, 309–328.

Festinger, L., Riecken, H. W., & Schachter, S. (1956). *When prophecy fails*. Minneapolis: University of Minnesota Press.

Foley, J. R. (2003). Mobilization and change in a trade union setting: Environment, structures and action. *Work, Employment, & Society, 17*, 247–268.

Fording, R. C. (1997). The conditional effect of violence as a political tactic: Mass insurgency, welfare generosity, and electoral context in the American States. *American Journal of Political Science, 41*, 1–29.

Freedman, J. L., & Fraser, S. C. (1966). Compliance without pressure: The foot-in-the-door technique. *Journal of Personality and Social Psychology, 4*, 195–202.

Giugni, M. (2004). *Social protest and policy change: Ecology, antinuclear, and peace movements in comparative perspective*. Lanham, MD: Rowman and Littlefield.

Greenaway, K., Quinn, E. A., & Louis, W. R. (2009). *Appealing to shared humanity: Sinister implications for forgiveness (expectations) and collective action (support) among victims and perpetrators of historical atrocities*. Manuscript in preparation.

Haslam, S. A., Ryan, M. K., Postmes, T., Spears, R., Jetten, J., & Webley, P. (2006). Sticking to our guns: Social identity as a basis for the maintenance of commitment to faltering organizational projects. *Journal of Organizational Behavior, 27*, 607–628.

Hornsey, M. J., & Hogg, M. A. (2000). Subgroup relations: A comparison of mutual intergroup differentiation and common ingroup identity models of prejudice reduction. *Personality and Social Psychology Bulletin, 26*(2), 242–256.

Hornsey, M. J., Blackwood, L., & O'Brien, A. (2005). Speaking for others: The pros and cons of group advocates using collective language. *Group Processes & Intergroup Relations, 8*, 245–257.

Iyer, A., Schmader, T., & Lickel, B. (2007). Why individuals protest the perceived transgressions of their country: The role of anger, shame, and guilt. *Personality and Social Psychology Bulletin, 33*, 572–587.

Jetten, J., Spears, R., & Postmes, T. (2004). Intergroup distinctiveness and differentiation: A meta-analytic integration. *Journal of Personality and Social Psychology, 86*, 862–879.

Klandermans, B. (1997). *The social psychology of protest*. Oxford: Blackwell.

Libby, L. K., Shaeffer, E. M., Eibach, R. P., & Slemmer, J. A. (2007). Picture yourself at the polls: Visual perspective in mental imagery affects self-perception and behavior. *Psychological Science, 18*, 199–203.

Lohmann, S. (1993). A signalling model of informative and manipulative political action. *American Political Science Review, 87*, 319–333.

Louis, W. R. (2008). Intergroup positioning and power. In F. M. Moghaddam, R. Harré, & N. Lee (Eds.), *Global conflict resolution through positioning analysis* (pp. 21–39). New York: Springer.

Louis, W. R. (2009). If they're not crazy, then what? The implications of social psychological approaches to terrorism for conflict management. In W. Stritzke, S. Lewandowsky, D. Denemark, F. Morgan, & J. Clare (Eds.), *Terrorism and torture: An interdisciplinary perspective* (pp. 125–153). Cambridge: Cambridge University Press.

Louis, W. R., & Taylor, D. M. (2002). Understanding the September 11th terrorist attack on America: The role of intergroup theories of normative influence. *Analyses of Social Issues and Public Policy, 2*, 87–100.

Louis, W. R., Mavor, K. I., & Terry, D. J. (2003). Reflections on the statistical analysis of personality and norms in war, peace, and prejudice: Are deviant minorities the problem? *Analyses of Social Issues and Public Policy, 3*, 189–198.

Louis, W. R., Taylor, D. M., & Neil, T. (2004). Cost-benefit analyses for your group and your self: The rationality of decision-making in conflict. *International Journal of Conflict Management, 15*(2), 110–143.

Louis, W. R., Taylor, D. M., & Douglas, R. L. (2005). Normative influence and rational conflict decisions: Group norms and cost-benefit analyses for intergroup behavior. *Group Processes and Intergroup Relations, 8*(4), 355–374.
Louis, W. R., Duck, J., Terry, D. J., Schuller, R., & Lalonde, R. (2007). Why do citizens want to keep refugees out? Threats, fairness and hostile norms in the treatment of asylum seekers. *European Journal of Social Psychology, 37*, 53–73.
Luders, J. (2006). The economics of movement success: Business responses to civil rights mobilization. *American Journal of Sociology, 111*, 963–998.
Manza, J., Cook, F. L., & Page, B. I. (2002). *Navigating public opinion: Polls, policy, and the future of American democracy*. Oxford: Oxford University Press.
McAdam, D., & Su, Y. (2002). The war at home: Antiwar protests and congressional voting, 1965 to 1973. *American Sociological Review, 67*, 696–721.
Mummendey, A., & Wenzel, M. (1999). Social discrimination and tolerance in intergroup relations: Reactions to intergroup difference. *Personality and Social Psychology Review, 3*(2), 158–174.
Ng, S.-H. (1982). Power and appeasement in intergroup discrimination. *Australian Journal of Psychology, 34*(1), 37–44.
Nickerson, A. M., & Louis, W. R. (2008). Nationality versus humanity? Personality, identity, and norms in relation to attitudes toward asylum seekers. *Journal of Applied Social Psychology, 38*, 796–817.
Oegema, D., & Klandermans, B. (1994). Why social movement sympathizers don't participate: Erosion and nonconversion of support. *American Sociological Review, 59*, 703–722.
Pharr, S. J., Putnam, R. D., & Dalton, R. J. (2000). Trouble in the advanced democracies? A quarter century of declining confidence. *Journal of Democracy, 11*, 5–25.
Piven, F. F., & Cloward, R. A. (1977). *Poor people's movements: Why they succeed, how they fail.* New York: Vintage Books.
Piven, F. F., & Cloward, R. A. (1991). Collective protest: A critique of resource mobilization theory. *International Journal of Politics, Culture and Society, 4*, 435–458.
Seel, B., & Plows, A. (2000). Coming live and direct! In B. Seel, M. Paterson, & B. Doherty (Eds.), *Direct action in British environmentalism* (pp. 112–132). New York: Routledge.
Skocpol, T., Abend-Wein, M., Howard, C., & Lehmann, S. G. (1993). Women's associations and the enactment of mothers' pensions in the US. *American Political Science Review, 87*, 686–701.
Simon, B., & Klandermans, B. (2001). Politicized collective identity: A social psychological analysis. *American Psychologist, 56*, 319–331.
Smith, J. R., & Louis, W. R. (2008). Do as we say and as we do: The interplay of descriptive and injunctive group norms in the attitude-behaviour relationship. *British Journal of Social Psychology, 47*, 647–666.
Soule, S. A., & Olzak, S. (2004). When do movements matter? The politics of contingency and the Equal Rights Amendment. *American Sociological Review, 69*, 473–497.
Spar, D. L. (1998). The spotlight on the bottom line: How multinationals export human rights. *Foreign Affairs, 77*, 7–12.
Stürmer, S., & Simon, B. (2005). Collective action: Towards a dual-pathway model. *European Review of Social Psychology, 15*, 59–99.
Tabachnick, B. G., & Fidell, L. S. (2007). *Using multivariate statistics*. Boston: Allyn and Bacon.
Tajfel, H., & Turner, J. C. (1979). An integrative theory of intergroup conflict. In W. G. Austin & S. Worchel (Eds.), *The social psychology of intergroup relations* (pp. 33–47). Monterey, CA: Brooks/Cole.
Tarrow, S. (1994). *Power in movement: Social movements and contentious politics*. New York: Cambridge University Press.
Turner, J., Hogg, M., Oakes, P., Reicher, S., & Wetherell, M. (1987). *Rediscovering the social group: A self-categorization theory*. Oxford: Blackwell.
van Zomeren, M., & Iyer, A. (2009). An introduction to the social and psychological dynamics of collective action. *Journal of Social Issues, 65*, 645–660.

van Zomeren, M., Spears, R., Fischer, A. H., & Leach, C. W. (2004). Put your money where your mouth is! Explaining collective action tendencies through group-based anger and group efficacy. *Journal of Personality and Social Psychology, 87*, 649–664.

Wohl, M. J. A., & Branscombe, N. R. (2005). Forgiveness and collective guilt assignment to historical perpetrator groups depend on level of social category inclusiveness. *Journal of Personality and Social Psychology, 88*, 288–303.

Wohl, M. J. A., Branscombe, N. R., & Klar, Y. (2006). Collective guilt: Emotional reactions when one's group has done wrong or been wronged. *European Review of Social Psychology, 17*, 1–37.

Wright, S. C., & Taylor, D. M. (1998). Responding to Tokenism: Individual action in the face of collective injustice. *European Journal of Social Psychology, 28*, 647–667.

Wright, S. C., & Tropp, L. (2002). Collective action in response to disadvantage: Intergroup perceptions, social identification, and social change. In I. Walker & H. Smith (Eds.), *Relative deprivation: Specification, development, and integration*. New York: Cambridge University Press.

Wright, S. C., Taylor, D. M., & Moghaddam, F. M. (1990). Responding to membership in a disadvantaged group: From acceptance to collective protest. *Journal of Personality & Social Psychology, 58*, 994–1003.

WINNIFRED R. LOUIS (PhD 2001, McGill University, Canada) is a senior lecturer in the school of psychology at the University of Queensland. She is a co-director of the Centre for Research on Group Processes at UQ, and a Research Associate of the Australian Centre for Peace and Conflict Studies. Her theoretical interests as well as experience as a community activist have led her to focus her research on decision making in intergroup conflict; social influence, norms, and identification; and collective action. This research was supported under the Australian Research Council's Discovery funding scheme (project number DP0663937).

Collective Action in Modern Times: How Modern Expressions of Prejudice Prevent Collective Action

Naomi Ellemers* and Manuela Barreto
Leiden University

This contribution addresses modern forms of group-based discrimination, and examines how these impact upon the likelihood that people engage in collective action. Based on a review of the relevant literature, we predict that modern expressions of prejudice are less likely to be perceived as indicating group-based disadvantage and hence elicit less anger, protest, and collective action than old-fashioned prejudice. We present three studies to offer empirical support for this prediction. In Study 1 (N = 116), female participants were led to believe that the general public endorses either old-fashioned or modern sexist views. In Study 2 (N = 44) and 3 (N = 37) female participants were exposed to a student supervisor who allegedly held either old-fashioned or modern sexist views. Results of all three studies indicate that modern sexism is less likely to be perceived as a form of discrimination, and as a result elicits less anger at the source and less support for collective action (Study 1), intentions to protest (Study 2), and collective protest behavior (Study 3) than old-fashioned sexism. In discussing the results of this research, we connect to current insights on antecedents of collective action, and identify conclusions from our analysis that are relevant for societal and organizational policy making.

Even though people tend to think that group-based prejudice and discrimination is a thing of the past, statistics show that equality between members of different groups has not been achieved. Importantly, attempts to account for such differences by referring to differential individual ability, motivation, or life choices

---

*Correspondence concerning this article should be addressed to Naomi Ellemers, Institutde for Psychological Research, Leiden University, P.O. Box 9555, 2300 RB Leiden, The Netherlands [e-mail: Ellemers@fsw.leidenuniv.nl].

This research was made possible through funding from the Dutch Science Foundation (NWO, Vernieuwingsimpuls) awarded to Manuela Barreto. We thank Dorien de Landstheer, Jeannette Honée, Angele Baas, Nicole Dujardin, Marian Hiekendorff, Dayanara Nijhoeve, Lenneke van Schoonhoven, Renee Verhaar, Renske Verweijen, and Ikram Yasbah for assistance with data collection. Manuela Barreto is currently employed at the Centre for Social Research and Intervention, Lisbon, Portugal.

do not appear to be tenable. Instead, there is ample evidence that group-based discrimination adversely affects the treatment, evaluation, and opportunities offered for instance to women as compared to men (e.g., Bartol, 1999; Crosby, Williams, & Biernat, 2004; Graves, 1999; Heilman, 2001). Nevertheless, special provisions for members of particular social groups tend to be considered unnecessary, unfair, or even illegal (see also Nielsen & Nelson, 2005). Thus, the evidence that group-based prejudice and discrimination continues to exist apparently does not result in the endorsement of collective action aiming to redress this. As a result, measures that might help provide equal opportunities for members of disadvantaged groups (affirmative action policies) have been terminated. Why? This is what we examine in the present contribution.

Our central proposition is that the way in which prejudice against certain social groups is expressed nowadays prevents members of these groups from engaging in collective action. Specifically, we posit that modern sexism is less likely to be perceived as a form of prejudice than old-fashioned sexism, and that as a result group members are less likely to experience anger at those who express modern sexism, which in turn prevents them from engaging in protest or collective action. We present evidence for this prediction from three studies, in which we compare the effects of old-fashioned versus modern expressions of sexism on the likelihood that women will engage in protest or collective action. We also examine the psychological process underlying these effects, in terms of the resulting levels of perceived prejudice and anger at the source.

Old-Fashioned and Modern Expressions of Prejudice

Our analysis builds on the notion that for people to engage in protest or collective action they first have to acknowledge that they and other members of their group are treated unjustly. Because prejudice is expressed nowadays in quite indirect and subtle ways (Swim, Aikin, Hall, & Hunter, 1995; Tougas, Brown, Beaton, & Joly, 1995), it has become more difficult to recognize instances of discrimination. We therefore focus on recognition of prejudice and discrimination (or the failure to do so) as an important factor in the emergence of collective action. Our reasoning is based on the proposition that the unwillingness to believe that sexism continues to be a problem in contemporary Western societies constitutes a form of prejudice in itself.

The term *prejudice* is often used in a traditional sense to refer to the explicit belief that members of certain groups are inherently inferior (such as that women are not capable of taking on leadership responsibilities, see Eagly & Karau, 2002; Eagly, Karau, & Makhijani, 1995). This is currently referred to as "old-fashioned" sexism. Nowadays, people tend to refrain from overtly expressing such blatantly prejudicial beliefs (Plant & Devine, 1998). Modern expressions of prejudice communicate these same beliefs but do so in more indirect ways

(Swim & Campbell, 2001; Swim et al., 1995), in which the failure to acknowledge group-based disadvantage is key. That is, "modern sexism" notes the systematic inequality in outcomes between members of different groups, while pointing out that this is not due to any form of systematic disadvantage (Swim et al., 1995). This then implicitly conveys that the inequality in outcomes must reflect some lack in deservingness among members of disadvantaged groups. Indeed, modern sexist views are further characterized by resentment of demands for equal treatment, and antagonism against special measures to ensure such treatment (Swim et al., 1995). Thus, denial of discrimination is a central aspect of modern sexism.

Previous research has shown that—compared to old-fashioned sexism—modern expressions of sexism make it more difficult to recognize that prejudicial beliefs are being conveyed (Barreto & Ellemers, 2005a, b). As a consequence, unfavorable individual outcomes as well as broader evidence of group disadvantage tend to be attributed to a lack of deservingness on the part of the individuals in question (see Crocker, Major, & Steele, 1998 for a review). The failure to recognize prejudicial beliefs—and the resulting conclusion that unfavorable outcomes can only be due to personal inadequacies—sets in motion a self-fulfilling cycle. That is, research has shown that the failure to recognize gender-based discrimination when this occurs in subtle ways matches the conviction that women are generally less deserving or able than men. As a result, women feel more uncertain and insecure and actually perform less well on relevant tasks, in effect confirming gender stereotypes (see Barreto, Ellemers, Cihangir, & Stroebe, 2008, for an overview). By contrast, unfavorable outcomes are more easily discounted when these can be seen to result from old-fashioned and more blatant forms of prejudice (Barreto & Ellemers, 2009; see also Major, Kaiser, & McCoy, 2003; Major, Quinton, & Schmader, 2003). Importantly the perception of discrimination mediated these different responses—not the negativity of the rejection experience nor participants' own agreement with different types of sexist views (Barreto et al., 2008).

Adverse Consequences of Exposure to Modern Sexism

More recently, research has elaborated on the diverging emotional consequences of different forms of sexism. So far this work has focused on the adverse consequences that subtle expressions of sexism can have for the self, for instance by examining how sexist beliefs or sexist treatment affect women's self-views and self-confidence. Across different studies it was observed that exposure to modern and more subtle forms of sexism caused women to report negative self-directed emotions (anxiety, insecurity; Barreto & Ellemers, 2005a, b). Modern sexism also elicited stereotype-consistent self-presentation and induced suboptimal task behavior (Cihangir, Barreto, & Ellemers, in press), setting in motion a cycle of stereotype-confirming and self-defeating behavior. By contrast, those who were exposed to more old-fashioned and blatant expressions of sexism displayed less evidence of self-defeating behavior. Our current aim is to elaborate on how modern versus old-fashioned expressions of sexism affect responses people direct toward others, and examine the behaviors they may show to challenge the prejudice they are exposed to. Specifically, we address the likelihood that modern versus old-fashioned expressions of sexism elicit anger toward those expressing such beliefs and raise intentions to protest or support for collective action.

Antecedents of Collective Action

Previous work on the antecedents of collective action has emphasized the social nature of this type of response, in that it has explicitly addressed collective action as a form of group behavior. For instance, researchers have examined the likelihood that people will join existing interest groups (e.g., Simon et al., 1998), or participate in an ongoing activity or protest (e.g., Reicher, 1984; Veenstra & Haslam, 2000; see Kelly & Breinlinger, 1996, for an overview). Thus previous work tends to address people's willingness to become involved in some form of action in situations in which the collective injustice is relatively clear. That is, there is some preexisting organization (e.g., gay movement, trade union) or ongoing activity (political protest, union march) to support the group's cause, in which individual group members can choose whether or not to participate.

In the present research we address the phase preceding the one examined in previous research. That is, we focus on the emergence of the awareness that collective action is in order. In doing this, we build on the literature on relative deprivation, which points to the acknowledgment of "fraternal deprivation" as an essential element in this process (see also Pettigrew, 2002; Tyler & Lind, 2002). According to this reasoning, rather than the personal experience of being disadvantaged, the recognition that the group as a whole suffers unjust disadvantage motivates people to engage in protest and collective action (Ellemers, 2002; Smith & Ortiz, 2002; Tyler, Boeckmann, Smith, & Huo, 1997; Wright & Tropp, 2002). Importantly, it has been emphasized that the conviction that group-level treatment is unfair—not the mere awareness that the group's outcomes are unfavorable—is key to the experience of group-level deprivation (Tyler & Lind, 2002). Accordingly, we argue that the awareness of group-based disadvantage (recognition of discrimination) that gives rise to the emotional experience of injustice (anger at the source of discrimination) is crucial in motivating group members toward collective action (see also Van Zomeren, Spears, Fisher, & Leach, 2004).

The Present Research

With the present research we connect current knowledge on relative deprivation and the antecedents of collective action to recent insights on the pernicious effects of modern expressions of prejudice. Based on previous research we predict that the way in which sexism is expressed determines the likelihood that group-level disadvantage is perceived. We argue that the explicit awareness of group-based disadvantage is a necessary precondition to be able to address the prejudicial views of others, instead of focusing on potential shortcomings of the self. We thus predict that perceived discrimination induces anger at the perpetrators of such discrimination, which in turn makes it more likely that people engage in some form of protest or collective action.

We present three studies on how modern expressions of sexism—characterized by a denial of group-based disadvantage—impact on the emergence of collective action. Specifically, we test whether modern (compared to old-fashioned) expressions of sexism undermine support for collective action (Study 1), intentions to protest (Study 2), and behavioral engagement in collective protest (Study 3). Additionally, we examine the psychological process underlying these effects, by testing our prediction that the way in which sexism is expressed determines the likelihood that group-based disadvantage is perceived, which in turn elicits anger at those expressing sexism and facilitates the emergence of collective action attempts. In Study 1, participants are exposed to the alleged results of a public opinion poll, expressing endorsement of either old-fashioned or modern sexist views. In Studies 2 and 3, we examine responses of participants to the (modern or old-fashioned sexist) opinions of a prospective supervisor for their student internship. Study 1 examines support for collective action. Study 2 assesses participants' intentions to protest. Study 3 focuses on actual protest behavior, distinguishing explicitly between individual and collective forms of protest, and additionally examines the degree to which participants identify with their gender group as a result of the modern versus old-fashioned sexist views they are exposed to.

Study 1

Method

Design and participants. Participants read about the prevalence of either old-fashioned or modern sexism in Dutch public opinion. Participants were 113 Dutch female undergraduate students, recruited at the University campus. Their age was not registered. All participants took part in a lottery, as a result of which 10 participants received 25 Euros.

Procedure. Participants received a package which contained the experimental manipulation as well as the dependent variables. On the first page, participants read that a prior study had revealed opinions about work and the workplace among a sample of the Dutch population. Some of these opinions were allegedly shown in the next paragraph. Depending on experimental condition, these opinions either consisted of old-fashioned sexist statements or of modern sexist statements. To manipulate old-fashioned sexism, we adapted five statements from the old-fashioned sexism scale by Swim et al. (1995). For instance, participants read that the men and women in the sample allegedly studied believe that women are less intelligent than men. For the modern sexist condition, we selected items from the subscale of denial of discrimination of the modern sexism scale by Swim et al. (1995). These communicate in more veiled ways that women are less worthy than men, for instance by stating that the fact that few women have high positions is not caused by discrimination. Participants were subsequently asked to indicate what they thought of these opinions and of the people who had allegedly expressed them.

Dependent measures. Perceived sexism was assessed by asking participants to indicate the extent to which they thought the people who had allegedly participated in the public opinion survey were prejudiced, sexist, and unfair (one factor explained 66% of variance, $\alpha = .90$). Following previous work (Barreto & Ellemers, 2005a, b) anger at the source was assessed by asking participants to indicate to what extent they experienced four negative emotions directed at people holding these beliefs (angry, indignant, frustrated, and disappointed; one factor explained 74% of variance, $\alpha = .88$). Support for collective action was assessed with two items (women should resist collectively, I am willing to join collective action in favor of equality between men and women, $r = .71, p < .001$). A principal components analysis confirmed that the items assessing these dependent variables loaded on three separate factors as intended, together explaining 79% of the variance in the individual items.

Results and Discussion

Effects of the manipulation. A MANOVA revealed a reliable multivariate main effect of type of sexism, $F(3, 109) = 18.62, p < .001,$ $_{partial}\eta^2 = .34$. At the univariate level this effect was reliable for perceived sexism, $F(1, 111) = 53,43, p < .001,$ $_{partial}\eta^2 = .33$, for anger, $F(1, 111) = 18.25, p < .001,$ $_{partial}\eta^2 = .14$, as well as for support for collective action, $F(1, 111) = 6.64, p < .01,$ $_{partial}\eta^2 = .06$. As expected, participants indicated that the source of old-fashioned sexism was more sexist than the source of modern sexism. Participants also expressed more anger at the source, and more support for collective action in favor of women, when exposed to old-fashioned sexism than when exposed to modern sexism (see Table 1 for all relevant means).

Mediation analyses. We predicted that the effect of type of sexism on support for collective action would be mediated by perceived sexism and anger, respectively (see Figure 1). We tested this prediction with a series of regression analyses (see also Taylor, MacKinnon, & Tein, 2008), following the steps

Table 1. Means and Standard Deviations for Perceived Sexism, Anger, and Support for Collective Action (Study 1), Intentions to Protest (Study 2), and Gender Identification (Study 3)

	Study 1		Study 2		Study 3	
	Type of Sexism		Type of Sexism		Type of Sexism	
	Old-Fashioned	Modern	Old-Fashioned	Modern	Old-Fashioned	Modern
Perceived sexism	5.16[a]	3.49[b]	6.14[a]	3.93[b]	5.72[a]	2.93[b]
	(1.03)	(1.36)	(.85)	(1.40)	(.79)	(.89)
Anger	3.42[a]	2.27[b]	4.65[a]	2.80[b]	4.61[a]	2.40[b]
	(1.60)	(1.25)	(1.22)	(1.11)	(.78)	(1.36)
Collective action	4.72[a]	3.96[b]				
	(1.40)	(1.68)				
Protest intentions			5.13[a]	2.65[b]		
			(1.09)	(1.28)		
Gender identification					5.44[a]	4.67[b]
					(.67)	(1.26)

Note. Standard deviations are presented within parentheses. In each row, means in the same study with a different superscript differ at $p < .05$.

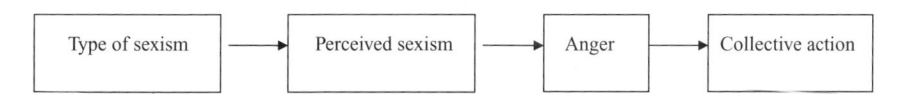

Fig. 1. Predicted model linking type of sexism to perceived sexism, anger, and collective action.

recommended by Baron and Kenny (1986). First, we established that the predictor (type of sexism; coded as $-1 =$ *old-fashioned sexism* and $+1 =$ *modern sexism*) significantly predicts the first mediator (perceived sexism; $\beta = -.56, p < .001$), as well as the outcome variable (support for collective action; $\beta = -.24, p < .01$), and that the first mediator (perceived sexism) reliably predicts the outcome variable (support for collective action; $\beta = .34, p < .001$). When the first mediator (perceived sexism) is entered in the equation together with the main effect of the predictor (type of sexism), the mediator (perceived sexism) is still reliably associated with support for collective action ($\beta = .30, p < .01$), while the main effect of the predictor (type of sexism) is no longer reliable ($\beta = -.08, p = .49$, Sobel $z = 2.56, p < .01$).

Second, we established that the predictor (type of sexism) significantly predicts the second mediator (anger; $\beta = -.36, p < .001$), and that the second mediator (anger) reliably predicts the outcome variable (support for collective action; $\beta = .38, p < .001$). When the second mediator (anger) is entered in the equation together with the main effect of type of sexism, anger is still reliably associated with support for collective action ($\beta = .34, p < .01$), while the main effect of type of sexism is no longer reliable ($\beta = -.11, p = .24$, Sobel $z = -2.69$, $p < .01$).

Finally, we examined whether the effect of type of sexism on perceived sexism results in anger, and anger in turn induces support for collective action (see Figure 1) with a regression analysis predicting support for collective action in three steps. The main effect of type of sexism was entered on the first step, perceived sexism was entered on the second step, and anger was entered on the third step. The results of the first and second step show that the prediction of support for collective action from type of sexism is significantly improved by adding perceived sexism as a predictor in the equation, R^2change $= .06$, $F(1, 110) = 7.65, p < .01$, and confirm that the main effect of type of sexism on support for collective action is reliably mediated by perceived sexism, as indicated above (Sobel $z = -2.59$, $p < .01$). When anger is entered as an additional predictor in the equation on the third step, neither the direct effect of type of sexism ($\beta = -.02$, ns), nor the effect of the first mediator perceived sexism ($\beta = .19$, ns) remain reliable, while the second mediator anger is reliably associated with support for collective action ($\beta = .28, p < .01$) R^2adj $= .15$, R^2change $= .06$, $F(1, 109) = 7.57, p < .01$. Sobel tests confirm that the relation between type of sexism and anger is reliably mediated by perceived sexism (Sobel $z = -3.50, p < .001$), and the reduction in the effect of perceived sexism on support for collective action due to the inclusion of anger as an additional predictor is also reliable (Sobel $z = 2.47, p < .05$). This is consistent with our reasoning that because modern sexism is less likely to be perceived as indicating prejudicial views, it raises less anger toward the source of sexism, which in turn results in less support for collective action.

Study 2

Method

Design and participants. The 44 Dutch female undergraduate student participants in this study were randomly allocated to one of two conditions: old-fashioned sexism or modern sexism. Participants were recruited on campus; their mean age was 20.61 (ranging from 18–27; $SD = 1.74$). At the end of the experiment participants were fully debriefed and received 4 Euros for their participation.

Procedure. Participants were seated in separate cubicles. The experiment took place via a computer and was introduced as an investigation about the expectations students have regarding their practical training. To support this cover story, participants were asked to answer several filler questions about what they expected from their training. Then we stated that we were also examining what students thought about the professionals from external institutions who frequently supervised students from this university. Participants read that they would be provided with some information about one of these supervisors, randomly chosen by the computer. In reality, all participants read about a Dr. Martin de Wit, who constituted the sexist source.

Subsequently, participants read some of the opinions that this supervisor held about work, five of which consisted the manipulation of sexism. To manipulate old-fashioned versus modern sexism, we used the same statements as in Study 1. This time, however, these statements were said to indicate the opinions of Dr. Martin de Wit. The focal statements were interspersed with additional information, representing 10 alleged opinions of Dr. Martin de Wit that were gender irrelevant (e.g., "He finds it important to reward a good performance in his workers"). As intended, no differences between experimental conditions were found in the time participants spent reading the opinions of the bogus supervisor (Overall $M = 25$ seconds), excluding the possibility that old-fashioned sexism has a larger impact on participants' responses because they pay more attention to this type of information. Participants were then led to anticipate that at the end of their studies they might be supervised by this particular supervisor. The dependent measures assessed how they would feel in that situation.

Dependent measures. As in Study 1 we examined perceived sexism, anger at the source, and support for collective action. However, this time we assessed participants' own intentions to protest with questions tailored to the experimental situation. Participants indicated their answer to all questions on 7-point Likert-type scales (from $1 = $ *not at all* to $7 = $ *very much*). Perceived sexism was assessed with two items (i.e., to what extent do you think Dr. Martin de Wit is prejudiced, to what extent do you find Dr. Martin de Wit sexist?), which formed a reliable scale ($r = .51$, $p < .001$). Four negative emotions focusing on the behavior of Dr. de Wit were included to assess anger at the source, as in Study 1 (see also Barreto & Ellemers, 2005a, b). Participants were asked to indicate the degree to which they felt angry, irritated, disappointed, and hostile at Dr de Wit ($\alpha = .89$). Intentions to protest were assessed with three items capturing the preconditions for the emergence of protest (see also Wright & Tropp, 2002), namely refusal to accept the situation (I would prefer not to work with Dr. de Wit), identification of the required change (I would not want to have Dr. de Wit as a supervisor), and action intention (I would object to having Dr. Martin de Wit as a supervisor), which together formed a reliable scale ($\alpha = .96$).

Results and Discussion

Effects of the manipulation. A MANOVA on perceived sexism, anger, and intentions to protest revealed a reliable multivariate main effect of type of sexism,

$F(3, 40) = 20.40$, $p < .001$, $_{\text{partial}}\eta^2 = .61$, as well as reliable univariate main effects for all dependent measures. As expected, when exposed to old-fashioned sexism participants perceived the source as more sexist, $F(1, 42) = 38.94$, $p < .001$, $_{\text{partial}}\eta^2 = .48$, reported more anger $F(1, 42) = 27.91$, $p < .001$, $_{\text{partial}}\eta^2 = .40$, and indicated stronger intentions to protest, $F(1, 42) = 48.46$, $p < .001$, $_{\text{partial}}\eta^2 = .54$, than when they were exposed to modern sexism (see Table 1).

Mediation analyses. We examined support for our prediction with the same analytical procedure as in Study 1, in which type of sexism was again coded as $-1 =$ old-fashioned sexism and $+1 =$ modern sexism. First, we established that type of sexism reliably predicted the first mediator, perceived sexism ($\beta = -.69$, $p < .001$), as well as the outcome variable, intentions to protest ($\beta = -.73$, $p < .001$), that perceived sexism also reliably predicted intentions to protest ($\beta = .69$, $p < .001$). The direct effect of type of sexism on intentions to protest reliably decreases when perceived sexism is entered in the equation (Sobel $t = -2.35$, $p < .05$).

Subsequently, we established that type of sexism reliably predicted the second mediator, anger ($\beta = -.63$, $p < .001$), and that anger also reliably predicted intentions to protest ($\beta = .87$, $p < .001$). The direct effect of type of sexism on intentions to protest reliably decreases when anger is entered in the equation (Sobel $t = -4.37$, $p < .001$).

Finally, we examined support for the hypothesized process (see Figure 1) in a three-step hierarchical regression, in which type of sexism was entered in the first step, perceived sexism was entered in the second step, and anger was entered in the third step. The results of the first two steps again show that the prediction of protest intentions from type of sexism is significantly improved when perceived sexism is entered in the equation together with the main effect of type of sexism (Sobel $t = -2.35$, $p < .05$), $R^2\text{adj} = .58$, $R^2\text{change} = .06$, $F(1, 41) = 6.45$, $p < .05$). Additionally, when anger is also entered in the equation, the direct effect of type of sexism on protest intentions is further reduced ($\beta = -.24$, $p < .05$; Sobel $t = -4.37$, $p < .001$). The relation between type of sexism and anger is reliably mediated by perceived sexism (Sobel $t = 2.09$, $p < .05$), and the effect of perceived sexism on protest intentions drops to non-significance when anger is included in the equation ($\beta = .12$, *ns;* Sobel $t = 4.32$, $p < .001$), while anger is reliably associated with intentions to protest ($\beta = .64$, $p < .001$) $R^2\text{adj} = .81$, $R^2\text{change} = .22$, $F(1, 40) = 48.60$, $p < .001$. These results are in line with predictions and converge with our reasoning that modern expressions of sexism are less likely to be recognized as sexist, and hence raise less anger and intentions to protest than old-fashioned sexism. However, with the present protest measure it is unclear whether participants would prefer collective action, or might also engage in more individual forms of protest. This is why we conducted a third study.

Study 3

Method

Design and participants. The 37 Dutch female undergraduate student participants in this study were randomly allocated to one of two conditions: old-fashioned sexism and modern sexism. Participants were recruited on campus; their mean age was 20.26 (ranging from 18–51, $SD = 4.60$). At the end of the experiment participants were fully debriefed and received 4 Euros for their participation.

Procedure and dependent measures. The procedure followed in this experiment was very similar to that followed in Study 2. Only the dependent measures were different. Participants indicated their answer to all questions on 7-point Likert-type scales (from $1 = $ *not at all* to $7 = $ *very much*). Perceived sexism was assessed with three items (I think that Dr. de Wit respects women, I think that Dr. de Wit is likely to discriminate against women, and I think that Dr. De Wit is fair; the first and last items were recoded, $\alpha = .89$). Anger at the source was assessed with five items (I feel angry, hostile, upset, frustrated, and disappointed at Dr. de Wit, $\alpha = .92$). Gender identification was measured with three items (being a woman is an important part of my self-concept, I identify with other women, I feel that people talk about me when they talk about women), to check whether old-fashioned sexism is more likely to make participants define themselves and think of their situation in group terms, which is thought to be an important precondition for collective action. Although reliability of this scale was relatively low ($\alpha = .56$), it is important to note that the scale only consisted of three items. Furthermore, analysis of the separate items showed parallel effects, so that there is no loss of information by presenting them together. Protest behavior was assessed by providing participants with the opportunity to write a protest message about Dr. de Wit. Participants were first asked to indicate whether or not they wished to write a message indicating any sort of dissatisfaction regarding Dr. de Wit. To explicitly distinguish between individual and collective protest, participants were told that they could choose to write a message on behalf of their individual interest (e.g., not wanting to have this training supervisor in the future). Alternatively, they could write a message on behalf of the collective interest (e.g., to indicate that other students should also not have this supervisor in the future). They could also choose to write two messages, one to voice an individual complaint, and one to voice a collective complaint. To measure collective protest we coded the behavior of participants who chose not to protest and of participants who protested only individually as 0, and the behavior of participants who chose to protest collectively or who chose to protest both individually and collectively as 1. To measure individual protest, we coded the behavior of participants who chose not to protest or to

Table 2. Protest Behavior: Number (and percentage) of Participants in Each Condition that Engaged in No Protest, Individual Protest, or Collective Protest (Study 3)

	Type of Sexism			
	Old-Fashioned		Modern	
No protest	1	(6%)	15	(79%)
Individual protest	6	(33%)	1	(5%)
Collective protest	11	(61%)	3	(16%)
Total	18	(100%)	19	(100%)

Note. Percentages of participants in each condition opting for a particular course of behavior are presented within parentheses.

protest only collectively as 0, and the behavior of participants who chose to protest solely individually, or who chose to protest both individually and collectively as 1. This is a less hypothetical and more publicly visible and effortful behavioral measure than was the case in the prior two studies—participants actually engaged in protest behavior.

Results and Discussion

Effects of the manipulation. A MANOVA on perceived sexism, anger, and gender identification revealed a multivariate main effect of type of sexism, $F(3, 33) = 32.73$, $p < .001$, $_{partial}\eta^2 = .75$. At the univariate level this effect was reliable for perceived sexism, $F(1, 35) = 99.73$, $p < .001$, $_{partial}\eta^2 = .74$, for anger, $F(1, 35) = 45.19$, $p < .001$, $_{partial}\eta^2 = .51$, as well as for gender identification, $F(1, 35) = 5.40$, $p < .05$, $_{partial}\eta^2 = .13$ (see Table 1). Replicating results of the two previous studies, participants perceived the source as more sexist and reported more anger at a source who expressed old-fashioned sexism than when it expressed modern sexism. Additionally, participants who were exposed to old-fashioned sexism reported stronger gender identification than when they had been exposed to modern sexism. This is in line with our reasoning and supports the notion that the denial of discrimination and the individual meritocracy ideology this implies makes it more likely that people think of themselves as a separate individual, instead of as a group member.

As predicted, our experimental manipulations also affected participants' displays of protest behavior. Of the 18 participants in the old-fashioned sexism condition 11 (61%) engaged in collective protest, while 6 (33%) protested individually. By contrast, in the modern sexism condition 15 of the 19 participants (79%) did not engage in any form of protest, and only 3 (16%) opted for collective protest (see Table 2). We performed logistic regression analyses in which collective protest was the dependent variable (coded as $0 = $ *no collective protest* and $1 = $ *collective protest*), the old-fashioned sexism condition was coded as -1 and the modern sexism condition was coded as $+1$. Consistent with predictions, these analyses revealed a reliable main effect of type of sexism indicating that more collective protest was chosen in the old-fashioned sexism condition than in the modern sexism condition ($\beta = -1.06$), Wald's chi-square $(1, N = 37) = 7.18$, $p < .01$. Thus, people were more likely to engage in actual protest behavior after exposure to old-fashioned sexism than modern sexism. Furthermore, this can be seen as indicating the propensity to engage in collective action, as the majority of these protest actions intended to address the treatment of the group as a whole, instead of focusing on individual outcomes.

Mediation analyses. We argued that the effect of type of sexism on collective protest emerges because people differ in the extent to which they perceive the source as sexist, and in the anger they experience as a result. To test this predicted mediation, we first established that the effect of type of sexism on collective protest ($\beta = -1.06$), Wald's chi-square $(1, N = 37) = 7.18$, $p < .01$, drops to non-significance ($\beta = .24$, Wald's chi-square $(1, N = 37) = .11$, *ns*), when the effect of perceived sexism ($\beta = 1.05$), Wald's chi-square $(1, N = 37) = 4.11, p < .05$, is entered into the equation. Likewise, when anger in entered in the equation together with the main effect of type of sexism, anger remains reliably associated with collective protest ($\beta = 1.58$) Wald's chi-square $(1, N = 37) = 6.41, p < .05$, whereas the effect of type of sexism on collective protest becomes nonsignificant ($\beta = .10$), Wald's chi-square $(1, N = 37) = .03$, *ns*. Then we conducted a logistic regression analysis in three steps, in which the main effect of type of sexism was entered in the first step, perceived sexism was entered in the second step, and anger was entered in the third step. Again, the main effect of type of sexism on collective protest is mediated by perceived sexism, as indicated above. When anger is also entered in the equation, neither the main effect of type of sexism ($\beta = .94$), Wald's chi-square $(1, N = 37) = .93$, *ns*, nor the effect of perceived sexism ($\beta = .81$), Wald's chi-square $(1, N = 37) = 1.46, p = .23$ remain reliable, while anger is reliably associated with support for collective action ($\beta = 1.44$), Wald's chi-square $(1, N = 37) = 5.35, p < .05$. This is consistent with our reasoning that the effect of type of sexism on collective protest through perceived sexism is further mediated by the anger invoked by the perception of sexism. Thus, our results support the notion that because modern sexism is less likely to be perceived as being sexist, people experience less anger at the source, and as a result are less likely to engage in collective protest. No such relation was observed between perceived sexism or anger and individual protest.

General Discussion

With the present work, we build on previous research suggesting that modern sexism elicits self-defeating responses (see also Barreto & Ellemers, 2009; Barreto et al., 2008) and connect to existing insights on relative deprivation and collective action. We have argued and shown across three studies that the failure to perceive group-based prejudice and discrimination in modern expressions of sexism impairs other-directed affective responses (anger at the source) and actions that might help redress systematic injustice (endorsement of collective action and collective protest behavior). The key factor in these findings is that whereas old-fashioned sexism is relatively easy to recognize, this is more difficult in the case of modern sexism. As a result, people who are exposed to modern sexism are less likely to address the possibility that the group as a whole is treated unjustly, and are less inclined to engage in any action that may counter or redress unjust treatment of the group. In this way then, modern sexism can render the social system more stable and resilient to change (Crosby, Pufall, Snyder, O'Connell, & Whalen, 1989; Major, 1994; Schmitt, Ellemers, & Branscombe, 2003; Wright, 2001).

With this research we extend existing models of collective action in that we focus on the emergence of the perceived need for collective action, instead of examining the willingness to become involved in existing interest groups or participate in ongoing protest activities. In doing this, we draw upon insights on relative deprivation indicating that the perception of group-level injustice is key to the emergence of collective action. We have argued that modern expressions of prejudice make it less easy to recognize the continued existence of group-based discrimination and reduce the emergence of collective action initiatives compared to more blatant expressions of prejudice. Thus, we have examined modern expressions of prejudice as an antecedent condition that has not been addressed before in this literature.

We think the connection between these different literatures is productive for further theory development and future research. That is, in their work on relative deprivation, Walker, Wong, and Kretzschmar (2002) have noted that the attributions people make for their current outcomes are relevant, as these will determine which course of action seems most appropriate in the future. Previous research examining the impact of exposure to modern prejudice on the self, has focused on attributions to discrimination as a focal variable of interest. The present research suggests that perceptions of discrimination, and the way these are affected by different expressions of prejudicial views, offer a concrete way to further current insights on how attributions relate to relative deprivation and collective action. Likewise, Tyler and Lind (2002) have argued that group-level procedural injustice, not group-level outcomes, is key in the experience of relative deprivation that is likely to lead to collective action. While in their analysis the distinction between outcomes and procedures may seem somewhat analytical, the current research suggests that perceptions of group-based prejudice and discrimination may offer a concrete example of how group-level procedural justice judgments may be expressed. Here too, we think the introduction of insights on modern prejudice and discrimination into the literature on relative deprivation and collective action may open up avenues for future research.

Limitations and Future Directions

Despite the convergence in the results we obtained, and the consistency between our findings and the theoretical analysis we developed, there are some limitations that might be addressed in future research. First, in theory our analysis should hold for all forms of modern prejudice. That is, the denial of any type of group-based discrimination should make it more difficult for those exposed to such views to realize that these represent prejudicial beliefs. Nevertheless, in the present research we only addressed modern sexism as a relevant example of modern prejudice. Further work is needed to establish whether similar effects are obtained with other types of prejudice, or whether other considerations come into play, for instance because people are more keenly aware of group-level differences in treatment (e.g., in the case of physically disabled people), because others are expected to hold stereotypical views of the ingroup, or are seen as having an obvious interest in downplaying and perpetuating existing intergroup differences.

Second, we have incorporated endorsement of collective action, protest intentions, and actual engagement in protest behavior as relevant dependent variables in the present research. Nevertheless, one may argue that these all refer to precursors of collective action in that they assess individual willingness to engage in some form of (collective) protest, rather than examining the actual emergence of collective action. Future research might address a broader range of behaviors, such as raising support for a joint protest, making public one's complaints, or undertaking legal action. We know from previous research that complaining about discrimination or confronting someone who expresses prejudicial views is seen as undesirable behavior, even if the complaint is justified (Kaiser & Miller, 2001; Major & Kaiser, 2005), and may cause the individual to be rejected by other members of their group. Therefore it would be important to asses which types of collective action would be most likely to emerge when people perceive discrimination, or be most quickly suppressed when perceptions are less clear.

Third, whereas Study 1 was a relatively larger questionnaire study, the number of participants in Studies 2 and 3 was limited, due to the more time-consuming nature of data collection using an experimental setup and the use of paid participants for these studies. While this would seem to call for a further examination of the robustness of these effects with other and broader samples, it is important to note that the smaller sample size also implies that there was lesser statistical power in these studies, making it all the more meaningful that we did find statistically reliable effects.

The fact that the present research—on the emergence of collective action— complements previous work on participation in existing forms of collective action, also offers interesting avenues for further research. For instance, the distinction between these two forms of collective action participation might be used to more explicitly compare the conditions under which people are likely to initiate some form of collective action with those under which they are willing to follow, or to engage in ongoing activities. Presumably, the threshold is highest when collective action needs to be initiated, so that modern expressions of prejudice might be most discouraging to undertake such action at this stage. As a result, the distinction between modern and old-fashioned prejudice may be less important in determining the engagement in activities or interest groups that already have been established.

Practical Consequences

The work presented here is not only interesting from a theoretical point of view, but also has important implications for societal and organizational policy. Despite the fact that systematic differences in level of education, career success and economic outcomes continue to exist between members of different social groups, there is a general belief that position improvement depends on individual merit only. The present research shows that modern expressions of prejudice affect the likelihood that people perceive discrimination or engage in some form of protest against their treatment. Denial of discrimination fosters the conviction that the achievement of desirable outcomes primarily depends on one's own abilities, motivation and life choices. Thus, the very notion that society offers equal opportunities to all individuals is an important factor in the suppression of collective action.

Thus, the problem of inequality in opportunities at least to some extent resides in the fact that "modern," more subtle expressions of prejudice have developed to replace more blatant and explicit group-based prejudice and discrimination, which has come to be regarded as "politically incorrect" behavior, due to social and legal sanctions. This raises the question of whether measures aiming to suppress blatant discrimination actually have the desired effect, if they only affect the way people express their views, without changing the content of their prejudicial beliefs. Aside from the thorny issue of whether such measures then do more harm than good in the end, the present research offers a clear reminder that simply prohibiting group-based discrimination is not sufficient to achieve the desired effect.

Indeed, the legal rights and equal opportunities provisions people can draw upon generally assume that those who suffer from discrimination are able to see that this is the case and will come forward to indicate this (Albiston, 2005). Thus, the responsibility for undertaking action and the burden of proof is on the victim of discrimination, instead of the perpetrator. At the same time, the present research reminds us that it is not always easy to recognize prejudicial views. This is why a proactive policy is needed, to put the responsibility for identifying and addressing group-based discrimination in the hands of work organizations and policy makers, instead of relying on potentially disadvantaged individuals to do this (see also Crosby, Iyer, Clayton, & Downing, 2003).

What might such a proactive policy look like? First, an organization or political institution can compile and examine comparative statistics on access to education, employment rates, career progress, or work compensation as a matter of course and actively search for evidence of group-based injustice. Second, it is possible to install preexisting interest groups that have the explicit responsibility to search for, identify, and collect instances of discrimination against members of particular groups. Third, members of potentially disadvantaged groups can explicitly be informed of their rights, and of the (legal) procedures available to exercise their rights, and they can be offered (free) legal support in case these rights are violated. Fourth, management of the institution can develop a climate in which discrimination complaints (even erroneous ones!) are seen as a source of institutional learning and improvement, instead of being covered up as a cause for embarrassment and shame. Fifth, in complaint procedures, the burden of proof can be put on the side of the perpetrator instead of the target in the case of suspected discrimination, with the target receiving explicit support and professional advice from the organization.

All these measures have in common that they intend to actively search for and draw out information about potential discrimination, in order to be able to more formally examine whether or not this has been the case, instead of relying on the spontaneous emergence of complaints or assuming that there is no discrimination when there are no such complaints. Furthermore, these measures take into account that prejudice can occur automatically and unintentionally (see also Ellemers & Barreto, 2008). In other words, people may discriminate without realizing that they do, and despite their best efforts not to do so. An institution that enables them to recognize and redress this, instead of disapproving of and sanctioning discrimination complaints, can then be seen as constructive and helpful and this seems to offer the most viable road toward achieving more equal opportunities for all individuals.

References

Albiston, C. R. (2005). Mobilizing employment rights in the workplace. In L. B. Nielsen & R. L. Nelson (Eds.), *Handbook of employment discrimination research: Rights and realities* (pp. 301–325). Dordrecht, The Netherlands: Springer.

Baron, R. M., & Kenny, D. A. (1986). The moderator-mediator variable distinction in social psychological research: Conceptual, strategic, and statisttical considerations. *Journal of Personality and Social Psychology, 51*, 1173–1182.

Barreto, M., & Ellemers, N. (2005a). The burden of "benevolent" sexism: How it contributes to the maintenance of gender inequalities. *European Journal of Social Psychology, 35*, 633–642.

Barreto, M., & Ellemers, N. (2005b). The perils of political correctness: Responses of men and women to old-fashioned and modern sexism. *Social Psychology Quarterly, 68*, 75–88.

Barreto, M., & Ellemers, N. (2009). Multiple identities and the paradox of social inclusion. In F. Butera & J. M. Levine (Eds.), *Coping with minority status: Responses to exclusion and inclusion* (pp. 269–292). Cambridge, UK: Cambridge University Press.

Barreto, M., Ellemers, N., Cihangir, S., & Stroebe, K. (2008). The experience of sexism in modern societies. In M. Barreto, M. Ryan, & M. Schmitt (Eds.), *Barriers to diversity: The glass ceiling after 20 years* (pp. 99–123). Washington, DC: American Psychological Association.

Bartol, K. M. (1999). Gender influences on performance evaluations. In G. M. Powell (Ed.). *Handbook of gender and work* (pp. 165–178). London: Sage.

Cihangir, S., Barreto, M., & Ellemers, N. (in press). The dark side of subtle discrimination: The moderating role of self-esteem in responses to subtle and blatant discrimination. *British Journal of Social Psychology*.

Crocker, J., Major, B., & Steele, C. (1998). Social stigma. In D. T. Gilbert, S. T. Fiske, & G. Lindzey (Eds.), *The handbook of social psychology* (Vol. 2, 4th ed., pp. 504–553). Boston: McGraw-Hill.

Crosby, F., Pufall, A., Snyder, R. C., O'Connell, M., & Whalen, P. (1989). The denial of personal disadvantage among you, me, and all the other ostriches. In M. Crawford & M. Gentry (Eds.), *Gender and thought* (pp. 79–99). New York: Springer-Verlag.

Crosby, F. J., Iyer, A., Clayton, S., & Downing, R. A. (2003). Affirmative action: Psychological data and the policy debates. *American Psychologist, 58*, 93–115.

Crosby, F. J., Williams, J. C., & Biernat, M. (2004). The maternal wall. *Journal of Social Issues, 60*, 675–682.

Eagly, A. H., & Karau, S. J. (2002). Role congruity theory of prejudice toward female leaders. *Psychological Review, 109*, 573–598.

Eagly, A. H., Karau, S. J., & Makhijani, M. G. (1995). Gender and the effectiveness of leaders: A meta-analysis. *Psychological Bulletin, 117*, 125–145.

Ellemers, N. (2002). Social identity and relative deprivation. In I. Walker & H. Smith (Eds.). *Relative deprivation: Specification, development, and integration* (pp. 239–264). Cambridge, UK: Cambridge University Press.

Ellemers, N., & Barreto, M. (2008). Putting your own down: How members of disadvantaged groups unwittingly perpetuate or exacerbate their disadvantage. In A. Brief (Ed.), *Diversity at work* (pp. 202–261). Cambridge, UK: Cambridge University Press.

Graves, L. M. (1999). Gender bias in interviewers' evaluations of applicants: When and how does it occur? In G. N. Powell (Ed.), *Handbook of gender and work* (pp. 145–164). Thousand Oaks, CA: Sage.

Heilman, M. E. (2001). Description and prescription: How gender stereotypes prevent women's ascent up the organizational ladder. *Journal of Social Issues, 57*, 657–674.

Kaiser, C. R., & Miller, C. T. (2001). Stop complaining! The social costs of making attributions to discrimination. *Personality and Social Psychology Bulletin, 27*(2), 254–263.

Kelly, C., & Breinlinger, S. (1996). *The social psychology of collective action: Identity, injustice, and gender*. London: Taylor & Francis.

Major, B. (1994). From social inequality to personal entitlement: The role of social comparisons, legitimacy appraisals, and group membership. In M. P. Zanna (Ed.), *Advances in experimental social psychology* (Vol.26, pp. 293–348). San Diego, CA: Academic Press.

Major, B., & Kaiser, C. R. (2005). Perceiving and claiming discrmination. In L. B. Nielsen & R. L. Nelson (Eds.). *Handbook of employment discrimination research: Rights and realities* (pp. 285–300). Dordrecht, The Netherlands: Springer.

Major, B., Kaiser, C., & McCoy, S. K. (2003). It's not my fault: When and why attributions to discrimination protect self-esteem. *Personality and Social Psychology Bulletin, 29*, 772–781.

Major, B., Quinton, W. J., & Schmader, T. (2003). Attributions to discrimination and self-esteem: Impact of group identification and situational ambiguity. *Journal of Experimental Social Psychology, 39*, 220–231.

Nielsen, L. B., & Nelson, R. L. (2005). Scaling the pyramid: A sociolegal model of employment discrimination litigation. In L. B. Nielsen & R. L. Nelson (Eds.). *Handbook of employment discrimination research: Rights and realities* (pp. 3–34). Dordrecht, The Netherlands: Springer.

Pettigrew, T. F. (2002). Summing up: Relative deprivation as a key social psychological concept. In I. Walker & H. Smith (Eds.), *Relative deprivation: Specification, development, and integration* (pp. 351–374). Cambridge, UK: Cambridge University Press.

Plant, E. A., & Devine, P. G. (1998). Internal and external motivation to respond without prejudice. *Journal of Personality and Social Psychology, 75*, 811–832.

Reicher, S. D. (1984). Social influence and the crowd: Attitudinal and behavioral effects of deindividuation in conditions of high and low group salience. *British Journal of Social Psychology, 23*, 341–350.

Schmitt, M. T., Ellemers, N., & Branscombe, N. (2003). Perceiving and responding to gender discrimination at work. In: A. Haslam, D. Van Knippenberg, M. Platow, & N. Ellemers (Eds.), *Social identity at work: Developing theory for organizational practice* (pp. 277–292). New York: Psychology Press.

Simon, B., Loewy, M., Stürmer, S., Weber, U., Freytag, P., Habig, C., et al. (1998). Collective identification and social movement participation. *Journal of Personality and Social Psychology, 74*, 646–658.

Smith, H. J., & Ortiz, D. J. (2002). Is it just me? The different consequences of personal and group relative deprivation. In I. Walker & H. Smith (Eds.), *Relative deprivation: Specification, development, and integration* (pp. 91–118). Cambridge, UK: Cambridge University Press.

Swim, J. K., & Campbell, B. (2001). Sexism: Attitudes, beliefs, and behaviors. In R. Brown & S. Gaertner (Eds.), *The handbook of social psychology: Intergroup relations* (Vol. 4, pp. 218–237). Oxford, UK: Blackwell Publishers.

Swim, J. K., Aikin, K. J., Hall, W. S., & Hunter, B. A. (1995). Sexism and racism: Old-fashioned and modern prejudices. *Journal of Personality and Social Psychology, 68*, 199–214.

Taylor, A. B., MacKinnon, D. P., & Tein, J. Y. (2008). Tests of the three-path mediated effect. *Organizational Research Methods, 11* (2), 241–269.

Tougas, F., Brown, R., Beaton, A. M., & Joly, S. (1995). Neosexism: Plus ça change, plus c'est pareil. *Personality and Social Psychology Bulletin, 21*, 842–849.

Tyler, T. R., & Lind, A. E. (2002). Understanding the nature of fraternalistic deprivation: Does group-based deprivation involve fair outcomes or fair treatment? In I. Walker & H. Smith (Eds.), *Relative deprivation: Specification, development, and integration* (pp. 44–68). Cambridge, UK: Cambridge University Press.

Tyler, T. R., Boeckmann, R. J., Smith, H. J., & Huo, Y. J. (1997). *Social justice in a diverse society*. Boulder, CO: Westview Press.

Van Zomeren, M., Spears, R., Fischer, A. H., & Leach, C. W. (2004). Put your money where your mouth is! Explaining collective action tendencies through group-based anger and group efficacy. *Journal of Personality and Social Psychology, 87*, 649–664.

Veenstra, K., & Haslam, S. A. (2000). Willingness to participate in industrial protest: Exploring social identification in context. *British Journal of Social Psychology, 39*, 153–172.

Walker, I., Wong, N. K., & Kretzschmar, K. (2002). Relative deprivation and attribution: From grievance to action. In I. Walker & H. Smith (Eds.), *Relative deprivation: Specification, development, and integration* (pp. 288–312). Cambridge, UK: Cambridge University Press.

Wright, S. C. (2001). Restricted intergroup boundaries: Tokenism, ambiguity, and the tolerance of injustice. In J. T. Jost & B. Major (Eds.), *The psychology of legitimacy: Emerging perspectives on ideology, justice, and intergroup relations* (pp. 223–256). Cambridge, UK: Cambridge University Press.

Wright, S. C., & Tropp, L. (2002). Collective action in response to disadvantage: Intergroup perceptions, social identification, and social change. In I. Walker & H. J. Smith (Eds.), *Relative deprivation: Specification, development, and integration* (pp. 200–238). Cambridge, UK: Cambridge University Press.

NAOMI ELLEMERS obtained her PhD in Social Psychology from the University of Groningen, the Netherlands. She currently is a Professor of Social and Organizational Psychology at Leiden University, the Netherlands. Her research, for which she received several substantial research grants and awards, covers a broad range of topics in the area of group processes and intergroup relations, and their effects on social behavior in organizations.

MANUELA BARRETO obtained her PhD in Social Psychology from the Free University, Amsterdam, the Netherlands, and was Associate Professor in Social and Organizational Psychology at Leiden University, the Netherlands. She currently works as a Researcher at the Centre for Social Research and Intervention, Lisbon, Portugal. She has been awarded several prizes and prestigious grants, and published extensively in peer reviewed journals and edited books. Her research interests are on the psychology of the disadvantaged, exemplified by her work on identity respect, reactions to prejudice, and the psychology of concealed identities.

Why Do the Privileged Resort to Oppression? A Look at Some Intragroup Factors

Tom Postmes[*]
University of Groningen
University of Exeter

Laura G. E. Smith
University of Queensland

This article shows that (intergroup) oppression can be strategically motivated by (intragroup) processes. It is often assumed that high-status groups oppress when their social position is declining (relative deprivation). Counterintuitively, research shows that oppression also occurs when their position is improving (gratification): a curvilinear relationship referred to as "the v-curve effect." We test the hypothesis that this relationship is due to intragroup processes within the high-status group: individuals respond strategically to elite norms. Two experiments manipulated participants' future prospects: to join the nation's elite in future (relative gratification), social stasis, or status decline (relative deprivation, Study 2). Elite norms toward immigrants (positive, negative) were manipulated independently. The curvilinear relationship was only found when norms were negative. In other words, those who anticipate joining the elite tailor their actions to the norms of their prospective in-group.

As is evident from the contributions to this special issue, the prime concern of students and scholars of collective action has been with the oppressed. Indeed, research has often focused on emancipation efforts (e.g., feminism, civil rights activism, social movement participation). However, although social revolutions

---

[*]Correspondence concerning this article should be addressed to Tom Postmes, Department of Social and Organizational Psychology, University of Groningen, Grote Kruisstraat 2/1, 9712 TS Groningen, The Netherlands [e-mail: t.postmes@rug.nl].

We thank Janelle Jones and Thomas Kessler for comments, and Helen McKean for her help with the data collection. The research was supported by a grant from the Economic and Social Research Council (ESRC) (RES-062-23-0135) to the first author, and a studentship from the ESRC to the second author.

are a familiar interlude, the pervasiveness of inequality suggests that the oppressive collective action of privileged groups is the depressing refrain of modern history (e.g., Hobsbawm, 1994). Questions about how such oppression is achieved, and to what extent it can be considered collective action, are rarely asked.

In the literature, there is a general assumption that oppression is a "normal," that is, functional response to threatened or illegitimate privilege. This article argues that oppression is more subtle and multifaceted, and hence theoretically interesting, than that. Oppression may often be more strategically motivated than collective actions of low-status groups. We present an analysis of different motives for participation in oppression. This is derived not just from intergroup relations, but also from the dynamics within groups (i.e., a group-level focus), and from the position of the perpetrating group member within the high-status group (i.e., an individual-level focus). As a test of this model, we present two empirical studies that illustrate how intragroup factors can affect oppressive action intentions with reference to a phenomenon that has recently attracted prominent attention in the research literature, the "v-curve hypothesis."

Collective Action by High- and Low-Status Groups

The focus of theorizing and research on collective action has been on the underdog. It is hard to think of good reasons why this would be so. One may define *collective action* as "as any action that aims to improve the status, power, or influence of an entire group" (van Zomeren & Iyer, 2009, p. 646). This definition elegantly allows us to include all those cases in which individuals stand up for their group's rights, thus undertaking actions on behalf of the collective. In the famous image of tanks rolling into Tiananmen square for instance, we understand the actions of the brave individual blocking their way as collective action. Ironically, the mass deployment of brute force he was up against has attracted much less attention in research, despite the fact that oppression (whether one considers genocides, prejudice against immigrants, ethnic minorities, or women, etc.) most unambiguously improves the outcomes of an entire group.

As a result we know a lot about what motivates collective action of the oppressed, much less about motives for oppression. This bias is present in both classic research as well as contemporary research. The classic study of crowds focused mainly on revolutionary crowds (e.g., Allport, 1924, p. 294; Le Bon, 1895/1995). A recent meta-analysis of contemporary literature on collective action found that only a very few studies concerned themselves with high-status groups' collective actions (van Zomeren, Postmes, & Spears, 2008). And this concern with low-status groups is not just empirical: contemporary theories of collective action are also focused mainly on low-status groups.

The three theoretical strongholds in collective action research are injustice (or relative deprivation), identification, and efficacy (Van Zomeren et al., 2008).

All three have been primarily concerned with low-status groups. This is obviously the case in research on injustice which has almost exclusively focused on (deprived) low-status groups (e.g., Runciman, 1966; Walker & Smith, 2002). Identification with the group is another strong predictor of collective action, and such identifications would appear to be important to high status as well as low-status groups. However, the original formulation of social identity theory (Tajfel & Turner, 1979) focused almost exclusively on the process by which low-status groups strive for social change, or not.[1] The key factors in this theory (permeability of group boundaries, legitimacy of intergroup inequalities, and security of status relations) are typically considered from below. Only recently have there been systematic attempts to apply these ideas to high-status groups (Haslam, 2001, pp. 37–40).

The third current perspective on collective action is derived from game theory (Olson, 1968). The individualistic underpinnings of game theory appear very consistent with the mind-set of elites: these, in some respects, are prone to the atomized perceptions of self and others (Lewin, 1948; Lorenzi-Cioldi, 2006) that make the mental calculations that are central to game theory possible. Nevertheless, the application of these ideas has been to deprived and disadvantaged groups, and the conditions that provide them with a sense of efficacy (Simon & Klandermans, 2001; see also Postmes & Brunsting, 2002). Again therefore, the high-status group's behavior is kept out of the frame.

Oppression as a natural outcome. At least part of the reason for this relative neglect for the motives of oppression is that it is often considered a normal or even natural phenomenon: where groups compete for scarce resources, oppression appears functional on both evolutionary and economic grounds. Indeed, the idea is common to perspectives in sociology, philosophy, political science, history, economics, and social psychology (Bobo, 1999; Sidanius & Pratto, 1999, for reviews). And it goes almost without saying that dominant groups' position provides them with privileged access to the necessary means, ensuring the efficacy of their enterprise.

Three contemporary perspectives are particularly relevant: social dominance theory (or SDT), systems justifications theory (SJT), and social identity theory (SIT).[2] They agree that intergroup threat produces oppression but advance

---

[1] There is a lot of research on bias displayed by high- versus low-status groups (Bettencourt, Dorr, Charlton, & Hume, 2001, for a review), showing that high-status groups display more bias overall. The question in this literature is when low-status group display as much or even more bias (which is taken as an indication of social competition). The behavior of high-status groups, if discussed, tends to be reflected on post hoc (cf. Turner & Brown, 1978).

[2] In order to be concise, numerous other theories are not discussed, including those about realistic group conflict, frustration–aggression, social learning, and modern racism.

different ideas about the processes involved. Briefly, SDT (Sidanius & Pratto, 1999) suggests that some people naturally hold the view that status differences are good—they have a "social dominance orientation." Individuals with such views would be more likely to endorse actions to preserve status differences when under threat. SJT is not incompatible with this idea. It proposes that humans tend to justify the current social system and the existing social structural conditions of their group within it (Jost & Banaji, 1994). For high-status groups, SJT implies that oppression is a straightforward way of satisfying a need to maintain the status quo (see also Blumer, 1958). Finally, SIT also sees threat as a natural precursor to oppression (Haslam, 2001; Tajfel & Turner, 1979). Although SIT is a more sophisticated in acknowledging that outright social competition is rare, and is but one strategy for combating (or presumably maintaining) inequality, it nevertheless proposes that threats to the status quo should result in a response from the high-status group to restore or preserve positive in-group distinctiveness. In sum, although these theories emphasize very different processes and variables, they all agree that oppression is a natural response to threat.

Empirical challenges. One problem for theories of oppression is that the empirical relationship between status threats and oppression is elusive. This raises the question whether the motives for oppression are as straightforward and self-explanatory as is often assumed. In Western society, traditionally dominant groups (White heterosexual men, upper and middle classes) still retain the upper hand, but they have clearly "lost" considerable economic and political power over the past century. Despite the fact that this should lead to increased threat levels according to the theories mentioned above, explicit oppression has tended to become rarer, not more frequent, and prejudice has become more subtle, not more blatant (e.g., Jackman, 1994; Kinder & Sears, 1981). In line with this, the relation between economic downturn and intergroup hostility is not as clear as some have suggested (Bonacich, 1972; Hovland & Sears, 1940). In fact, there is an inconsistent relation between economic indicators and prejudicial behavior (Green, Glaser, & Rich, 1998), and this suggests that a closer look at the psychological experience of threat is warranted.

The complex relationship between threat and prejudice is also evident in recent experimental research. High-status group members who are threatened with future deprivation show some oppressive tendencies, but when they look forward to future gratification (status increases!) oppression increases more sharply (Dambrun, Taylor, McDonald, Crush, & Meot, 2006; Guimond & Dambrun, 2002). This finding resonates with historical research suggesting that intergroup struggles are particularly acute when the economic tide is rising after having been low (Rudé, 1964; Tilly, Tilly, & Tilly, 1975). In sum, the relation between threat and prejudice is not as straightforward as is often assumed. One reason for this, we suggest, is that there are multiple motives for oppression.

Strategies of Oppression and Group Outcomes

Oppression is not only the unjust exercise of authority or power. It includes a range of actions to keep low-status groups in subjection and hardship. High-status groups can maintain the status quo by engaging in overt and pervasive exclusion of the low-status group, but this may be rare. Outright oppression and systematic exclusion[3] disadvantages the out-group in a visible (possibly violent) fashion. Although such exclusion can maintain inequality for a long time (i.e., "effectively" from a high-status viewpoint), it also risks undermining the long-term stability of the system through its illegitimacy. Such oppression is highly visible for the low-status group and can thus form a clear target for resistance and a powerful source of solidarity (see also Reicher, 1996; Turner, 2005). Long-term, overt, and systematic oppression may thus inadvertently undermine the status quo. Furthermore, these strategies may divide the high-status group itself—especially when questions about the legitimacy of oppression are raised (Mummendey & Otten, 1998; Smith & Postmes, 2009).

A more common and familiar pattern of oppression occurs when the majority of the high-status group does not itself resort to visible and overt oppression but merely endorses and supports actions and/or policies which have such effects. Ad hoc and incidental acts of exclusion (e.g., isolated incidents of discrimination, failure to punish bullying by a few "rotten apples," support for a xenophobic speech by a politician; Killen, Rutland, & Jampol, 2008, for a review) may at first blush appear to be less harmful. Similarly, political parties may propose policies which systematically disadvantage and exclude certain groups from fully participating in society. However, such acts and policies can be extremely pernicious for a low-status group, to the extent that supporting them becomes normative for the high-status group as a whole. As these acts of exclusion are ad hoc, there is less risk of them reflecting badly on the high-status group as a whole. This "deniability" undermines low-status groups' emancipatory efforts. As an instrument of oppression, therefore, tacit support for discriminatory policies and actions can be quite effective: it signals the high-status group's superiority without threatening its morality.

The Intragroup Dimension of Oppression

One key difference between oppression and the actions of low-status groups, is that the scope for participating in oppression for opportunistic reasons is far greater. Many of the participants in oppression may do so without having any express aims to improve the status of their group (i.e., for intergroup reasons)

---

[3] *Social exclusion* is used here broadly as excluding from a place or society, and keeping from resources. This is an ongoing strategy rather than a one-off display of in-group bias.

but for other reasons, such as advancing their own interests within the high-status group (i.e., for intragroup reasons). Intragroup factors are often ignored in research on collective action and intergroup relations (although there are exceptions, e.g., Reicher, 1996). In low-status groups, the individual typically makes short-term sacrifices for the potential future benefit of the collective (e.g., there appears to be a negative interdependence between the interests of the individual and those of the collective; Klandermans, 1997).[4] For example, a woman who chooses to fight discrimination at work typically suffers personal setbacks for some idealized collective benefits. In high-status groups, however, oppression can serve the interests of the individual and the group in parallel ways. As a consequence, there can be a positive interdependence such that discriminatory actions are not just rewarding for the group, but also for individual perpetrators. Consider for example a man working in a slightly sexist environment: For this person, committing a visible act of oppression can have positive consequences for the group (maintenance of status quo), as well as for himself (within-group status, trust and influence).

The participation in institutionalized exclusion may bring individual rewards. Those with moral reluctance to engage in such acts may be compelled to participate in order to avoid being excluded themselves. Those with more opportunistic motives are likely to lead from the front as a way of increasing their own status within the in-group. Although there are risks associated with this (e.g., Enoch Powell's ousting from the British conservative party after his famous "rivers of blood" speech) there are also potential rewards (e.g., the success of politicians such as Pim Fortuyn in the Netherlands or Pauline Hanson in Australia). Similar to bullying in schools (Killen et al., 2008, for a review), their actions may be less about maintaining the status quo than about demonstrating their in-group credentials, or about their desire to gain influence over and redefine in-group norms (Postmes, Haslam, & Swaab, 2005).

In such cases, we can see that acts of oppression are not just motivated by intergroup relations (conflict, threat), by cognitive factors (prejudice, social identity salience), or by material considerations (profit). Oppression also happens because individuals act strategically to achieve certain objectives within (or with) the in-group.[5] Obviously, such strategic considerations should be highly sensitive to the prevalent normative climate within the in-group. If one finds, for example, that relatively gratified high-status group members are more likely to be prejudiced (Dambrun et al., 2006; Guimond & Dambrun, 2002), this may reflect the strategic considerations of those high-status group members that displaying prejudice may be normative within their in-group. It is this hypothesis which is tested in the

---

[4] As one would expect, such sacrifices are most likely to come from those who see inequality as structural, who are highly identified, and who see possibilities for social change. Contrary to economic theses, these are not the most deprived or disaffected.

[5] The more general process at work here is that oppression can play a role in the preservation and/or creation of a sense of unity and belongingness.

present article. One advantage of such a normative explanation is that it does not just predict the occurrence of oppression, but also its dissipation. When considering the changing pattern in discriminatory practices toward women and ethnic minorities during the past century, it is clear that ideological and normative factors have played a prominent part: Pressures for "political correctness" have increasingly marginalized the expression of blatant prejudices. Although an important question is how such norms form and change in the first place, the present article is devoted to providing the "groundwork" demonstration that intragroup processes and norms have an important part to play.

Moving toward the design of the present research, we anchored our studies to one puzzling finding in the literature, which we believe could be explained by some of the intragroup processes mentioned above. Guimond and Dambrun (2002) manipulated relative "deprivation" (bad future prospects) and "gratification" (good future prospects) of university students and examined their prejudice toward immigrants. This is a high-status group who discriminate and oppress an immigrant minority—a phenomenon which has become commonplace in Europe. Their results show that prejudice is somewhat elevated when the high-status group feels deprived, compared with the control condition—a finding that confirms the widespread assumption that threat is a key factor in oppression. However, those who feel gratified (i.e., whose perspectives are improving) are especially prejudiced. The authors thus found a curvilinear association between deprivation–control–gratification and prejudice, which they refer to as the "v-curve hypothesis."

Later research suggested that in-group identification plays a role in this process (Dambrun et al., 2006). The effect of identification could be consistent with various explanations: People who are highly identified with their privilege may have a greater sense of entitlement (Blumer, 1958), or a stronger need to positively differentiate their in-group through discrimination (Turner & Brown, 1978). Alternatively, we propose that the prospect of attaining a privileged position also triggers strategic considerations, such that those who anticipate joining the privileged elite in the future are more likely to attune their behaviors, intentions, and expressions to the norms of their prospective in-group. If such norms are hostile toward immigrants this could potentially explain the v-curve effect.[6] This article presents two studies that test this hypothesis.

Overview of the Present Research

Based on the studies of Guimond and Dambrun (2002), Study 1 compared a no-feedback control condition with manipulations of whether university students

---

[6]Indeed, there are indications that such hostile norms existed in all contexts in which the v-curve has been found thus far. This is elaborated in the discussion.

expect their future prospects to be better than expected. Study 2 examined the full factorial design, allowing a test of the v-curve hypothesis (relative gratification vs. relative deprivation vs. control).

To examine the hypothesis that oppressive intent may be at least partly strategic, we manipulated the norms of participants' prospective in-group.[7] We know from the group socialization literature (e.g., Moreland & Levine, 1982) that new members are more keen to display "good citizenship" by adhering to group norms. Both studies therefore manipulated the norm of the privileged elite that these students might one day belong to. In Study 1, the manipulated norm was one of benevolence versus selfishness. Study 2 manipulated anti- versus proimmigration norms. The key dependent variables focused on oppressive intent and included support for anti-immigration policies and anti-immigration action intentions. Control variables that were included to test for alternative explanations were social dominance orientation (cf. Guimond & Dambrun, 2002) and entitlement (Blumer, 1958). Predictions were that the v-curve hypothesis would be confirmed only when the group norms of the elite were selfish. In other words, the content of group norms of a prospective in-group would moderate the effect of relative gratification on oppressive action intentions.

Study 1

Method

Participants and design. Participants were 150 undergraduates ($M_{age} = 19.8$, $SD = 2.18$, 83 females), randomly allocated to conditions. All participants were British students at Exeter University. The study had a 2 (norm: selfish vs. benevolent toward immigrants) × 2 (prospects: relatively gratified vs. no feedback control) between-participants factorial design.

Independent variables and procedure. In order to manipulate independent variables, the experiment ostensibly consisted of three separate studies. The first two surreptitiously manipulated the norm and social prospects, respectively. Participants were told that the "first study" was about politics in Britain and differences between rich and poor. To manipulate the norm, participants were given fictional feedback about "affluent people, with influence and advantage over others." They were told that these affluent people either do (or do not) "Use their wealth and status as a way of helping those less fortunate than themselves." They were given three examples to support this statement, one of which was germane to

---

[7]Manipulating the norms of the prospective group rather than the in-group has the considerable advantage that one can test the hypothesis that this is strategic behavior, because all rewards of such behavior are anticipated in the future.

immigrants. This was designed to manipulate the norm that privileged people are either selfish or benevolent toward immigrants. Participants were asked to respond a manipulation check embedded in a series of questions about politics.

The feedback materials for "Study 2" manipulated prospects. It stated that, "A recent survey... has found that students graduating from Exeter University now have the same job prospects as Oxbridge graduates." Participants were also asked to examine a graph which showed the projected income of Exeter graduates overtaking that of Oxbridge graduates (traditionally higher status) and rising significantly above that of graduates from lower status universities. In the control condition, no such feedback was provided. Participants were asked to respond to a manipulation check item, embedded among a few questions about student prospects. Participants then continued onto the "third study," which consisted of a questionnaire. Finally, participants were fully debriefed.

Dependent measures. Dependent measures were in the form of statements with which participants indicated agreement (1 = *disagree strongly*, 7 = *agree strongly*). The manipulation check for the norm was "In Britain today, rich people believe they ought to do their best to help others." The manipulation check for prospects was "I think that the prospects for Exeter University students are improving over time." The main dependent measure was a 4-item anti-immigration policy scale ($\alpha = .75$) adapted from Pettigrew and Meertens (1995) and included the items, "Send back only those immigrants who do not make an economic contribution to this country," "Send back only those immigrants who have broken the law and committed serious offences," "Send back only those immigrants who do not have a legal right to be in Britain," and "The government should not send back any immigrants" (reverse-coded). Also included (for control purposes) were a Social Dominance Orientation (SDO) scale (6 items, $\alpha = .75$) adapted from Sidanius and Pratto (1999; $\alpha = .71$), containing the items, "If certain groups stayed in their place, we would have fewer problems," "Some groups of people are simply inferior to other groups," "It is probably a good thing that certain groups are at the top and other groups are at the bottom," "It would be good if all groups could be equal but this would not be practically possible," and the reverse-coded items, "We would have fewer problems if we treated people more equally," and "Group equality should be our ideal."

In addition, a 4-item scale ($\alpha = .83$) of social entitlement of the British in-group over immigrants was included, "The British ought to have priority in matters of employment," "The British are entitled to have priority over immigrants in receiving social security benefits," "The British ought to have priority in matters of government housing," and "Immigrants in Britain should have the right to vote" (reverse-coded).

Finally, a 4-item scale measured *identification with Britain* ($\alpha = .87$). Items were, "I identify strongly with traditional British beliefs and values," "Being

British is an important aspect of my identity," "I feel a sense of pride when I think about Britain and British history," and "I identify with Britain."

Results and Discussion

Manipulation checks. Results were analyzed with 2 × 2 ANOVAs. Checks indicated that both manipulations were successful. The norm check, $F(1, 144) = 3.54, p = .06, \eta^2 = .02$, showed participants thought the rich were more benevolent in that condition ($M = 3.97, SD = 1.23$) than in the selfish norm condition ($M = 3.61, SD = 1.19$). There was also a significant social prospects main effect on prospects check, $F(1, 139) = 3.90, p = .05, \eta^2 = .03$, with greater endorsement that prospects were good in the relatively gratified condition ($M = 5.27, SD = .96$) than in the control condition ($M = 4.92, SD = 1.15$).

Condition effects. On the anti-immigration policy scale, there were no main effects, norm $F(1, 137) = 0.06, p = .81$; prospects $F(1, 137) = 1.38, p = .24$. However, the predicted 2-way interaction was significant, $F(1, 137) = 5.20, p = .02, \eta^2 = .04$ (Figure 1). Further analyses showed that only when supported by a selfish in-group norm was there greater anti-immigration political intent when participants were relatively gratified ($M = 5.11, SD = 1.11$) than in the control condition ($M = 4.35, SD = 1.34$), $F(1, 137) = 5.78, p = .02, \eta^2 = .04$. When the norm was benevolent, there was no difference between the gratified ($M = 4.56$,

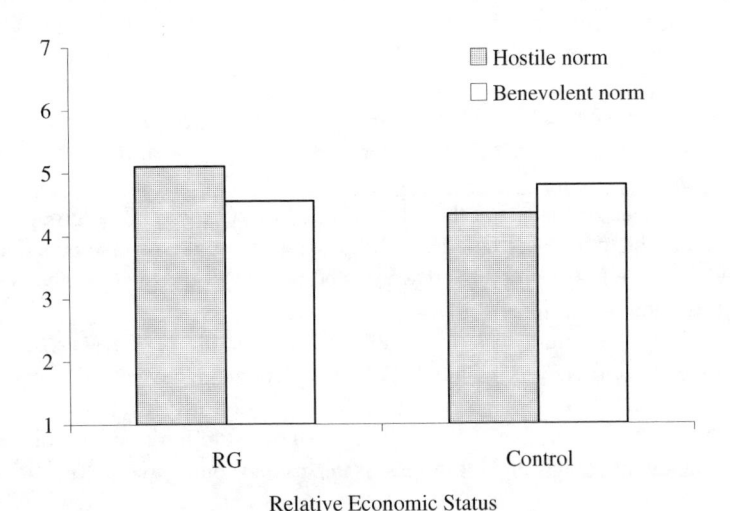

Fig. 1. Effects of anticipated relative economic status (gratification versus control) on support for anti-immigrant policies depend on the elite's norms.

$SD = 1.48$) and control ($M = 4.80$, $SD = 1.25$) conditions, $F(1, 137) = 0.63, p = .43$. Within the gratified condition, the difference between norm conditions was marginally significant, $F(1, 137) = 3.06, p = .08, \eta^2 = .02$. Within the no feedback control condition, there was no effect of norms, $F(1, 137) = 2.16, p = .14$.

This result is consistent with predictions. In the selfish norm condition, we replicated previous research that participants who had prospects to improve their station in life displayed more prejudice (Guimond & Dambrun, 2002) and had clear intent to oppress the immigrant out-group. This is especially noteworthy given that such positive expectations of future gratification should reduce any economic or socioevolutionary need for competition. However, this effect occurred only in the condition where the norms of the prospective in-group encouraged such actions. When these norms were more benevolent, in contrast, there was no significant effect of relative gratification.

Further analyses explored effects on potential process variables. A multivariate 2 × 2 ANOVA was conducted on responses to the scales which measured SDO, entitlement, and British identification (Table 1). None of the multivariate effects was significant, nor were any of the univariate effects. For SDO, there was neither a norm main effect, $F(1, 138) = 1.44, p = .23$, nor a social prospects main effect, $F(1, 138) = .43, p = .51$, nor a 2-way interaction, $F(1, 138) = 0.01, p = .94$. This was also the case for entitlement: there was no norm main effect, $F(1, 138) = 0.04, p = .85$, no social prospects main effect, $F(1, 138) = 1.56, p = .21$, and no 2-way interaction, $F(1, 138) = .07, p = .80$. Finally, there was no significant norm main effect, $F(1, 138) = 0.18, p = .67$, no social prospects main effect, $F(1, 138) = .46, p = .50$, nor a 2-way interaction, $F(1, 138) = 0.13, p = .72$, for British identification.

Table 1. Means in the Selfish ($N = 72$) and Benevolent Norm ($N = 70$) Conditions for Relatively Gratified ($N = 68$) and Control ($N = 74$) Participants

		Selfish Norm		Benevolent Norm	
		RG	Control	RG	Control
Support for anti-immigration policies	M	5.11	4.35	4.56	4.80
	SD	1.11	1.34	1.48	1.25
SDO	M	2.73	2.85	2.96	3.11
	SD	1.13	1.28	1.32	1.07
British identification	M	4.86	4.93	4.67	4.92
	SD	1.37	1.27	1.53	1.46
Entitlement	M	4.42	4.17	4.53	4.16
	SD	1.45	1.72	1.14	1.16

Note. A higher score indicates a greater propensity on each measure.

In sum, the process variables did not show any significant effects. Although we confirmed the main hypothesis, some residual questions remained. We conducted a follow-up that improved the design in two ways: one was to add a relative deprivation condition, so that we could test the full v-curve hypothesis. The second was to make the prospective in-group norms more specific to immigrants: this would allow for a more precise test of predictions (and should boost power because the normative incentive is more targeted).

Study 2

Method

Participants and design. Participants were 147 (M_{age} 20.95, $SD = 2.29$, 100 female) undergraduate volunteers. All were British students at Exeter University. The design was between subjects: 2 (norm: prejudiced toward immigrants vs. no norm control) × 3 (social prospects: relative gratification [RG] vs. no feedback control vs. relative deprivation [RD]). Participants were randomly assigned to conditions.

Procedure and independent variables. The procedure was similar to Study 1 in most respects. The norm manipulation was very similar, but the content of the feedback about the privileged group's attitudes was specific to immigrants. Thus, participants received fictional feedback that a "Recent survey by the government body *National Statistics*, regarding attitudes toward immigration" found significantly higher levels of concern about immigration among those who were on higher salaries. They also heard that research has found that affluent jurors were most likely to find Black defendants guilty. The third piece of research ostensibly showed that "The decline of the corner shop" was due to "the mistrust... in those areas... of shops and businesses that are run by people of a different ethnic background." Participants in the control condition were not provided with feedback about the norm.

The prospects manipulation was as in Study 1, except that a third condition was added, in which feedback showed that Exeter earnings were decreasing relative to Oxbridge (relative deprivation). The rest of the procedure was identical to Study 1.

Dependent measures. Two items were manipulation checks for the social prospects manipulation, "Exeter University students have good job opportunities compared with students from Oxford and Cambridge" and "Compared with the prospects for students from Cambridge and other top universities, the prospects for Exeter graduates are improving over time."

The main dependent variables were measured using standardized 7-point scales (1 = *Do not agree at all*, 7 = *Agree completely*). Three measures assessed participants' support for anti-immigrant policies and practices. We used the same anti-immigration policy scale as in Study 1 ($\alpha = .68$) but selected the more harsh policies only, to send back: "... all immigrants [...], including those who were born in Britain," "[...] only those immigrants who were not born in Britain," and "[...] only those immigrants who do not have a legal right to be in Britain." The second scale measured support for anti-immigrant prejudicial practices. This was measured through an adapted scale of generalized prejudice (Guimond & Dambrun, 2002; $\alpha = .62$), retaining five items that reflect support for hostile actions and policies toward immigrants, for example, "I cannot understand violence toward ethnic minorities" (recoded) and "Immigration laws should be more stringent." A final 6-item scale measured support for ethnocentric practices ($\alpha = .82$): "Immigrants' primary loyalty should be with the country they have moved to," "Immigrants should be made to learn English," "Immigrants should promise allegiance to the country they move to," "The number of immigrants who are granted asylum should be reduced," "The sheer number of immigrants that are legally allowed to stay is a major problem," and "Immigrants should not be given responsibility or positions of authority over the British."

The same SDO scale was used as in Study 1 ($\alpha = .71$). A 4-item entitlement scale ($\alpha = .80$, see Study 1) was also included. Finally, British identification was measured as potential process variable (see Study 1, $\alpha = .87$).

Results and Discussion

Manipulation checks. A 2×3 ANOVA on the first manipulation check showed a main effect of social prospects, as predicted, $F(2, 141) = 8.57, p = .001, \eta^2 = .11$. Highest scores were found in the gratified condition ($M = 4.73, SD = 1.24$) and lowest in the deprived condition ($M = 3.61, SD = 1.48$). Responses to the second check which measured improvements over time also showed a significant prospects main effect, $F(2, 141) = 4.88, p = .01, \eta^2 = .07$. The mean in the relatively gratified condition was again the highest ($M = 4.98, SD = 1.41$) and the relatively deprived condition the lowest ($M = 4.14, SD = 1.42$). These results suggest that the social prospects variable was successfully manipulated.

Condition effects. First, we report the results of a multivariate 2×3 ANOVA, which is followed by tests of the specific hypothesis (v-curve). Please refer to Table 2 for means. A multivariate analysis across the three measures of support for anti-immigrant policies and practices indicated there were significant main effects of group norm, $F(3, 139) = 4.42, p = .005$, and of prospects, $F(3, 140) = 6.03, p = .001$, as well as a trend for the interaction to be significant, $F(3, 140) = 2.47, p = .07$.

Table 2. Means in the Prejudiced Norm ($N = 70$) and No Norm Control ($N = 77$) Conditions for Relatively Gratified ($N = 52$), Control ($N = 51$) and Relatively Deprived ($N = 44$) Participants

		Prejudiced Norm			No Norm Control		
		RG	Control	RD	RG	Control	RD
Support for:							
Anti-immigration	M	4.03$_a$	2.97$_b$	2.89$_b$	3.27$_b$	3.12$_b$	2.74$_b$
policies	SD	1.34	.64	1.03	1.43	.99	1.11
Prejudicial treatment	M	4.76$_a$	3.64$_b$	4.26$_{ab}$	3.85$_b$	3.71$_b$	3.62$_b$
	SD	1.01	.85	1.43	.95	.89	.87
Ethnocentric policies	M	4.90$_a$	3.99$_b$	4.51$_{ab}$	3.70$_b$	3.75$_b$	3.83$_b$
	SD	1.30	.92	1.69	1.30	1.05	1.00
Entitlement	M	4.35	3.91	4.58	3.75	3.66	3.57
	SD	1.27	1.22	1.40	1.39	1.65	1.38
SDO	M	2.90	2.82	2.83	2.89	2.44	2.72
	SD	.96	.79	.94	.86	.86	1.01
British identification	M	5.72$_c$	4.84$_{bc}$	4.39$_{ab}$	4.51$_{ab}$	3.67$_a$	5.25$_{bc}$
	SD	.94	1.64	1.27	.86	1.70	1.50

Note. A higher score indicates a greater propensity on each measure. Means with different subscripts differ significantly from each other according to Student–Newman–Keuls post hoc comparisons, $p < .05$. If no subscripts are given, there are no significant differences.

Tests of hypotheses: the moderated v-curve. We conducted tests of the v-curve hypothesis using contrasts in a one-way ANOVA (e.g., Rosenthal & Rosnow, 1985). The hypotheses addressed in these analyses are (1) whether there was an overall between-condition difference, (2) whether there was overall support for the moderated v-curve hypothesis. This was tested with a contrast specifying the predicted v-curve in the prejudiced norm conditions (RG, control and RD condition contrast: 2 −1 2), and a "flat line" no difference pattern in the control norm condition (−1 −1 −1). (3) Whether the v-curve was significant in the prejudiced norm conditions, and (4) whether there was any support for a v-curve in the nonprejudiced control norm conditions (prediction being that the pattern would not be found in this condition).

For support of anti-immigration policies, the overall between-conditions difference was highly significant, $F(5, 141) = 3.77$, $p = .003$, $\eta^2 = .12$, confirming hypothesis 1. There was also significant support for hypothesis 2: the contrast which tested the entire predicted pattern of a moderated v-curve was significant, $F(1, 141) = 4.58$, $p = .03$, $\eta^2 = .03$. More specific tests of Hypotheses 3 and 4, respectively, showed that there was trend toward a v-curve in the prejudiced norm condition, $F(1, 141) = 3.03$, $p = .08$, $\eta^2 = .02$, but not in the control norm condition, $F(1, 141) = 0.33$, ns, $\eta^2 = .00$. Closer inspection of the means (Figure 2)

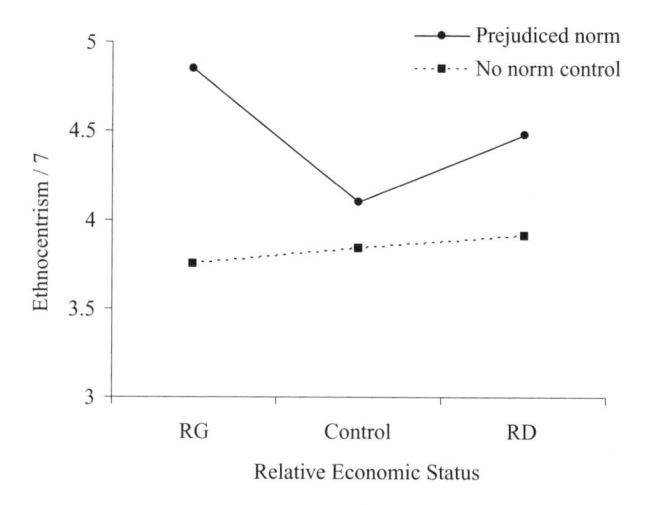

Fig. 2. Effects of anticipated relative economic status (gratification vs. control vs. deprivation) on support for ethnocentric policies depend on the elite's social norms: The moderated "v-curve."

reveals that the v-curve in the prejudiced norm conditions did not completely hold up because, contrary to expectations, there was no significant increase of support for anti-immigrant policies when participants felt deprived. The prediction of an elevated level of support for anti-immigrant policies in the gratification condition was upheld.

With regard to the participants' support for prejudicial practices, all hypotheses were confirmed. The overall between-groups difference was significant, $F(5, 141) = 4.65, p = .004, \eta^2 = .14$. Moreover, the overall test of the predicted contrast was highly significant, too, $F(1, 141) = 19.80, p < .001, \eta^2 = .12$. As predicted by hypotheses 3 and 4, there was a significant "v-curve" in the prejudiced norm condition, $F(1, 141) = 11.90, p = .001, \eta^2 = .08$, but not in the control norm condition, $F(1, 141) = 0.24, ns, \eta^2 = .00$.

For ethnocentrism, all hypotheses were also confirmed. The overall between-groups difference was significant, $F(5, 141) = 3.70, p = .004, \eta^2 = .12$, as was the test of the predicted contrast, $F(1, 141) = 12.53, p < .001, \eta^2 = .08$. There was a significant "v-curve" in the prejudiced norm condition, $F(1, 141) = 5.48, p = .02, \eta^2 = .08$, but not in the control norm condition, $F(1, 141) = 0.34, ns, \eta^2 = .00$. Results on these three variables, overall, replicated and extended the findings of Study 1 as predicted, although the effects in the relative deprivation condition appeared to be somewhat smaller than before.

For SDO and entitlement, the tests of the hypotheses faltered at Step 1. There was no overall between-condition difference either for SDO, $F(5, 140) = 0.95, ns, \eta^2 = .03$, or for entitlement, $F(5, 141) = 1.95, p = .09, \eta^2 = .06$.

For British identification, finally, the overall between-groups difference was highly significant, $F(5, 141) = 6.75, p < .001, \eta^2 = .19$. The predicted contrast was also significant, $F(1, 141) = 3.98, p = .048, \eta^2 = .03$. The trend for the "v-curve" was marginally significant in the prejudiced norm condition, $F(1, 141) = 2.76, p = .09, \eta^2 = .02$. Contrary to expectations, the "v-curve" pattern was highly significant in the control norm condition, $F(1, 141) = 13.54, p < .001, \eta^2 = .09$. Inspection of the means reveals that identification was significantly lower in the condition in which participants were not given any information about prospects.

Mediation. In order to investigate the process behind the moderated v-curve pattern, we examined whether the relation between predicted between-condition differences (the moderated v-curve hypothesis) and dependent measures was mediated by British identification (cf. Dambrun et al., 2006). First, the condition contrast (Hypothesis 2, above) led to more identification, $ß = .18, p = .045$. Second, analyses of the direct effect confirmed that there was a significant relationship between the condition contrast and support for anti-immigration policies, $ß = .14, p = .046$. When support for anti-immigrant policies was regressed on the condition contrast and British identification simultaneously, only the relationship between identification and support was significant, $ß = .23, p < .001$; the relationship between the condition code and support became non-significant, $ß = .10, ns$. The bootstrap confidence interval revealed the indirect effect of identification to be significant (.0033 to 0.0879). This provides evidence that identification mediated the effect of condition on support.

Support for prejudicial treatment revealed a similar direct effect, $ß = .27, p < .001$. When support was regressed on condition contrast and British identification simultaneously, the relationship between identification and support was significant, $ß = .15, p = .009$. Although the relationship between the condition code and support was somewhat attenuated, it remained significant, $ß = .24, p < .001$. The bootstrap confidence interval revealed that the indirect effect of identification was not significant ($-.0001$ to 0.0623). There was no evidence that identification mediated the effect of condition on support for prejudicial treatment.

Finally, a mediation analysis of support for ethnocentric treatment also revealed a direct effect, $ß = .30, p < .001$. When support was regressed on condition contrast and British identification simultaneously, the relationship between identification and support was significant, $ß = .33, p < .001$, and the relationship between condition and support was attenuated, though still significant, $ß = .24, p < .001$. The bootstrap confidence interval revealed that the indirect effect of identification was significant (.0049 to 0.1248). Thus, identification mediated the effect of condition on support for ethnocentric treatment.

In sum, identification mediated (at least partially) the effect for two out of three key dependent variables and can thus be said to play a key role, as hypothesized by Dambrun et al. (2006). Such identification effects are, of course, completely consistent with a social identity interpretation of these effects, which would suggest that an increase in status through gratification (as well as an increase in threat through deprivation) can affect identification and concurrently affect normative behavior. The fact that identification did not mediate in Study 1 could have been caused by the slightly different manipulation of group norms: In the present study, this emphasized the intergroup dimension explicitly and this may explain why national identification effects were found (rather than, for instance, identification with the elite).

General Discussion

Results of two studies show that the "v-curve effect" demonstrated by Guimond and Dambrun (2002) is moderated by the content of the prospective in-group's norm. In both studies there was more hostility toward immigrants (support for anti-immigrant policies in both studies, support for prejudicial treatment and ethnocentric policies in Study 2) when participants anticipated future gratification—that is, when their future prospects were good, and when there was less chance of economic competition from immigrants. Study 2 also showed some evidence to suggest that anticipated deprivation increased such hostility, although this was a much less consistent and strong pattern.

Importantly, however, there was no evidence to support the v-curve hypothesis when the norms of the elite (the prospective in-group, for those who expected future gratification) were neutral. The strong evidence for the v-curve only emerged when the elite condoned hostility. When we examine other research that has reported a v-curve, it could reasonably be argued that the elites under observation there were also hostile toward the low-status groups: studies focused on French elites (Guimond & Dambrun, 2002) and South African elites (Dambrun et al., 2006), both of which have a reputation for hostility toward immigrants. The third v-curve was demonstrated among the White residents of a segregated 1960s town in Midwest United States that experienced racial tensions (Grofman & Muller, 1973), another context in which hostility toward African Americans was overt.

The design of the studies ensured that the gratification that participants were confronted with was anticipated (as was the case in Grofman & Muller, 1973; Guimond & Dambrun, 2002). Coupled with the manipulation of social norms for the elite only (i.e., for the prospective in-group of gratified participants) this makes for a strong test of the hypothesis that there are not just intragroup processes at work here, but that the motives of participants were strategic with respect to future prospects. In the gratified condition (Studies 1 and 2) participants in effect expressed support for the actions that they believed their prospective in-group to be responsible for. They thus adapted their personal preferences to suit the expectations of their future station in life.

It should be emphasized that this support was expressed in private toward the experimenters only, making it unlikely that this was a mere compliance effect, and more likely that it was either willing conformity to a behavioral pattern that was consistent with the entry into a new group, or strategic self-presentation (Moreland & Levine, 1982). It is important to note too that identification partially mediated the effects in Study 2 (as in Dambrun et al., 2006), but that it did not in Study 1. This is relevant because high identifiers should be most prone to willingly conform to the norms of the prospective in-group. This (coupled with the lack of any entitlement effects) provides further (indirect) support for the idea that strategic factors could have been responsible for these effects.

But irrespective of whether this endorsement of intergroup hostility was the result of purely strategic processes, or reflective of some "real" normative influence of the in-group, it is clear that the present results are far removed from the intergroup considerations that are traditionally considered the predictors of oppression in theories of intergroup relations. There is no evidence that people support hostile actions toward immigrants merely because of a sense of threat. In fact, effects in relative deprivation condition (Study 2) were not showing consistent increases in hostility, compared with a control condition. There was no evidence either that potential process variables identified by other theories (SDO, entitlement) played a prominent role. Instead, it is very clear that intragroup factors such as norms and individuals' (strategic) responses to them are of central importance (see also Amiot & Bourhis, 2005; Smith & Postmes, 2009).

There is strong evidence for the claim that intragroup processes are at work because both studies directly manipulated norms of the prospective in-group. It is worth noting that such manipulations of the process variable provide more direct and incontrovertible evidence of causality than mediation with measured process variables does. Methodological issues for future research would be to facilitate generalization to actual intergroup behavior by inclusion of a broader range of dependent variables. Needless to say, measurement of actual oppressive behavior is ethically dubious, but the generalizability of present findings to real-life oppression would be easier if future research could focus on certain mild forms of hostility or concrete intentions to engage in them.

Implications and Conclusions

The present research shows that acts of oppression need not be motivated by intergroup factors such as conflict and threat, nor do they necessarily feed on cognitive precursors such as pervasive prejudice or hostile stereotypes. Instead, the results underline the importance of the intragroup dimension of intergroup behavior. Oppression occurs because individuals act strategically to achieve certain objectives within (or with) the in-group. This finding affirms that oppression is indeed genuine collective behavior in the sense that it is grounded in processes of social influence and collective co-ordination of actions. However, it also underlines the importance of considering the intergroup and intragroup dimension of collective action in interaction with each other. Indeed, as argued elsewhere, the present-day hostility toward immigrants appears to be driven primarily by intragroup processes (Smith & Postmes, 2008), and the aims of their oppression consequently have less to do with keeping them down, so much as advancing the positions of particular subgroups within the high-status majority (see also Morton, Postmes, & Jetten, 2007).

There are practical implications of the present research in its optimistic outlook on the amelioration of intergroup relations. Far from being an inevitable outcome of threatened status or entrenched entitlement, the present results suggest that patterns of oppression are highly responsive to in-group norms (see also Smith & Postmes, 2009). Such norms, however, are highly permeable and changeable: There is considerable evidence that practitioners can do a lot to change group norms in general (Cialdini & Goldstein, 2004). Hostile norms and stereotypes are similarly subject to intragroup social influences (Haslam, 1997; Postmes et al., 2005). A key role in this process of norm change is played by the intragroup dynamics of high-status groups: to challenge the legitimacy of inequity and to encourage debate about this within the high-status group would appear to be a positive first step toward the eradication of oppression.

In conclusion, the prime concern of the collective action literature tends to be with low-status groups' actions. Among high-status groups, the assumed drivers of collective action tend to be individual and "group-level" (or intergroup) factors. At the individual level, the concern is with factors such as prejudice or social dominance orientation. At the intergroup level the concern is with the impact of intergroup threat, and with psychological processes of justice, efficacy and identity. In the present article, we advance the idea that it is also important to attend to the "intermediate" level of intragroup processes, because this is likely to be the source of profound influences to support and initiate oppressive actions. We also propose that it may be worthwhile, in future research, to examine a broader range of oppressive actions than institutionalized and pervasive exclusion alone. A study of a broad spectrum of oppressive actions is likely to reveal that in addition to individual and intergroup factors, there are various strategic reasons for participation in collective action, both at an intergroup (Reicher, Spears, & Postmes, 1995) and an intragroup level. Such strategic and intragroup factors are more likely to play a key role in high-status groups: Among the privileged, actions that benefit the group tend to also be beneficial for more personal reasons.

References

Allport, F. H. (1924). *Social psychology*. New York: Houghton Mifflin.
Amiot, C. E., & Bourhis, R. Y. (2005). Discrimination between dominant and subordinate groups: The positive-negative asymmetry effect and normative processes. *British Journal of Social Psychology, 44*, 289–308.

Bettencourt, B. A., Dorr, N., Charlton, K., & Hume, D. L. (2001). Status differences and in-group bias: A meta-analytic examination of the effects of status stability, status legitimacy, and group permeability. *Psychological Bulletin, 127*, 520–542.

Blumer, H. (1958). Race prejudice as a sense of group position. *Pacific Sociological Review, 1*, 3–7.

Bobo, L. D. (1999). Prejudice as group position: Microfoundations of a sociological approach to racism and race relations. *Journal of Social Issues, 55*, 445–472.

Bonacich, E. (1972). A theory of ethnic antagonism. *American Sociological Review, 77*, 547–559.

Cialdini, R. B., & Goldstein, N. J. (2004). Social influence: Compliance and conformity. *Annual Review of Psychology, 55*, 591–621.

Dambrun, M., Taylor, D. M., McDonald, D. A., Crush, J., & Meot, A. (2006). The relative deprivation-gratification continuum and the attitudes of South Africans toward immigrants: A test of the V-curve hypothesis. *Journal of Personality And Social Psychology, 91*, 1032–1044.

Green, D. P., Glaser, J., & Rich, A. (1998). From lynching to gay bashing: The elusive connection between economic conditions and hate crime. *Journal of Personality and Social Psychology, 75*, 82–92.

Grofman, B. N., & Muller, E. N. (1973). Strange case of relative gratification and potential for political violence–V-curve hypothesis. *American Political Science Review, 67*, 514–539.

Guimond, S., & Dambrun, M. (2002). When prosperity breeds intergroup hostility: The effects of relative deprivation and relative gratification on prejudice. *Personality and Social Psychology Bulletin, 28*, 900–912.

Haslam, S. A. (1997). Stereotyping and social influence: Foundations of stereotype consensus. In R. Spears, P. J. Oakes, N. Ellemers, & S. A. Haslam (Eds.), *The social psychology of stereotyping and group life* (pp. 119–143). Oxford: Blackwell.

Haslam, S. A. (2001). *Psychology in organizations: The social identity approach.* London: Sage.

Hobsbawm, E. (1994). *Age of extremes: The short 20th century, 1914–1991.* New York: Pantheon.

Hovland, C. I., & Sears, R. R. (1940). Minor studies of aggression: VI. Correlation of lynching with economic indices. *Journal of Psychology, 9*, 301–310.

Jackman, M. R. (1994). *The velvet glove: Paternalism and conflict in gender, class, and race relations.* Berkeley: University of California Press.

Jost, J. T., & Banaji, M. R. (1994). The role of stereotyping in system-justification and the production of false consciousness. *British Journal of Social Psychology, 33*, 1–27.

Killen, M., Rutland, A., & Jampol, N. S. (2008). Social exclusion in childhood and adolescence. In K. H. Rubin, W. Bukowski, & B. Laursen (Eds.), *Handbook of peer relationships, interactions, and groups* (pp. 249–266). New York: Guilford.

Kinder, D. R., & Sears, D. O. (1981). Prejudice and politics–symbolic racism versus racial threats to the good life. *Journal of Personality and Social Psychology, 40*, 414–431.

Klandermans, B. (1997). *The social psychology of protest.* Oxford: Blackwell.

Le Bon, G. (1995). *The crowd: A study of the popular mind.* London: Transaction Publishers. (Original work published in 1895).

Lewin, K. (1948). *Resolving social conflicts: Selected papers on group dynamics.* Washington, DC: APA.

Lorenzi-Cioldi, F. (2006). Group status and individual differentiation. In T. Postmes & J. Jetten (Eds.), *Individuality and the group: Advances in social identity* (pp. 93–115). London: Sage.

Moreland, R. L., & Levine, J. M. (1982). Socialization in small groups: Temporal changes in individual-group relations. In L. Berkowitz (Ed.), *Advances in experimental social psychology* (Vol. 15, pp. 137–192). New York: Academic Press.

Morton, T. A., Postmes, T., & Jetten, J. (2007). Playing the game: When group success is more important than downgrading deviants. *European Journal of Social Psychology, 37*, 599–616.

Mummendey, A., & Otten, S. (1998). Positive-negative asymmetry in social discrimination. In W. Stroebe & M. Hewstone (Eds.), *European review of social psychology* (Vol. 9, pp. 107–143). Chichester, UK: Wiley.

Olson, M. (1968). *The logic of collective action: Public goods and the theory of groups.* Cambridge, MA: Harvard University Press.

Pettigrew, T. F., & Meertens, R. W. (1995). Subtle and blatant prejudice in Western Europe. *European Journal of Social Psychology, 25*, 57–75.
Postmes, T., & Brunsting, S. (2002). Collective action in the age of internet: Mass communication and online mobilization. *Social Science Computer Review, 20*, 290–301.
Postmes, T., Haslam, S. A., & Swaab, R. I. (2005). Social influence in small groups: An interactive model of social identity formation. *European Review of Social Psychology, 16*, 1–42.
Reicher, S. (1996). "The Battle of Westminster": Developing the social identity model of crowd behaviour in order to explain the initiation and development of collective conflict. *European Journal of Social Psychology, 26*, 115–134.
Reicher, S., Spears, R., & Postmes, T. (1995). A social identity model of deindividuation phenomena. In W. Stroebe & M. Hewstone (Eds.), *European review of social psychology* (Vol. 6, pp. 161–198). Chichester, UK: Wiley.
Rosenthal, R., & Rosnow, R. L. (1985). *Contrast analyses: Focused comparisons in the analysis of variance*. Cambridge: Cambridge University Press.
Rudé, G. (1964). *The crowd in history: A study of popular disturbances in France and England, 1730–1848*. New York: Wiley.
Runciman, W. G. (1966). *Relative deprivation and social justice: A study of attitudes to social inequality in twentieth-century England*. Berkeley: University of California Press.
Sidanius, J., & Pratto, F. (1999). *Social dominance: An intergroup theory of social hierarchy and oppression*. New York: Cambridge University Press.
Simon, B., & Klandermans, B. (2001). Politicized collective identity—a social psychological analysis. *American Psychologist, 56*, 319–331.
Smith, L. G. E., & Postmes, T. (2008). *The power of talk: Legitimizing hostile social action*. Unpublished manuscript, Exeter.
Smith, L. G. E., & Postmes, T. (2009). Obstructed ingroup advancement and the development of norms which reverse the positive-negative asymmetry effect. *European Journal of Social Psychology, 39*, 130–144.
Tajfel, H., & Turner, J. C. (1979). An integrative theory of intergroup conflict. In S. Worchel & W. G. Austin (Eds.), *The psychology of intergroup relations* (pp. 33–47). Monterey, CA: Brooks-Cole.
Tilly, C., Tilly, L., & Tilly, R. (1975). *The rebellious century: 1830–1930*. Cambridge, MA: Harvard University Press.
Turner, J. C. (2005). Explaining the nature of power: A three-process theory. *European Journal of Social Psychology, 35*, 1–22.
Turner, J. C., & Brown, R. (1978). Social status, cognitive alternatives and intergroup relations. In H. Tajfel (Ed.), *Differentiation between groups: Studies in the social psychology of intergroup relations* (pp. 201–234). London: Academic Press.
van Zomeren, M., & Iyer, A. (2009). An introduction to the social and psychological dynamics of collective action. *Journal of Social Issues, 65*, 645–660.
van Zomeren, M., Postmes, T., & Spears, R. (2008). Toward an integrative social identity model of collective action: A quantitative research synthesis of three socio-psychological perspectives. *Psychological Bulletin, 134*, 504–535.
Walker, I., & Smith, H. J. (2002). *Relative deprivation: Specification, development, and integration*. Cambridge: Cambridge University Press.

TOM POSTMES is professor of Social Psychology at the University of Groningen and the University of Exeter. He received his PhD in social psychology from the University of Amsterdam in 1997, where he went on to become a lecturer and research fellow of the Royal Netherlands Academy of Arts and Sciences. In 2001, he joined the University of Exeter as senior lecturer, where he was promoted to reader (2003) and full professor (2004). While at Exeter, he was awarded a research fellowship of the Economic and Social Research Council (ESRC) and numerous grants from various funding bodies. In 2007, he moved back to the Netherlands to join the University of Groningen. His research is concerned with social identity, intragroup processes, intergroup relations, and communication. In 2006, he edited a book with Jolanda Jetten titled *Individuality and the Group: Advances in Social Identity* (Sage).

LAURA G. E. SMITH is a postdoctoral research fellow at the University of Queensland, Australia. She received her PhD in social psychology from the University of Exeter, United Kingdom, in 2008, funded by an Economic and Social Research Council (ESRC) scholarship. Her thesis examined the effect of small-group interaction on identity and intergroup action. Smith spent 6 months at the University of Queensland in 2007, collaborating with senior colleagues on a project on rumor transmission. She was an Associate Research Fellow at the University of Exeter (2007) working on the impact of group norms on the inter-group behavior of high-status group members. She is currently investigating the development of organizational identification over time. Her main research interests are social identity formation in interactive small groups, and the development of norms for intergroup behavior.

# Why Do Men and Women Challenge Gender Discrimination in the Workplace? The Role of Group Status and In-group Identification in Predicting Pathways to Collective Action

Aarti Iyer[*]
The University of Queensland

Michelle K. Ryan
University of Exeter

Group status and group identification were hypothesized to moderate the predictors of collective action to challenge gender discrimination against women. Higher identifiers were expected to respond to the inequality through the lens of their in-group's interests. Among highly identified women, collective action was predicted by appraisals of illegitimacy and feelings of anger, suggesting that they felt a sense of solidarity with the victims and experienced the justice violation as personally relevant. In contrast, higher identification with the high-status group should reflect more investment in the advantaged in-group, relative to the interests of the victimized out-group members. Thus, among highly identified men, collective action intentions were predicted by perceiving the inequality as pervasive (i.e., not limited to a few cases) and feelings of sympathy for victims. This suggests that highly identified men did not experience the inequality as self-relevant until they saw it as too widespread to be ignored. In contrast, men and women with lower gender group identification demonstrated more similar pathways to collective action, where sympathy was the main predictor. Theoretical and practical implications are discussed.

---

[*]Correspondence concerning this article should be addressed to Aarti Iyer, School of Psychology, University of Queensland, McElwain Building, St. Lucia QLD 4072, Australia [e-mail: a.iyer@uq.edu.au].

We thank Clara Kulich, Jamie Mason, and Mette Hersby for help with data collection and management. This research was jointly supported by the Economic and Social Research Council (RES 062 23 0135) and a RCUK Academic fellowship awarded to the second author.

History suggests that challenges to social inequality and injustice are typically led by groups that occupy low-status positions in the status hierarchy. Thus, for example, it is primarily racial minority groups in the United States, Australia, and South Africa who have taken action to claim their civil rights; and it is mostly women who have struggled to expand their gender group's restricted legal rights in various domains (see Tilly, 2004). However, there are also notable cases where advantaged groups (who collectively benefit from the status quo) have also acted to challenge the status quo. Indeed, the power, influence, and resources held by advantaged groups can even help social movements achieve their aims (Iyer & Leach, 2010).

Although social change arguably could not occur without support and participation from those advantaged by systems of inequality, early social psychological approaches typically focused on groups' efforts to improve their own status position. Theoretical frameworks, such as relative deprivation theory (Runciman, 1966) and social identity theory (Tajfel & Turner, 1979), primarily consider the structural perspective of the disadvantaged. Empirical research that has developed from these approaches has also focused on members of low-status groups (for a review, see van Zomeren, Postmes, & Spears, 2008).

In contrast, early work on advantaged groups typically considered their tendency to ignore instances of intergroup inequality or legitimize it (for reviews, see Iyer & Leach, 2010; Leach, Snider, & Iyer, 2002). More recently, however, social psychologists have taken a broader view of those who might participate in collective action. Work on group-based emotions has considered how members of structurally advantaged groups become involved in collective action on behalf of another group's interests (for reviews, see Iyer & Leach, 2010; Iyer & Leach, 2008). However, this line of research has remained relatively independent of the work investigating collective action by disadvantaged groups. In other words, researchers tend to focus on explaining either collective action by disadvantaged groups (e.g., van Zomeren, Postmes, & Spears, 2008) or by advantaged groups (e.g., Iyer & Leach, 2010).

Indeed, very little empirical work has (to our knowledge) directly compared how members of advantaged and disadvantaged groups come to participate in collective action. As we discuss in the following sections, some work has considered how group status moderates rates of participation in collective action, but little is known about the processes that underlie participation by individuals from different status groups. This question is the focus of the present article: We investigate the predictors of participation by high- and low-status groups and examine how these predictors may be moderated by level of identification with the in-group. Within the context of gender inequality, we consider how men (i.e., members of the advantaged group) and women (i.e., members of the disadvantaged group) think and feel about a specific type of gender discrimination, and how these perceptions and emotions are related to their willingness to take action challenging such discrimination. Below, we briefly review the literatures on group status and collective action participation. We then outline how level of identification with the in-group might moderate reasons for collective action.

Comparing Advantaged and Disadvantaged Groups' Rates of Participation in Collective Action

Early theoretical frameworks such as relative deprivation theory (Runciman, 1966) and social identity theory (Tajfel & Turner, 1979) proposed that, relative to members of advantaged groups, members of disadvantaged groups should be more likely to participate in collective action to challenge the status quo. This is because occupying a position of (undeserved) relative disadvantage hurts the material interests of the group (Guimond & Dubé-Simard, 1983) as well as its members' social identities, because low-status positions are typically not valued in society (Tajfel & Turner, 1979). As a result, the disadvantaged should have a vested interest in challenging the status quo.

Subsequent empirical work has demonstrated that individuals who perceive an inequality to be illegitimate and unstable are most likely to participate in efforts to challenge it, whether they are members of low-status groups (for a review, see Wright, 2001) or high-status groups (for a review, see Leach et al., 2002). However, few lines of empirical research have directly investigated the role of group status in moderating rates of participation in collective action.[1] A key exception is the work examining the role of group identification in predicting collective action intentions, which we review below.

Group identification and participation in collective action. Work in the social identity tradition has long argued that all group members do not necessarily respond to inequality in the same way. Rather, individuals' level of group identification—or psychological attachment to the group—should influence these responses. More specifically, lower identifiers should focus on their individual prospects, whereas higher identifiers should care more about the prospects of the group (see van Zomeren & Spears, this volume). This is because higher identifiers

---

[1] Various lines of research may appear at first glance to be relevant to this question but turn out to be tangential for one of two reasons. First, the dependent measures included in comparisons of high-status and low-status groups are not typically relevant to the concept of collective action to achieve social equality. For instance, early laboratory experiments manipulated group status and examined its impact on group bias in the allocation of points or resources (e.g., Sachdev & Bourhis, 1987; Turner & Brown, 1978). Second, theoretical and empirical work on intergroup helping (e.g., Levine, Prosser, Evans, & Reicher, 2005; Stürmer, Snyder, & Omoto, 2005) and collective action (e.g., van Zomeren, Spears, Fischer, & Leach, 2004, Study 1) has used membership in a social group to explain willingness to take action. Such group membership, however, is not necessarily equivalent to membership in high-status and low-status groups within a system of inequality.

are more likely to define themselves as group members rather than as individuals (Spears, Doosje, & Ellemers, 1999), and their perceptions, feelings, and actions are more likely to be in line with group interests and goals (see Ellemers, Spears, & Doosje, 2002). Indeed, empirical work has demonstrated that members of disadvantaged groups are more likely to participate in collective action when they report higher levels of identification with the disadvantaged group in general (see Kelly, 1993), with a particular social movement (see Stürmer & Simon, 2004) or with an emergent social identity developed in the context of crowds (Drury & Reicher, 2000; for a review and meta-analysis, see van Zomeren, Postmes, & Spears, 2008). Moreover, work with members of advantaged groups suggests that those who are less identified with their groups are more willing (in some circumstances) to acknowledge the illegitimacy of their group's position and to challenge it (e.g., Doosje, Branscombe, Spears, & Manstead, 1998).

To our knowledge, only one study (Gordijn, Yzerbyt, Wigboldus, & Dumont, 2006) has considered how levels of group identification influence responses to inequality among members of high-status groups and low-status groups. Results showed that members of a victim group who demonstrated higher levels of group identification saw the harm as more illegitimate, felt angrier about it, and were more likely to participate in collective action to address the situation, compared to those who were less identified with the group. In contrast, it was lower identifiers among the perpetrator group (whose representatives caused the harm) who saw the harm as more illegitimate. Thus, challenges to the status quo were more likely to come from higher identifiers of the victim (i.e., low-status) group, and lower identifiers of the perpetrator (i.e., high-status) group due to different levels of perceived legitimacy and reported anger.

However, the existence of mass social movements suggests that challenges to the status quo are undertaken by more than a subset of high-status and low-status groups. That is, participation in collective action does occur (at least sometimes) among lower identified members of the low-status group, and higher identifiers in the high-status group. How might this participation be explained, if these individuals do not exhibit high levels of the standard appraisals (i.e., perceived legitimacy) and emotions (i.e., felt anger) that have most frequently been proposed as predictors of collective action?

Previous work focusing on action among low-status groups suggests that the less identified members have different reasons for participating in collective action, such as beliefs about their ability to achieve the goals of the action (e.g., van Zomeren, Spears, & Leach, 2008) or more individual goals (e.g., Klandermans, 1984, Simon et al., 1998). In line with this work, we propose that less identified members of low-status groups may make additional appraisals of the inequality (e.g., pervasiveness, or the extent to which the inequality extends beyond a few isolated cases) and experience additional emotions (e.g., sympathy) that better explain their intentions to challenge the status quo. We also extend this analysis to the other set of individuals who are unlikely candidates for collective action: highly identified members of the high-status group.

In-group Identification and Reasons for Collective Action Participation

As noted earlier, individuals who are more identified with their group are more likely to self-define as group members, and to view the world through the lens of this group perspective (see Ellemers et al., 2002). Such a chronic awareness of group-level (identity and material) interests should make any specific instance of group-based inequality more relevant to the individual, even if s/he is not directly affected by it. As a result, higher identifiers should be more likely to notice instances of group-based inequality as self-relevant, to feel emotional reactions about them, and to evaluate them in terms of the implications for the group (see Iyer & Leach, 2008). This should have different implications for members of different status groups, as we outline below.

Identification with the Low-Status Group

Those who are highly identified with a low-status or victimized group are likely to see the inequality as violating important principles of justice and fairness, and therefore as illegitimate. We also expect them to perceive the inequality as pervasive. That is, they should see the inequality as a widespread phenomenon that represents a real problem, rather than as a small issue affecting only a few individuals. Previous work suggests that these high identifiers are also more likely to feel an increased sense of connectedness and solidarity with victims of the discrimination (Kelly, 1993). This suggests an increase in justice-relevant emotions such as anger, which is typically experienced when one's goals and interests are unfairly undermined (Frijda, Kuipers, & ter Shure, 1989). This should also increase sympathy for the victims of the inequality, as this emotion is typically experienced in response to those who are suffering illegitimate harm (Leach et al., 2002). Taken together, then, we expect high identifiers to report high levels of perceived illegitimacy and pervasiveness, and high levels of justice-relevant emotions (i.e., anger and sympathy). As a result, they should also be willing to participate in collective action to challenge the inequality.

We also expect specific patterns of associations between these variables, including the appraisals that predict the emotions, and the emotions that predict willingness to participate in collective action. Compared to appraisals of pervasiveness, appraised illegitimacy is hypothesized to be a stronger predictor of anger and sympathy among this subset of the low-status group. This is because we expect the mere fact of a justice violation to elicit emotional reactions among higher identifiers, more so than considerations of how widespread or pervasive this phenomenon is. In other words, the existence of illegitimacy may be sufficient to elicit justice-relevant emotions such as anger among these group members.

What of the predictors of collective action? Theoretical frameworks of emotion in intergroup relations suggest that both anger and sympathy could motivate participation in collective action (see Leach et al., 2002; Smith & Kessler, 2004). Anger has been shown to predict willingness to participate in collective action among disadvantaged groups (e.g., van Zomeren et al., 2004) and sympathy to increase helping behavior directed at disadvantaged individuals (e.g., Batson, Chang, Orr, & Rowland, 2002). Although individuals who are highly identified with a low-status group should experience both anger and sympathy about its disadvantaged position, we propose that anger is the emotion that should more strongly predict their participation in collective action. The increased solidarity that these individuals feel with the victims of discrimination suggests that they are likely to take action to defend their group's interests and express their beliefs that the discrimination is unfair. These appraisals and goals have been linked to anger in the interpersonal emotions literature, rather than to sympathy (see Frijda et al., 1989; Roseman, Wiest, & Swartz, 1994). This suggests that anger should play a key role in predicting collective action among these individuals.

Members of low-status groups should exhibit a different pattern of responses when they are less identified with the group. Such individuals are less likely to view the inequality in group terms and thus should be less focused on the group's interests (Ellemers et al., 2002). As such, they should differ from the more highly identified members of their groups with respect to (1) the mean levels of reported appraisals, emotions, and collective action intentions; (2) the unique predictors of emotion; and (3) the unique predictors of collective action.

First, following previous work (e.g., Gordijn et al., 2006), we propose that lower identifiers should perceive the inequality as less of a problem (i.e., as less illegitimate and less pervasive) compared to higher identifiers. Similarly, they should also report feeling lower levels of justice-relevant emotions such as anger and sympathy. As a result of these lower appraisals and emotions, lower identifiers should also be less willing than higher identifiers to participate in collective action to challenge the status quo.

Second, given that beliefs about the legitimacy of the group's position are not as salient or relevant to these individuals' worldview, these beliefs should not be the sole basis for their emotional responses to the inequality (e.g., anger or sympathy). Rather, if the inequality becomes self-relevant or important to the individual, it is likely to be due to another appraisal, such as the size of the phenomenon being so large that it cannot be ignored or explained away. This increased self-relevance may then serve as an additional basis of emotional reactions to the inequality (see Iyer & Leach, 2008). Thus, we propose the beliefs about the pervasiveness of the inequality—that is, how widespread it is perceived to be—should be positively associated with feelings of anger and sympathy.

Third, we hypothesize that collective action among the lower identifiers will be predicted more strongly by sympathy than by anger. This is because individuals who are less identified with the low-status group should feel less invested in the interests of their fellow group members who are victimized by the inequality. As such, when they do take action to challenge the inequality, it may be driven more by a sympathetic concern for victims of inequality, rather than by feelings of anger experienced on behalf of the victims' illegitimately violated interests (see Wispé, 1986).

Identification with the High-Status Group

Individuals whose groups either benefit from, or have perpetuated, social inequality may also perceive it to be unjust (Doosje et al., 1998; Iyer, Schmader, & Lickel, 2007; Leach, Iyer, & Pedersen, 2006) and experience anger (Iyer et al., 2007; Leach et al., 2006) and sympathy (e.g., Harth, Kessler, & Leach, 2008) about the inequality. However, identification should also play an important role in moderating the responses, and the pathways to collective action, among members of the high-status group. Interestingly, we expect these results to take the opposite pattern of those found in the low-status group.

As with a low-status group, members of a high-status group who are less identified with the group tend to see themselves as individuals, rather than as group members. As a result, their perceptions and emotions are not necessarily guided by the group norms and goals, and they are less likely to be invested in this group's material and identity interests (Branscombe, Ellemers, Spears, & Doosje, 1999; Doosje et al., 1998). Thus, they may respond with appraisals, emotions, and actions that limit, or perhaps even contradict, their group's self-interest (Gordijn et al., 2006).

Following this logic, we expect that lower identifiers of high-status groups should be willing to perceive an inequality that privileges their own group as illegitimate and pervasive. These individuals should also be likely to experience emotional reactions to the violation of justice principles (e.g., anger) as well as the undeserved suffering of the victims (e.g., sympathy). And they should be willing to engage in collective action to challenge the status quo. Thus, less identified members of the high-status group may respond in similar ways as highly identified members of the low-status group.

Given that members of the high-status group are likely to experience group-based privilege, however, we expect that their ability to empathize with victims of inequality will be somewhat limited. Their structural position makes them less likely to feel a sense of connection or solidarity with members of the low-status group. Thus, we expect that the predictors of their emotions and collective action intentions will be similar to lower-identified members of the low-status group. More specifically, we propose that appraised illegitimacy may not be sufficient to promote feelings of anger and sympathy about the inequality. Members of the high-status group may need to be convinced that the phenomenon is a widespread and pervasive one before they respond to it. Similarly, anger on behalf of those whose interests have been illegitimately violated may not be sufficient to promote action. Rather, it is likely that feelings of sympathy for the (somewhat distanced) suffering of these victims should also predict collective action intentions, a pattern akin to that expected for the less identified members of the low-status group.

Just as for the low-status group, individuals who are highly identified with the high-status group should also view an inequality in group-based terms. In this case, however, the group's (material and identity) interests lie in maintaining the status quo, rather than challenging it (see Branscombe et al., 1999; Leach et al., 2002). As in the low-status group, we propose that the responses of highly identified members of the high-status group should differ in three ways from their less identified counterparts.

First, we expect individuals who are highly identified with the high-status group to perceive the inequality as less illegitimate and pervasive in order to maintain their own group's positive image (Branscombe et al., 1999). These high-status group members are also hypothesized to feel lower levels of justice-based emotions such as anger and sympathy about the inequality. And, they should be less willing to participate in collective action to challenge the status quo.

Second, beliefs about illegitimacy should not be the sole basis for the emotions of anger and sympathy. Rather, as for less identified members of the low-status group, it is likely that such emotions will be elicited when the inequality is too large to be explained away, and therefore must be a "real" problem that is relevant to the individual. Thus, we propose that beliefs about the pervasiveness of the inequality—or how widespread it is perceived to be—should be positively associated with feelings of anger and sympathy.

Third, we expect individuals who are highly identified with the high-status group to feel less invested in the interests of those victimized by the inequality (see Doosje et al., 1998). Thus, their willingness to take action to challenge the inequality may be driven more by sympathy for victims, rather than by anger *on behalf of* victims. It may even be the case that appraised pervasiveness is a direct predictor of collective action. In other words, high identifiers in the high-status group may be willing to act to challenge inequality only when they see it as a pervasive and widespread phenomenon.

Present Research

The present research investigates the role of group status and group identification in moderating the predictors of participation in collective action to combat gender discrimination. We present working men and women with a specific example of gender discrimination in the workplace (where women are disadvantaged compared to men). We then assess their perceptions (of illegitimacy and pervasiveness) and emotional reactions (anger and sympathy) as predictors of intentions to participate in collective action to address this gender discrimination.[2]

Method

Participants and Procedure

Working adults were recruited to complete an online survey about "Hiring and Promotion in the Workplace" using three strategies. First, an open invitation to participate (which contained a link to the survey) was posted on various research web sites that are visited by individuals who are willing to participate in psychological research. Second, the invitation was posted in various chat rooms and discussion groups focusing on workplace issues. Third, the invitation was emailed to informal networks of colleagues and acquaintances (who were unfamiliar with the research questions).

In all, 364 questionnaires were downloaded, of which 352 (97%) were completed sufficiently to be usable. Participants included 176 women and 176 men with working experience. More than half of the participants (60.2%) were located in the United States and Canada. Residents of the United Kingdom made up 31.8% of sample, and the rest were from Australia (4.7%), other European countries (1.9%), and various Asian countries (1.4%). Most of the sample (85%) self-identified as White, while 8% self-identified as Black, and 5.6% as Asian. Participants' ages ranged from 23 to 65 years ($M = 38.40$, $SD = 7.2$). Participants reported a range of occupations, including attorney, teacher, manager, civil servant, and sales. In terms of the level of seniority they held in their current job, 74 (21.1%) reported being "quite junior," 88 (25%) reported being "intermediate," 68 (19.3%) reported being "senior," 52 (14.7%) reported being "very senior," and 70 (19.8%) reported that this question was "not applicable" to their current position.

Materials and Measures

Gender group identification. Participants were first asked to complete a three-item measure of gender group identification (adapted from Doosje, Spears, & Ellemers, 1995; $\alpha = .78$; $M = 5.07$, $SD = 1.02$). A sample item read: "I feel strong ties to other members of my gender group."

Description of gender discrimination in the workplace. A potential danger in studying responses to social issues such as gender discrimination is that

---

[2] Feelings of guilt about the inequality were not investigated, as previous work has shown that this emotion does not independently explain willingness to participate in collective action (see Iyer et al., 2007; Leach et al., 2006).

participants' behavior may be dictated by social desirability norms to respond in a politically correct way. For instance, participants may report that they believe discrimination to be illegitimate, despite their private views. In order to reduce this possibility, we presented participants with an example of gender discrimination that has recently been documented—the "glass cliff" (Ryan & Haslam, 2005). Extending the metaphor of the glass ceiling, the glass cliff describes the phenomenon whereby women are more likely to be appointed to risky or precarious leadership positions than are men (for a review of archival and experimental evidence, see Ryan & Haslam, 2007). A recent study (Ryan, Haslam, & Postmes, 2007) showed that men and women were willing to question the existence of the glass cliff, as well as its characterization as an example of illegitimate gender discrimination. As such, we can be reasonably sure that people will respond honestly to this example of gender discrimination.

Participants read an article from the BBC News web site (Ryan & Haslam, 2004) that presented an account of the glass cliff phenomenon. The article reviewed archival and experimental evidence to demonstrate that women are more likely than are men to be appointed to risky leadership positions in the workplace. It concluded that women leaders are thus more likely to be put in a position to fail, compared to their male counterparts.

Appraisals of gender discrimination. After reading the article, participants were asked to indicate their level of agreement with a number of statements about the glass cliff (1 = *disagree completely*, 7 = *agree completely*).

Six items ($\alpha = .81$; $M = 4.21$, $SD = 0.81$) assessed the perception that the glass cliff phenomenon was illegitimate or unfair to women (e.g., "I think the glass cliff phenomenon reflects unjust hiring and promotion practices").

Six items ($\alpha = .87$; $M = 4.24$, $SD = 1.00$) assessed the extent to which participants saw the glass cliff phenomenon as pervasive or widespread, rather than confined to a few organizations or employment sectors (e.g., "I think that most women in leadership have to deal with the glass cliff phenomenon").

Emotions. Participants were next asked, "After reading the article, how do you feel about the 'glass cliff' phenomenon?" They were presented with a series of emotion terms and were asked to use a six-point scale (0 = *not at all*, 5 = *extremely*) to indicate how much they felt each one. Following previous research (e.g., Iyer, Leach, & Crosby, 2003; Leach et al., 2006) anger was assessed with three items (angry, furious, frustrated; $\alpha = .89$; $M = 2.29$, $SD = 1.25$) and sympathy was assessed with three items (concerned, sympathetic, compassionate; $\alpha = .86$; $M = 2.93$, $SD = 1.34$).

Collective action intentions. The final section of the survey asked participants, "How willing would you be to become involved in the following collective action strategies in your organization?" Using a seven-point scale (1 = *very unwilling*, 7 = *very willing*), participants responded to a list of seven actions, which aimed to monitor the glass cliff phenomenon and take steps to reduce its negative impact. Sample strategies included implementing Equal Employment/Affirmative Action program to monitor the number of men and women appointed to risky and safe leadership positions, developing a mentoring system to help women develop professional contacts and networks, and preparing a report outlining the "glass cliff" phenomenon to educate the general public. The seven items formed a reliable uni-dimensional measure of collective action intentions ($\alpha = .93$; $M = 3.82$, $SD = 1.70$).

Results

Mean Differences

As a preliminary step, a one-way ANOVA was conducted to examine gender differences in levels of gender group identification. Women were marginally significantly more identified with their gender group ($M = 5.19$, $SD = 1.09$) than were men with their gender group ($M = 4.94$, $SD = 0.92$), $F(1, 239) = 3.68$, $p = .056$, $\varepsilon^2 = .02$. This is consistent with arguments that, relative to members of low-status groups, members of high-status groups tend to be less aware of, and identified with, their groups (see Leach et al., 2002).

We next sought to test our general hypothesis that men and women who are more or less identified with their gender group should differ in their mean levels of responses to the inequality. A series of hierarchical multiple regression analyses were conducted, with gender (contrast coded: men = -1, women = 1) and (mean centered) identification entered as predictors in Step 1, their interaction entered as a predictor in Step 2, and each dependent variable in turn as the criterion (Aiken & West, 1991).

Appraisals of illegitimacy and pervasiveness. Appraised illegitimacy was predicted by gender ($\beta = .32$, $t = 5.22$, $p < .01$) and (marginally) by identification ($\beta = -.18$, $t = 1.85$, $p = .07$). Thus, women were more likely to view the glass cliff phenomenon as illegitimate than were men, and those who were more strongly identified with their gender group were less likely to view the glass cliff phenomenon as illegitimate than were those with lower levels of gender group identification. These effects were qualified by the interaction between gender and identification: $\beta = .22$, $t = 2.13$, $p = .03$. This interaction is displayed in Figure 1. Among women, higher identifiers were significantly more likely than lower identifiers to see the glass cliff as illegitimate: $\beta = .32$, $t = 5.24$, $p < .01$. Among men, in contrast, higher identifiers were significantly less likely than lower identifiers to see the glass cliff as illegitimate: $\beta = -.31$, $t = -2.06$, $p = .04$.

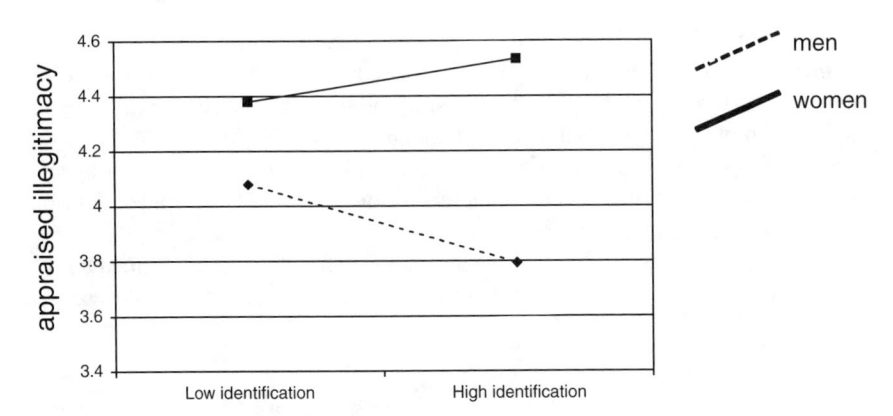

Fig. 1. Perceived illegitimacy as a function of gender and identification with gender group.

Appraised pervasiveness was only significantly predicted by gender: $\beta = .32$, $t = 5.17$, $p < .01$. Thus, women were more likely than men to perceive the glass cliff phenomenon as a widespread phenomenon. Unexpectedly, there was no effect of the interaction between gender and gender group identification. Thus, identification did not moderate men's and women's appraisals of pervasiveness.

Felt anger and sympathy. Anger was predicted by gender ($\beta = .25$, $t = 4.06$, $p < .01$) and (marginally) by identification ($\beta = -.18$, $t = -1.80$, $p = .07$). Thus, women were more likely than men to feel angry about the glass cliff phenomenon, and those who were more strongly identified with their gender group were less likely to feel angry about the glass cliff than were those with lower levels of gender group identification. These effects were qualified by the interaction between gender and identification: $\beta = .27$, $t = 2.70$, $p = .007$. This interaction is displayed in Figure 2. Among women, higher identifiers were significantly more likely than lower identifiers to feel angry about the glass cliff: $\beta = .25$, $t = 4.06$, $p < .01$. Among men, higher identifiers were as likely as lower identifiers to feel angry about the glass cliff: $\beta = -.08$, $t = .92$, $p = .36$.

Sympathy was only significantly predicted by gender: $\beta = .32$, $t = 5.17$, $p < .01$. Thus, women were more likely than men to feel sympathy about the glass cliff phenomenon. Unexpectedly, there was no effect of the interaction between gender and gender group identification.

Collective action intentions. Collective action intentions were only significantly predicted by gender: $\beta = .19$, $t = 2.92$, $p < .01$. Thus, women were more likely than men to intend to take action about the glass cliff in their workplace. Unexpectedly, there was no effect of the interaction between gender and gender group identification.

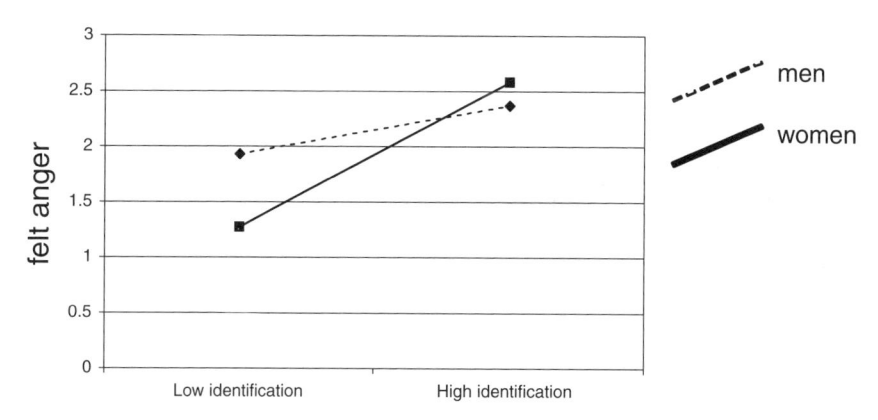

Fig. 2. Anger as a function of gender and identification with gender group.

Summary. The results for appraised illegitimacy and felt anger supported our hypotheses. Within the low low-status group, higher identifiers reported higher means on these two measures than did lower identifiers. The opposite pattern was found with members of the high-status group, with lower identifiers reporting higher means. Surprisingly, this pattern of results was not found on our measures of appraised pervasiveness, felt sympathy, or willingness to participate in collective action. We return to this issue in the Discussion.

Predictive Models Testing Relationships between Variables

We next investigated our hypothesis that the predictors of emotions and collective action intentions should be different for higher and lower identified members of the different status groups. To examine the relationships between appraisals, emotions, and collective action intentions, we used EQS software to test a series of structural models with measured variables. As a first step, we conducted a multiple-sample analysis to investigate whether the predictive relationships between variables were significantly different for men and women at different levels of gender group identification (high or low). Next, we examined the direction and magnitude of these relationships for each of the four groups separately. At each step, we report standard indicators of fit (e.g., χ^2, Comparative Fit Index [CFI], Incremental Fit Index [IFI], Goodness of Fit Index [GFI], standardized root mean residual [RMR], and root mean square error of estimation [RMSEA]; see Hu & Bentler, 1999) to assess how well the model accounts for relationships in the data.

Our hypothesized models specified the appraisals as predictors of emotions, which, in turn, were specified as direct predictors of collective action intentions. Following appraisal theories of emotion (e.g., Frijda, 1986), we also expected emotions to fully mediate the relationships between appraisals and collective action intentions, rather than appraisals serving as the mediator, or collective action intentions being the predictor variable. Previous research on emotion in intergroup relations provides support for this choice: regression analyses have shown that emotions fully mediate the relationship between appraisals and action intentions (e.g., Gordijn et al., 2006). Another set of studies has shown models specifying emotions as predictors of action intentions to fit significantly better than models specifying action intentions as predictors of emotions (Iyer et al., 2007). Thus, we can be reasonably confident in the theoretical and empirical basis of the proposed model.

Preliminary analyses. In order to compare patterns of predictive relationships between higher and lower identified men and women, it was necessary to create these four separate groups. Thus, men and women who were high or low in gender group identification were divided into four groups of equal size. A median split was not used, because this strategy would produce groups of unequal sizes. Rather, we identified the point on the 7-point response scale that divided each gender group into two equal halves—lower and higher identifiers. For men, this cutoff point was 3.67 and for women, this cutoff point was 4. Thus four groups were created for these analyses: male higher identifiers, male lower identifiers, female higher identifiers, and female lower identifiers.

Multi-sample analysis. We hypothesized that emotions and collective action intentions should be predicted by different variables among higher and lower identified members of different status groups. To assess whether these relationships differed for the four groups, we conducted a multisample analysis. This involves testing a model that constrains the relationships between variables to be equal for all groups. If the fit of this constrained model meets standard thresholds for acceptable fit, this indicates that the pattern of associations in the model is essentially the same for the four groups. However, if the constrained model does not fit the data well, it suggests that there are statistically reliable differences in patterns of associations for the four groups (see Kline, 2005).

The constrained model did not meet the standards for acceptable fit (see Hu & Bentler, 1999). The χ^2 value was large and statistically reliable, $\chi^2(8\ df, N = 236) = 42.712, p < .001$, the incremental fit indices were below the threshold of .95 (CFI = .84, IFI = .80, GFI = .84), and the residual fit indices were above the threshold of .08 (standardized RMR = .10, RMSEA = .10). The LaGrange Multiplier test for model modification indicated that overall model fit would be reliably improved ($p < .01$) if six equality constraints were removed from the model.[3] This indicates

---

[3] The six constraints that could be released to improve overall fit represented five direct predictive paths and one correlation. The direct predictive paths were: anger → collective action, sympathy →

(a)

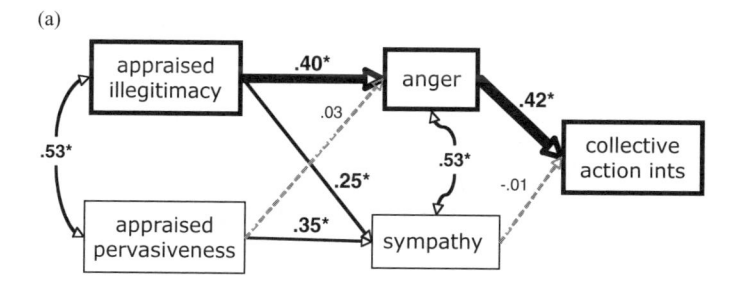

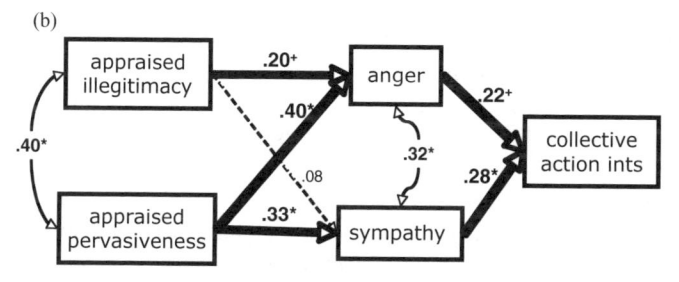

[Figure 3a: Path diagram with appraised illegitimacy, appraised pervasiveness, anger, sympathy, collective action ints. Coefficients: .53*, .40*, .03, .25*, .35*, .53*, .42*, -.01]

(b)

[Figure 3b: Path diagram with appraised illegitimacy, appraised pervasiveness, anger, sympathy, collective action ints. Coefficients: .40*, .20+, .40*, .08, .33*, .32*, .22+, .28*]

Note. Standardized parameter estimates shown. $^+p < .10$, $^*p < .05$. Dashed lines indicate relationships that are not statistically reliable. Thick solid lines indicate relationships of interest.

Fig. 3. (a) Structural model of relationships between appraisals, emotions, and collective action intentions—women with higher levels of gender group identification. (b) Structural model of relationships between appraisals, emotions, and collective action intentions—women with lower levels of gender group identification.

that six associations between variables were reliably different between the four groups. Thus, the next step was to test the model separately for each group to examine the magnitude and direction of all the relationships between variables.

Model for women with higher gender group identification. The hypothesized model provided excellent fit for the data: χ^2 (2 df, $N = 60$) = 2.91, $p = .233$; CFI = .96, IFI = .96, GFI = .97, std. RMR = .07, RMSEA = .06. Standardized parameter estimates for this model are shown in Figure 3a. Many of the estimated parameters in this model were statistically reliable and in the expected directions. Given our interest in pathways to collective action, we focus on those variables that directly or indirectly predict collective action intentions. These central variables and predictive paths are highlighted in Figure 3a with thick boxes and arrows.

---

collective action, appraised pervasiveness → collective action, appraised illegitimacy → sympathy, appraised pervasiveness → sympathy. The correlation was between anger and sympathy.

Collective action intentions in this group had only one statistically reliable predictor: anger. Anger, in turn, was predicted only by perceived illegitimacy. Thus, consistent with hypotheses, women with higher gender group identification who perceived the glass cliff as illegitimate, and who felt angry about it, were more likely to participate in collective action to address this form of gender discrimination. As expected, appraised pervasiveness was not a reliable predictor of anger. Appraised pervasiveness did predict feelings of sympathy, but this is irrelevant to the pathway to action, as sympathy was not a reliable predictor of collective action.

Model for women with lower gender group identification. The hypothesized model provided excellent fit for the data: $\chi^2(2\ df, N = 60) = 2.90, p = .234$; CFI = .96, IFI = .99, GFI = .98, std. RMR = .06, RMSEA = .08. Standardized parameter estimates for this model are shown in Figure 3b. Again, given our interest in pathways to collective action, we focus on those variables that directly or indirectly predict collective action intentions (highlighted with thicker boxes and arrows in Figure 3b).

Starting at the righthand side of the figure, collective action intentions had two direct predictors: anger (which was marginally significant) and sympathy. Consistent with hypotheses, women with lower levels of gender group identification were more willing to take collective action to address the glass cliff when they felt angry and sympathetic about it. Anger was predicted by appraised illegitimacy and pervasiveness, and sympathy by appraised pervasiveness alone. As expected, emotional responses to gender inequality were driven not only by perceptions that it is unfair, but that it is also a widespread phenomenon. Thus, taken together, lower identified women differed from higher identifiers in the expected ways: appraised pervasiveness was a significant predictor of anger and sympathy, and both of these emotions predicted collective action intentions.

Model for men with lower gender group identification. The model provided excellent fit for the data: $\chi^2(2\ df, N = 58) = 3.211, p = .148$; CFI = .95, IFI = .95, GFI = .96, std. RMR = .07, RMSEA = .20.[4] Standardized parameter estimates for this model are shown in Figure 4a. Thicker boxes and arrows indicate the variables that directly or indirectly predict collective action intentions.

As expected, collective action intentions among this group were predicted by both anger and sympathy. Somewhat surprisingly, however, both emotions were predicted only by perceived illegitimacy. Contrary to hypotheses, appraised

---

[4] The RMSEA fit index did not meet Hu and Bentler's (1999) cutoff criteria for good model fit. However, Hu and Bentler (1999) point out that the RMSEA index tends to over-reject true population models in small samples ($N < 250$). Given that the other indices indicate good model fit, it seemed appropriate to overlook the RMSEA index in this case.

(a)

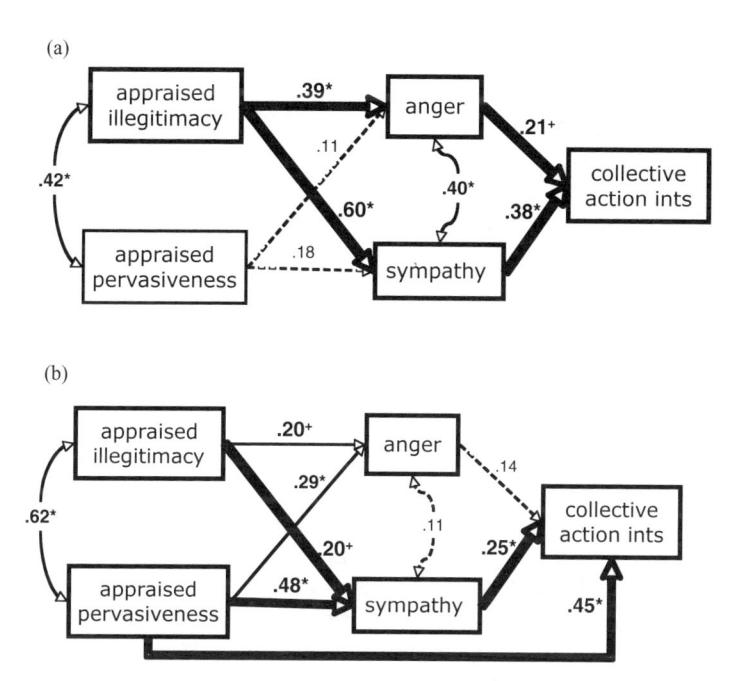

Fig. 4. (a) Structural model of relationships between appraisals, emotions, and collective action intentions—men with lower levels of gender group identification. (b) Structural model of relationships between appraisals, emotions, and collective action intentions—men with higher levels of gender group identification.

Note. Standardized parameter estimates shown. $^+p < .10$, $^*p < .05$. Dashed lines indicate relationships that are not statistically reliable. Thick solid lines indicate relationships of interest.

pervasiveness was not a significant predictor of anger or sympathy. Thus, the model for men with lower gender group identification looked similar to the models for both groups of women: both anger and sympathy predicted collective action (similar to women with lower gender group identification), but only perceived illegitimacy predicted anger and sympathy (similar to women with higher gender group identification).

Model for men with higher gender group identification. The hypothesized model did not quite meet the thresholds for acceptable fit: $\chi^2(2\ df, N = 58) = 4.61, p = .11$; CFI $= .92$, IFI $= .91$, GFI $= .91$, std. RMR $= .09$, RMSEA $= .21$. The LaGrange Multiplier test for model modification indicated that the overall fit would be reliably improved ($p < .01$) with the addition of a direct predictive path from appraised pervasiveness to collective action intentions. This modified model provided excellent fit for the data: $\chi^2(1\ df, N = 58) = 2.90, p = .10$; CFI $= .98$, IFI $= .98$, GFI $= .98$, std. RMR $= .03$, RMSEA $= .19$.[4] Standardized parameter estimates for this model are shown in Figure 4b. Again, thicker boxes and arrows indicate the variables that directly or indirectly predict collective action intentions.

Collective action intentions among this group were directly predicted by feelings of sympathy and appraised pervasiveness. Thus, the more these men felt sympathetic about the glass cliff, and the more they perceived it to be a widespread phenomenon, the more likely they were to participate in strategies to address it. Sympathy was directly predicted by both appraised illegitimacy and appraised pervasiveness. The results provide support for our hypotheses, such that anger was not a predictor of collective action intentions among men with higher gender group identification, and appraised pervasiveness was a direct (as well as indirect) predictor of collective action intentions.

Discussion

The present study demonstrates that the structural position occupied by one's group, as well as one's level of identification with that group, has important implications for how people respond to intergroup inequality. Consistent with previous work (Gordijn et al., 2006), our survey of working adults' responses to a novel form of gender discrimination against women (the glass cliff) found differences in the mean-level responses of higher and lower identifiers. As expected, women who were more highly identified with their gender group perceived the glass cliff as more illegitimate and felt more anger about it relative to lower identifiers. Among men, lower identifiers perceived the glass cliff as more illegitimate relative to higher identifiers, again consistent with expectations and previous research.

However, the resultant difference in reported anger was not found: contrary to hypotheses, higher and lower identified men reported the same levels of anger in response to the glass cliff. This may be because the anger reported by male participants was not necessarily based in appraisals of illegitimacy. Research among advantaged groups has demonstrated a prosocial anger that is based in appraisals of illegitimate inequality (Leach et al., 2006), as well as a prejudiced anger that is based in negative appraisals of the low-status group (Leach, Iyer, & Pedersen, 2007). Future work should include the target of anger when assessing this emotional response to inequality.

We also found only a main effect of gender on appraised pervasiveness and felt sympathy about the glass cliff phenomenon. Gender group identification did not have any additive or interactive effects on these variables. These results are somewhat surprising, and our data does not account for them in any clear way. However, one plausible explanation is that our operationalization of these variables does not clearly differentiate between the individual-based views and group-based views that characterize lower and higher identifiers. Participants may have perceived the glass cliff phenomenon to be widespread, regardless of their beliefs about its underlying cause (i.e., holding individual women responsible for their own position, or blaming systemic discrimination). Similarly, participants could express sympathy toward the women victimized by the glass cliff, regardless of whether they were focusing on their group (i.e., at higher levels of group identification) or on individuals (i.e., at lower levels of group identification).

Results from the path analyses indicated that group identification also influenced the reasons underlying participants' collective action intentions. More specifically, men and women who were highly identified with their respective gender groups displayed markedly different pathways to action. Women with higher levels of gender identification wished to take action to address the glass cliff phenomenon when they perceived it to be unfair and felt angry about it. In contrast, men with higher levels of gender group identification wished to take action when they perceived the glass cliff phenomenon to be pervasive, and when they felt sympathy for those victimized by it.

This sharp contrast in pathways to action underscores the distinction between experiences of inequality among members of low-status groups and members of high-status groups. Higher identification reflects a relatively strong investment in the interests of the fellow group members (Ellemers et al., 2002). In the case of highly identified women, then, the violation of justice is likely to be experienced as one's own, and the resulting collective action is driven by feelings of anger. In contrast, higher identification with a high-status group suggests more investment in the high-status in-group, relative to the interests of the out-group members being victimized (see Doosje et al., 1998). Thus, collective action is undertaken when inequality is believed to be pervasive (i.e., too widespread to be ignored) and by feelings of sympathy for the victims.

In contrast, men and women low in gender group identification demonstrated more similar pathways to collective action. For both these groups, sympathy was the only significant predictor of collective action intentions. We argue that this is because lower identifiers with both groups tended to see the group's goals and interests as less relevant to themselves. Interestingly, appraised legitimacy predicted this sympathy for lower identified men, whereas appraised pervasiveness predicted sympathy for the lower identified women. The result for women is consistent with van Zomeren, Spears, and Leach (2008), who showed that collection action among less identified members of a disadvantaged group were predicted by instrumental concerns such as group efficacy beliefs, rather than by emotions such as anger.

Implications and Future Directions

Empirical work in social psychology has demonstrated that increased levels of identification should increase collective action intentions (among disadvantaged groups). To our knowledge, no work has considered whether group identification moderates the reasons underlying willingness to participate in collective action among both low-status and high-status groups (although some work has considered this question among low-status groups alone; e.g., Klandermans, 1984; Simon et al., 1998; van Zomeren, Spears, & Leach, 2008). Our results have important implications for theories of collective action, as they suggest that no single set of predictors will satisfactorily explain the attitudes and behaviors of higher and lower identifiers of high-status and low-status groups. We have proposed one explanation for why this might be the case (focusing on the salience and relevance of the inequality) but the current data-set did not provide direct evidence for this process. Future work should investigate the possibilities further.

The present research indicates that emotions play an important role in participation in collective action, even after perceptions about the inequality are taken into account. In addition, there is support for the idea that specific emotional responses to inequality can shape people's willingness to take collective action. In particular, for higher identified women, anger was a unique predictor of such willingness for action, above and beyond the effect of sympathy. In contrast, for lower identified men, sympathy was the unique predictor, even after controlling for anger. This pattern of results underscores the importance of including multiple justice-focused emotions as predictors when assessing their role in explaining collective action.

That anger about discrimination against women did not always lead to collective action is especially interesting, because this result is not consistent with previous work. Research on anger about in-group advantage (e.g., Leach et al., 2006) and anger about out-group advantage (e.g., van Zomeren et al., 2004; Gordijn et al., 2006) has shown that anger is a reliable predictor of willingness for collective action. There are a number of possible explanations for this divergence in results. First, the aforementioned studies did not assess sympathy, and thus did not directly compare the predictive effects of sympathy and anger. Second, the present sample of working men and women may have represented a broader range of age and political orientation relative to the samples of university students and activists used in the aforementioned studies. There may have been more variability in attitudes toward discrimination and disadvantage, and it is also more likely that participants in our study honestly felt that it is legitimate and appropriate to treat men and women differently in the workplace. As a result, their anger may have been directed at different targets. Future work should investigate the explanation(s) underlying these different results.

The present research also highlights the important role that beliefs and perceptions about inequality play in explaining people's willingness to challenge the status quo. Consistent with social identity theory and relative deprivation theory, perceptions of illegitimacy were related to justice-focused emotions among most of the sample, which in turn increased intentions to participate in collective action. However, in some cases, collective action intentions were a reflection of more practical concerns about the extent to which the inequality reflected a pervasive or widespread phenomenon. This supports the social identity theory claim that perceptions of instability (such that the inequality seems to be changeable) and impermeable group boundaries (such that members of the disadvantaged group may not move into the advantaged group) are important predictors of social change (e.g., Wright, Taylor, & Moghaddam, 1990). It is also consistent with recent work on the dual-pathway model of collective action (van Zomeren et al., 2004), which proposes that problem-focused instrumental beliefs (such as group efficacy; van Zomeren, Spears, & Leach, 2008) may serve as an important predictor of collective action.

Future work could also pursue questions raised by our finding that identification did not predict or moderate appraisals of pervasiveness. For instance, more specific operationalizations of this construct could be used, in order to identify what the term means for lower and higher identifiers in different status groups. It would also be useful to consider whether higher identifiers disregard issues of pervasiveness entirely when forming their responses to an instance of inequality.

Taken together, our results provide support for the broader claim that identification with a group may shape individuals' responses (including perceptions, emotion, and behavior) to an intergroup context. Indeed, various frameworks have proposed that identification with one's group is one component of a politicized identity that increases the likelihood of engaging in collective action (e.g., Simon & Klandermans, 2001). However, it is important to note that identification may also serve as a dependent variable, as it may be shaped by people's perceptions, emotions, and actions. For instance, the rejection-identification model (e.g., Branscombe, Schmitt, & Harvey, 1999) proposes that disadvantaged group members' perceptions of discrimination can shape their levels of group identification. Future work should continue to explore the dynamic relationship between identification and responses to intergroup inequality.

The constraints posed by the methodology of Internet survey research resulted in at least two major limitations of the present work. First, we assessed collective action intentions rather than actual behavior. Second, space limitations and the sample size kept our research questions fairly simple, and thus we focused solely on the social identity of gender, without considering how additional group memberships (e.g., race, age, or level of seniority) may have influenced responses to inequality. Future work should address these questions.

Taken together, the results from the present research indicate that group status and group identification should be treated as important moderators of the factors explaining collective action. An important practical implication is that appeals for collective action and political participation should be framed in different ways to target various groups. In particular, it appears that attempts to motivate members of low-status groups to challenge their own collective disadvantage would focus on the illegitimacy of group differences, and the self-relevance of this inequality for one's own experiences (i.e., to elicit anger). In contrast, motivating members of high-status groups to take action on behalf of another group's disadvantage might focus more on the illegitimacy and pervasiveness of the problem (i.e., to elicit sympathy). In this way, appeals and campaigns may need to employ varied and targeted strategies in order to effectively motivate more individuals—including those with power and influence—to become involved in efforts to achieve social justice.

References

Aiken, L. S., & West, S. G. (1991). *Multiple regression: Testing and interpreting interactions.* Thousand Oaks, CA: Sage.

Batson, C. D., Chang, J., Orr, R., & Rowland, J. (2002). Empathy, attitudes, and action: Can feeling for a member of a stigmatized group motivate one to help the group? *Personality and Social Psychology Bulletin, 28,* 1656–1666.

Branscombe, N. R., Ellemers, N., Spears, R., & Doosje, B. (1999). The context and content of social identity threat. In N. Ellemers, R. Spears, & B. Doosje (Eds.), *Social identity: Context, commitment, content* (pp. 35–58). Oxford: Blackwell.

Branscome, N. R., Schmitt, M. T., & Harvey, R. D. (1999). Perceiving pervasive discrimination among African-Americans: Implications for group identification and well-being. *Journal of Personality and Social Psychology, 77,* 135–149.

Doosje, B., Branscombe, N. R., Spears, R., & Manstead, A. S. R. (1998). Guilty by association: When one's group has a negative history. *Journal of Personality and Social Psychology, 75,* 872–886.

Doosje, B., Ellemers, N., & Spears, R. (1995). Perceived intragroup variability as a function of group status and identification. *Journal of Experimental Social Psychology, 31,* 410–436.

Drury, J., & Reicher, S. (2000). Collective action and psychological change: The emergence of new social identities. *British Journal of Social Psychology, 39,* 579–604.

Ellemers, N., Spears, R., & Doosje, B. (2002). Self and social identity. *Annual Review of Psychology, 53,* 161–186.

Frijda, N. H. (1986). *The emotions.* Cambridge: Cambridge University Press.

Frijda, N. H., Kuipers, P., & ter Shure, E. (1989). Relations among emotion, appraisal, and emotional action readiness. *Journal of Personality and Social Psychology, 57,* 212–228.

Gordijn, E. H., Yzerbyt, V., Wigboldus, D., & Dumont, M. (2006). Emotional reactions to harmful intergroup behavior. *European Journal of Social Psychology, 36,* 15–30.

Guimond, S., & Dubé-Simard, L. (1983). Relative deprivation and the Quebec nationalist movement: The cognition-emotion distinction and the personal-group deprivation issue. *Journal of Personality and Social Psychology, 44,* 526–535.

Harth, N. S., Kessler, T., & Leach, C. W. (2008). Advantaged group's emotional reactions to inter-group inequality: The dynamics of pride, guilt, and sympathy. *Personality and Social Psychology Bulletin, 34,* 115–129.

Hu, L., & Bentler, P. M. (1999). Cutoff criteria for fit indexes in covariance structure analysis: Conventional criteria versus new alternatives. *Structural Equation Modeling, 6,* 1–55.

Iyer, A., & Leach, C. W. (2008). Emotion in inter-group relations. *European Review of Social Psychology, 19,* 86–125.

Iyer, A., & Leach, C. W. (2010). Helping disadvantaged groups challenge unjust inequality: The role of group-based emotions. In S. Stürmer & M. Snyder (Eds.), *The psychology of prosocial behavior: Group processes, intergroup relations, and helping* (pp. 337–353). Chichester, UK: Wiley-Blackwell.

Iyer, A., Leach, C. W., & Crosby, F. J. (2003). White guilt and racial compensation: The benefits and limits of self-focus. *Personality and Social Psychology Bulletin, 29,* 117–129.

Iyer, A., Schmader, T., & Lickel, B. (2007). Why individuals protest the perceived transgressions of their country: The role of anger, shame, and guilt. *Personality and Social Psychology Bulletin, 33,* 572–587.

Kelly, C. (1993). Group identification, inter-group perceptions, and collective action. *European Review of Social Psychology, 4*, 59–83.
Klandermans, B. (1984). Mobilization and participation: Social-psychological expansions of resource mobilization theory. *American Sociological Review, 49*, 583–600.
Kline, R. B. (2005). *Principles and practice of structural equation modelling* (2nd ed.). New York: Guilford Press.
Leach, C. W., Snider, N., & Iyer, A. (2002). "Poisoning the consciences of the fortunate": The experience of relative advantage and support for social equality. In I. Walker & H. J. Smith (Eds.), *Relative deprivation: Specification, development, integration* (pp. 136–163). New York: Cambridge University Press.
Leach, C. W., Iyer, A., & Pedersen, A. (2006). Anger and guilt about ingroup advantage explain the willingness for political action. *Personality and Social Psychology Bulletin, 32*, 1232–1245.
Leach, C. W., Iyer, A., & Pedersen, A. (2007). Angry opposition to government redress: When the structurally advantaged perceive themselves as relative deprived. *British Journal of Social Psychology, 46*, 191–204.
Levine, M., Prosser, A., Evans, D., & Reicher, S. (2005). Identity and emergency interventions: How social group membership and inclusiveness of group boundaries shape helping behavior. *Personality and Social Psychology Bulletin, 31*, 443–453.
Roseman, I. J., Wiest, C., & Swartz, T. S. (1994). Phenomenology, behaviors, and goals differentiate discrete emotions. *Journal of Personality and Social Psychology, 67*, 206–221.
Runciman, W. G. (1966). *Relative deprivation and social justice: A study of attitudes to social inequality in twentieth-century England.* Berkeley: University of California Press.
Ryan, M. K., & Haslam, S. A. (2004, May 29). Introducing the glass cliff. *News online.* Retrieved 25 March 2008, from http://news.bbc.co.uk/1/hi/magazine/3755031.stm
Ryan, M. K., & Haslam, S. A. (2005). The glass cliff: Evidence that women are over-represented in precarious leadership positions. *British Journal of Management, 16*, 81–90.
Ryan, M. K., & Haslam, S. A. (2007). The glass cliff: Exploring the dynamics surrounding the appointment of women to precarious leadership positions. *Academy of Management Review, 32*, 549–572.
Ryan, M. K., Haslam, S. A., & Postmes, T. (2007). Reactions to the glass cliff: Gender differences in the explanations for the precariousness of women's leadership positions. *Journal of Organizational Change Management, 20*, 182–197.
Sachdev, I., & Bourhis, R. Y. (1987). Status differentials and intergroup behaviour. *European Journal of Social Psychology, 17*, 277–293.
Simon, B., & Klandermans, B. (2001). Politicized collective identity: A social psychological analysis. *American Psychologist, 56*, 319–331.
Simon, B., Loewy, M., Stürmer, S., Weber, U., Freytag, P., Habig, C., et al. (1998). Collective identification and social movement participation. *Journal of Personality and Social Psychology, 74*, 646–658.
Smith, H. J., & Kessler, T. (2004). Group-based emotions and inter-group behavior: The case of relative deprivation. In L. Z. Tiedens & C. W. Leach (Eds.), *The social life of emotions* (pp. 292–313). New York: Cambridge University Press.
Spears, R., Doosje, B., & Ellemers, N. (1999). Commitment and the context of social perception. In N. Ellemers, R. Spears, & B. Doosje (Eds.), *Social identity: Context, commitment, content* (pp. 59–83). Oxford: Blackwell.
Stürmer, S., & Simon, B. (2004). Collective action: Towards a dual-pathway model. *European Review of Social Psychology, 15*, 59–99.
Stürmer, S., Snyder, M., & Omoto, A. M. (2005). Prosocial emotions and helping: The moderating role of group membership. *Journal of Personality and Social Psychology, 88*, 532–546.
Tajfel, H., & Turner, J. C. (1979). An integrative theory of intergroup conflict. In W. G. Austin & S. Worchel (Eds.), *The social psychology of intergroup relations* (pp. 33–47). Monterey, CA: Brooks/Cole.
Tilly, C. (2004). *Social movements: 1768–2004.* Boulder, CO: Paradigm.

Turner, J., & Brown, R. (1978). Social status, cognitive alternatives, and intergroup relations. In H. Tajfel (Ed.), *Differentiation between social groups: Studies in the social psychology of intergroup relations* (pp. 201–234). London: Academic Press.

van Zomeren, M., Spears, R., Fischer, A. H., & Leach, C. W. (2004). Put your money where your mouth is! Explaining collective action tendencies through group-based anger and group efficacy. *Journal of Personality and Social Psychology, 84*, 649–664.

van Zomeren, M., Postmes, T., & Spears, R. (2008). Toward an integrative social identity model of collective action: A quantitative research synthesis of three socio-psychological perspectives. *Psychological Bulletin, 134*, 504–535.

van Zomeren, M., Spears, R., & Leach, C. W. (2008). Exploring psychological mechanisms of collective action: Does relevance of group identity influence how people cope with collective disadvantage? *British Journal of Social Psychology, 47*, 353–372.

Wispé, L. (1986). The distinction between sympathy and empathy: To call forth a concept, a word is needed. *Journal of Personality and Social Psychology, 50*, 314–321.

Wright, S. C. (2001). Strategic collective action: Social psychology and social change. In R. Brown & S. Gaertner (Eds.), *Blackwell handbook of social psychology: Intergroup processes* (Vol. 4, pp. 409–430). Oxford: Blackwell.

Wright, S. C., Taylor, D. M., & Moghaddam, F. M. (1990). Responding to membership in a disadvantaged group: From acceptance to collective action. *Journal of Personality and Social Psychology, 58*, 994–1003.

AARTI IYER received her PhD in Social Psychology from the University of California, Santa Cruz (2004). She is currently a faculty member at the University of Queensland (Australia). Her research investigates (1) challenges to group-based inequality by individuals (e.g., through collective action) and organizations (e.g., through affirmative action) and (2) individual and government responses to different representations of terrorism. Her doctoral dissertation, which examined how White Americans and non-Indigenous Australians come to participate in political action to achieve racial equality, won second prize in the 2005 competition for SPSSI's Dissertation Award. In 2008, she was awarded the Jos Jaspars Early Career Award by the European Association of Social Psychology.

MICHELLE K. RYAN obtained her PhD from The Australian National University (2004). She is currently an Associate Professor at the University of Exeter, holding a 5-year Academic Fellowship from the Research Council of the UK. She is a member of the Centre for Identity, Personality and Self in Society, and specializes in research into gender and gender differences. With Alex Haslam, she has uncovered the phenomenon of the glass cliff, whereby women (and members of other minority groups) are more likely to be placed in leadership positions that are risky or precarious. Research into the glass cliff is funded by a large grant from the Economic and Social Research Council (UK) and was named by the *New York Times* as one of the ideas that shaped 2008.

Context Matters: Explaining How and Why Mobilizing Context Influences Motivational Dynamics

Jacquelien van Stekelenburg,[*] Bert Klandermans, and Wilco W. van Dijk
VU University Amsterdam

The emphasis in the social-psychological collective action literature is on why individuals take part in collective action; however, it does not elaborate on how different mobilizing contexts may appeal to distinct motivational dynamics to participate. The present study connects the microlevel of motivational dynamics of individual protesters with the mesolevel of social movement characteristics. To do so a field study was conducted. Protesters were surveyed in the act of protesting in two different demonstrations in two different town squares simultaneously organized by two social movements at exactly the same time against the same budget cuts proposed by the same government. But with one fundamental difference, the movements emphasized different aspects of the policies proposed by the government. This most similar systems design created a unique natural experiment, which enabled the authors to examine whether the motivational dynamics of individual protesters are moderated by the social movement context. Previous research suggested an instrumental path to collective action, and the authors added an ideology path. The authors expected and found that power-oriented collective action appeals to instrumental motives and efficacy and that value-oriented collective action appeals to ideological motives, and, finally, that efficacy mediates on instrumental motives and motivational strength, but only so in power-oriented action.

The general picture of Dutch society has been one of steady progress, up to 2001 the Dutch were happy and satisfied people (Social and Cultural Planning Office, 2004). However, a break in this trend occurred, and since 2001 the Dutch social and political climate has been characterized by unrest. A number of notable events took place, including acts of international terrorism and a political (Pim Fortuin) and radical religious (Theo van Gogh) assassination within The

---

[*]Correspondence concerning this article should be addressed to Jacquelien van Stekelenburg, VU University Amsterdam, FSW/Sociology, Boelelaan 1081c, 1081 HV Amsterdam, The Netherlands [e-mail: j.van.stekelenburg@fsw.vu.nl].

Netherlands, with serious social and political consequences, and on top of this, the economy deteriorated. All in all, Dutch society appeared to be in relatively rough weather, and Dutch people turned from happy and satisfied people into more dissatisfied and indignant people. A climate of social and political unrest increases people's demands on the government, because the population seeks greater protection against perceived risks (Social and Cultural Planning Office, 2004). Political protest is one way to address demands to the government.

Indeed, both willingness to participate and actual participation in political protest increased after a relatively quiet period. On Saturday, October 2, 2004, for instance, more than 300,000 people took to the streets in Amsterdam to protest against austerity plans regarding early retirement rights. This demonstration formed the stage for the present field study. Most of these protesters (about 250,000) were mobilized by the labor union, whereas the remaining 50,000 were mobilized by an alliance called "Keer het Tij" (Turn the Tide, TTT), an anti-neo-liberalism alliance. What motives do people have to participate in this demonstration? Moreover, do unionists have different motives to participate compared to the anti-neo-liberals? And if so, can this be explained by differences in the mobilizing context which appeal to distinct motivational dynamics to protest?

These questions relate to the dynamics between the individual protester and mobilization strategies of movement organizations. Such dynamics are at the core of the social psychology of protest: individual participation and social movements in society. Individuals participate in collective action when they act as representative of their group and the action is directed at improving the conditions of the entire group (Wright, Taylor, & Moghaddam, 1990). However, although typically many members of disadvantaged groups are dissatisfied with their in-group's situation and thus strongly sympathize with the goals of collective actions, often only a small proportion of them actually participate in protest to achieve these goals (e.g., Klandermans, 1997; Marwell & Oliver, 1993). In collective action research the motives underlying participation have therefore become a key issue (Klandermans, 1997). Over the last two decades, social psychologists investigated participation motives and demonstrated that instrumental reasoning (Klandermans, 1984), identification (e.g., Simon et al., 1998), and group-based anger (van Stekelenburg, Klandermans, & van Dijk, 2008; van Zomeren, Spears, Fischer, & Leach, 2004) influenced people's participation in collective action. Surprisingly, ideological factors until recently were absent in explanations of collective action participation (for exceptions, see Hornsey et al., 2006; van Stekelenburg et al., 2008, van Zomeren & Spears, this issue).

Although the emphasis in the social psychology of protest is on the individual level, protest participation takes place in a wider context (Klandermans, 1997; van Stekelenburg & Klandermans, 2007). The current social psychological literature on protest participation, however, does not elaborate on how different social contexts may appeal to distinct motivational dynamics to participate in protest. Yet variation in the social context may be attractive to different protesters with distinct motivational dynamics (Klandermans, 1997, 2004), and social movements are important actors in the social context. Indeed, participation because of common interests requires a shared interpretation and social movements do their utmost to communicate how they interpret a social, political, or economic change (its diagnosis) and what should be done (prognosis) as a reaction to perceived losses or unfulfilled aspirations (Benford & Snow, 2000). Besides this so-called consensus mobilization, social movements gear up for "action mobilization" (Klandermans, 1984), a process in which they aim to activate people to participate in the actions staged by movements. In the process of consensus and action mobilization, movements emphasize different reasons as to why people should participate. For a theoretical distinction on these different reasons we will build on Turner and Killian's (1987) notion that demonstrations have different action orientations. In the present research we investigated whether the motivational make-up of individual protesters is contingent on the action orientation of the social movement involved. In the remainder of this introduction we will elaborate on the motivational dynamics of individual protesters[1] and the moderating role of social movement context. Subsequently, we will present and discuss results of a field study.

Instrumental Path to Collective Action Participation

Instrumentality became the focus of the sociological literature on collective action participation when resource mobilization (e.g., McCarthy & Zald, 1976) and political process approaches (e.g., McAdam, 1982) became the dominant paradigms of the field. It was emphasized that collective action participation is as rational or irrational as any other behavior. Participants are regarded as people who believe that a situation can be changed through collective action at affordable costs. The social-psychological literature emphasized efficacy as a key variable in this respect. That is, people's willingness to protest collectively is a direct reflection of their estimates of success or efficacy (Finkel & Muller, 1998; Klandermans, 1984; Simon et al., 1998; van Zomeren et al., 2004). Hence, when people take the instrumental path to political protest they are involved in problem-focused coping oriented toward instrumental strategies expected to improve their situation (e.g., van Zomeren et al., 2004) and participate "for the purpose of changing reality" (Lazarus, 1991, p. 48). Previous studies have provided empirical support for this instrumental path to collective action in collectives as varied as the labor union (Klandermans, 1984), university students (van Zomeren et al., 2004), and obese, gay, and elderly people (Simon et al., 1998).

---

[1] Although we acknowledge the influence of identification and group based anger on collective action participation, in this article we will focus on instrumental and ideological factors.

Ideology Path to Collective Action Participation

Very little systematic empirical work is available on ideology and on the way people's ideas and values generate passionate politics (Klandermans, 2004). Indeed, the role beliefs, values, and ideologies play in motivating protest participation has recently received more attention (Hornsey et al., 2006; Jasper, 2007; Klandermans, 2004). Nevertheless, more systematic and empirical research is required. In the present research we try to fill this gap by examining an ideology path to collective action participation. More specifically, we investigate whether wanting to express one's views after violated values motivates people to participate in protest.

Values, according to Schwartz (1992, p. 4), "(1) are concepts of beliefs, (2) pertain to desirable end states or behaviors, (3) transcend specific situations, (4) guide selection or evaluations of behavior and events, and (5) are ordered by relative importance." Moreover, violated values are "worth challenging, protesting, and arguing about" (Rokeach, 1973, p. 13; see also Feather & Newton, 1982) let alone violated "sacred" values that arouse moral outrage responses (see van Zomeren and Spears, this issue). Hence, conceptualized in this manner, values are individual phenomena about which people usually feel strongly. A violation of these values instigates a motivation to express one's view and protest participation is one way to do so. People's value systems influence to what extent social or political situations are evaluated or perceived as illegitimate, unjust, unfair, and thus "wrong." This personal set of values functions as a compass in determining directions to people in complicated and sometimes foggy social and political matters. Like a real compass, values help us to find where we stand, where others stand, where we want to go, and as such reveal discrepancies between actual and ideal situations. The larger these discrepancies or the more they stem from a violation of central values, the more strongly people will be motivated to express their view. Therefore, value violation plays a key role in the ideological path to collective action.

Social Movement Context

If one considers an instrumental and ideological path to collective action, the question arises as to what factors determine which path is taken. Social movements work hard to create moral outrage and anger and to provide a target against which these can be vented. They must weave together a moral, cognitive, and ideological package of attitudes and communicate a specific appraisal of the situation. However, they may emphasize different aspects of the situation or the solution. In doing so, social movement organizations play a significant role in the selective process of construction and reconstruction of collective beliefs and in the transformation of individual discontent into collective action.

Individual members of a collectivity incorporate a smaller or larger proportion of the interpretations provided by "their" collectivities; but there is an abundance of frames in our social and political environment, so why would people adopt certain frames rather than others? Benford and Snow (2000) propose that the underlying process is frame alignment, whereby individual orientations, values, and beliefs become congruent (or aligned with) activities, goals, and ideologies of social movement organizations. A successful process of frame alignment results in a fit between the collective action frame of an organization and that of an individual, and this enhances the likelihood that this individual will participate in a protest event staged by this organization. In case of successful frame alignment, that is when ideas of individuals and movements line up, we expect to ascertain shared action orientations and thus a motivational constellation that inspires and legitimates the reasons why people should take part in protest.

Following Klandermans (1993) we argue that different social movements may appeal to different participation motives. In a comparison of three movements (the labor movement, the women's movement, and the peace movement) Klandermans was able to show that the action for which each of the three movements was mobilizing—a strike, women's groups in the community and a peace demonstration—appeals to different participation motives. He defined action orientation in terms of Turner and Killian's (1987) description of action orientations that can determine the course of a mobilization campaign. Turner and Killian distinguish three action orientations of which the first two may be relevant in the context of the present research: (1) power orientation, or an orientation toward acquiring and exerting influence; (2) value orientation, or an orientation toward the goals and the ideology of the movement; and (3) participation orientation, whereby collective action activities are satisfying in and of themselves.[2] Because strikes are power oriented Klandermans expected and found that the expectancy component was important in explaining trade unionists' willingness to strike. While in participation-oriented actions like the women's groups, women participated because participation in itself was perceived as satisfying. In the value-oriented demonstration of the peace movements, the value component rather than the expectancy component carried great weight.

Because instrumentally oriented participation implies that participation is seen as an opportunity to change a state of affairs at affordable costs, we assume that a power-oriented protest event will be appealing to people who take the instrumental pathway. Moreover, we assume that feelings of efficacy impact on motivational strength in the context of power-oriented rather than value-oriented protest. After all, "the more power-oriented a campaign is, the more strongly it will emphasize the movement's effectiveness, its ability to exert influence. Therefore, a

---

[2] In our studies we did not assess participation orientation, and therefore we will not elaborate this orientation further.

movement must convince the individual that the planned action will be successful" (Klandermans, 1993, p. 389).

"The more value-oriented a campaign is, the more it will emphasize the importance of its goals and the ideology behind them" (Klandermans, 1993, p. 389) and the more it will give participants the opportunity to express their discontent with a given state of affairs. Because participation on the basis of an ideology motive is aimed at expressing one's views and venting one's anger against a target that has violated one's values, we assume that protest events with a value-action orientation will be appealing to people with ideology motives.

The Present Research

To test these contentions we conducted two surveys among participants in two different demonstrations. These demonstrations were in two different town squares organized by the labor movement and TTT at exactly the same time against the same budget cuts proposed by the same government. But there was one fundamental difference: the movements emphasized different aspects of the policies proposed by the government. This most similar systems design (Przeworski & Teune, 1970, p. 32) created a unique natural experiment. Indeed, these two cases are similar with respect to crucial variables such as time, place, issue at stake, and opponent but differ in the variable we wish to explain: mobilizing context. This natural experiment enabled us to examine whether the motivational dynamics of individual protesters are moderated by the social movement context. In doing so, the present study replicates and extends the findings of Klandermans (1993) that motivational dynamics are contingent on mobilizing context. However, due to the most similar systems design, the present study can be seen as a more robust test to demonstrate that context indeed matters. What makes the design of the present study so robust? First of all, take Klandermans' 1993 paper as a comparison: The three social movements acted at different points in time, against different issues, against different authorities, and employing different activities. In the design of the present study all these matters are identical whereas the variable of interest—social movement context—differs. This reduces the possibility of alternative explanations and thus achieves a large measure of control to test our claim that context matters. A second point relates to coalition formation. To mobilize large numbers of participants, individual movement organizations must build coalitions. In order to do so they must set aside their differences and speak with one voice. Such an emphasis on similarities rather than diversity may blur possible differences present in the mobilizing contexts of the individual movements that form a coalition. As a consequence, coalition formation may hide from view differences between movement organizations (e.g., ideological, instrumental, or more practical organizational differences) and thus obscure how context relates to motivational dynamics. In the present study the movements did not form a coalition, but communicated their own diagnostic, prognostic and motivational frames (Benford & Snow, 2000) and in doing so made it possible to test our argument that different mobilizing contexts appeal to different motivational dynamics in a powerful way.

Mobilizing Context

The aim of the present research is to provide empirical support for our contentions regarding instrumentally and ideologically motivated protest participation as a function of mobilizing context. However, first we will provide background information on the mobilizing context. Our intention here is not to analyze deeply the social and political setting (as it is the same for the two movements) but rather to provide some background information on the mobilizing context that is needed to appreciate the argument.

Labor movement. In a reaction to the deterioration of the economy, the government announced a comprehensive package of severe cost-cutting measures (most notably the austerity plans regarding early retirement rights), which worsened the relation between employers and labor unions. The controversy resulted in a breakdown of the consultations between government and employers and unions and eventually the government "arrogantly" (van Leeuwen, 2004) exclaimed that it would put its own plans through. This is notable in a consensus democracy as The Netherlands. Indeed, one of the characteristics of a consensus democracy is an almost continuous process of consensus-oriented consultation between employers' associations, unions, and the government. The labor movement declared that although they support the Dutch "consultative model," at the moment that consultation with the government no longer seems fruitful, they saw no other alternative than to launch collective action. In their mobilization campaign the labor movement did its utmost to emphasize its effectiveness and ability to exert influence via collective action since consensus-oriented consultation seems no longer effective. Therefore, we assume that the labor movement demonstration fits the description of action that is predominantly power oriented.

Turn the tide alliance. TTT was the second movement staging for collective action. TTT is an alliance founded by organizations that were active earlier in the antiglobalization movement. They were founded in 2002 in reaction to a stark shift to the right in the political climate, during the 2002 national election campaign. These tumultuous times witnessed the rise of anti-immigrant politician Pim Fortuyn, and his assassination, just a few days before the election. The alliance has made it its goal to oppose the harsh right-wing climate in the country and the antisocial government policies. At the moment of the mobilization against the austerity of early retirement rights, this alliance consisted of 550 political and civil organizations staging collective action twice a year. By stressing anti-neoliberal and progressive policies the organizers emphasized the ideology behind their claims, thus giving participants an opportunity to express their discontent and indignation with proposed government policies. Therefore, we assumed that this social movement context was value oriented.

Two movements simultaneously organizing a value- and a power-oriented demonstration provided us with a unique opportunity to examine which path would prevail as a result of power- and value-oriented mobilizing context. We expected that the instrumental rather than the ideological path would prevail in the power-oriented context, whereas in the value-oriented context the ideological path would dominate the instrumental path.

Motivational Strength

The instrumental and ideological paths aim to account for motivational strength, that is, the strength of the motivation to participate. Theoretically, motivational strength ranges from 0 to infinite with a normal distribution, whereby zero motivational strength concerns people who will never ever participate in protest and infinite motivational strength concerns people who are impatiently waiting for just another call for action. Motivational strength can be seen as motivation to participate in protest in general but can also be motivation for an action with a specific goal or as is the case in the present study motivation for a specific action (Klandermans & Goslinga, 1996). In the remainder of this article, we report a study in which we examine the motivational strength of people actually participating. Sampling those people who actually participate implicates that these people are motivated, and they fall necessarily on the right side of the normal distribution. This does not necessarily imply that all participants were identically motivated. On the contrary, one may assume that the motivational strength and—important for our study—the motivational configuration of these people vary. It is this variation that we are interested in.

Method

Procedure

Data were collected during the demonstrations. This kind of field research implies that it is conducted in a crowded, unpredictable, and erratic environment. In order to guarantee the representativeness of the findings we relied on two techniques employed by Walgrave and colleagues (van Aelst & Walgrave, 2001). Although obtaining data by using a protest survey is not new, this systematic application is. So, we outline its basic principles.

The first technique is a device to guarantee that every protester in the area where the protest event was taking place had an equal chance of being selected by one of the interviewers with the request to complete a survey and mail it back to the researchers in a postage-paid envelope. Interviewers were equally distributed around the square on the outer edge of the protest event. The interviewers were instructed to hand a questionnaire to a protester on the outer circle, followed by another, 10 steps inwards, and so on until the centre of the circle was reached. The second technique was to conduct, in addition to the postal survey, face-to-face interviews before the protest event set off. After introducing themselves the interviewers asked approximately 10 waiting protesters whether they would like to take part in a study which investigates why people protest. After confirmation the interviewer posed a short set of questions concerning the main predictor variables and some demographics. We reached a response rate of close to 100% for the face-to-face interviews. Hence, provided proper sampling, these face-to-face interviews can serve to assess the reliability of the postal survey data. These short, face-to-face interviews were used primarily to evaluate the representativeness of the postal survey.

The organizers planned the demonstrations on two different squares in Amsterdam. Therefore, we collected data on these two squares. For the face-to-face interviews, two times 10 interviewers posed 123 (TTT) and 115 (labor movement) protesters a short set of questions. Subsequently, 500 questionnaires were handed out twice of which 442 questionnaires (209 TTT and 233 labor movement) were returned. The overall response rate was 44% (42% TTT and 47% labor union). Comparisons with the face-to-face interviews revealed no significant difference between the two samples. Hence, we concluded that the postal sample provides a fair approximation of the population of protesters.

Participants

In the value-oriented protest event 56% of the participants were men. Mean age of these participants was 44 years, and the level of education was high (1% primary school, 11% lower secondary, 5% middle secondary, 29% higher secondary university preparatory, 11% nonuniversity higher education, 42% university). Fifty-six percent of these participants were members of an organization affiliated to the social movement that organized the protest event. In the power-oriented protest event 48% of the participants were men. The mean age of these participants was 52 years, and the level of education was high as well (2% primary school, 19% lower secondary, 19% middle secondary, 30% higher secondary university preparatory, 7% nonuniversity higher education, 22% university). Eighty-one percent of these participants were members of an organization affiliated to the trade union federation. All but one of the participants were of Dutch nationality (the remaining participant was from Spain).

Measures

Data for the analyses were taken from the postal survey questionnaires.

Instrumental motives. Instrumental motives were assessed by averaging participants' responses on the following two items (Cronbach's $\alpha = .79$): "To what extent is your personal situation affected by the government plans concerning early retirement rights?" and "To what extent is the situation of relatives affected by the government plans concerning early retirement rights?" These items were measured on a Likert-type scale ranging from 1 (*not at all*) to 7 (*very much*).

Efficacy. Perceived efficacy was assessed with one item: "To what extent do you think that this protest event will contribute to persuading the government not to implement its plans concerning early retirement rights?" The efficacy item was measured on a Likert-type scale ranging from 1 (*not at all*) to 7 (*very much*).

Ideology motives. Ideological participation motives were assessed by averaging participants' responses on the following four items ($\alpha = .80$): I am protesting because: "I want to take my responsibility," "The proposed government policy is against my principles," "I find the proposed government policy unfair," "I find the proposed government policy unjust." The ideology items were measured on a Likert-type scale ranging from 1 (*not at all*) to 7 (*very much*).

Motivation to participate in the protest. Respondents indicated the strength of their motivation to participate with the following item: "How determined were you to participate in this protest event?" Motivational strength was measured on a Likert-type scale ranging from 1 (*not at all determined*) to 7 (*very much determined*).

Typically, gender, age, and education are the most important demographic predictors of protest participation (e.g., van Aelst & Walgrave, 2001). Higher educated, male, and young to middle-aged are most prone to participate in protest. Therefore gender, age, and education will be controlled for in our statistical analyses.

Results

Preliminary Analyses

Table 1 provides the correlation matrices, means, and standard deviations of the value- and power-oriented protest event of the variables measured in this study. Correlation analyses showed that instrumental and ideological motives were positively correlated with motivational strength in the context of the power-oriented protest. In contrast, in the value-oriented protest only ideological motives were

Table 1. Correlations, Means, and Standard Deviations for Instrumental Motives, Efficacy, Ideology, and Motivational Strength

Value Oriented	M	SD	1	2	3	4
1. Instrumental motive	4.19	2.43	–			
2. Efficacy	4.37	1.70	.20***	–		
3. Ideology	6.42	0.77	.08	.14*	–	
4. Motivational strength	6.29	1.27	.11	.05	.52***	–

Power oriented	M	SD	1	2	3	
1. Instrumental motive	4.93	2.42	–			
2. Efficacy	4.51	1.82	.27***	–		
3. Ideology	6.40	0.74	.18***	.21***	–	
4. Motivation strength	6.51	0.83	.12°	.21***	.33***	–

Note. Valid N (listwise) Value oriented = 209, Power oriented = 238; all variables on a scale ranging from 1 = *not at all*—7 *very much* °$p < .10$, *$p < .05$, **$p < .01$, ***$p < .001$.

positively related to motivational strength. Both in the context of value and power-oriented protest, efficacy appeared to be positively correlated to instrumental and ideological motives. Important for our hypothesis, however, only in the context of power-oriented protest efficacy was related to motivational strength. This is in contrast to the value-oriented protest, where efficacy was not related to motivational strength.

The motivational strength in the value-oriented protest of actual protesters varied from 1 to 7 (on a 7-point scale), the mean was 6.29, and the standard deviation was 1.27. In the power-oriented protest the motivational strength varied from 2 to 7, the mean was 6.51, and the standard deviation 0.83. This indicates that despite the fact that all the respondents took part in the collective action (and apparently were sufficiently motivated) they happened to diverge in their motivational strength.

The Instrumental and Ideological Path as a Function of Mobilizing Context

To test whether participants' instrumental motives and efficacy affected their motivation in the context of power-oriented protest, whereas ideological motives affected motivation in the context of value-oriented protest, two separate hierarchical regressions were conducted (see Table 2). For both mobilizing contexts gender, age, and education were entered first (Step 1), followed by instrumental motives and efficacy (Step 2), and ideological motives (Step 3).

Concerning the analysis for the value-oriented protest, results revealed that educational level was a significant predictor of motivational strength, indicating

Table 2. Hierarchical Regressions of Motivation to Participate in Power- and Value-Oriented Protest Events on Instrumental and Ideology Motives

	\multicolumn{6}{c}{Motivational Strength}
	\multicolumn{3}{c}{Value Oriented}	\multicolumn{3}{c}{Power Oriented}
	Step 1 β	Step 2 β	Step 3 β	Step 1 β	Step 2 β	Step 3 β
Gender	.04	.04	−.03	.11	.14*	.09
Age	.13	.12	.04	.31***	.30***	.29***
Education	−17*	−.16*	−.15*	.02	.05	.03
Instrumental motive		.08	.07		.12°	.08
Efficacy		.03	−.04		.15*	.11°
Ideology			.53***			.26***
Model F	4,04***	2.71*	15.51***	7,22***	6,61***	8,64***
df	(3, 189)	(5, 187)	(6, 186)	(3, 212)	(5, 210)	(6, 209)
Adjusted R^2	.05	.05	.33	.08	.12	.18
R^2 change		.00	.27***		.04***	.07***

Note. Coefficients are standardized regression weights (betas).
°$p < .10$, *$p < .05$, **$p < .01$, ***$p < .001$.

that a higher level of education was associated with less motivational strength. Furthermore, results showed that neither instrumental motives ($\beta = .08$, *ns*) nor efficacy ($\beta = .03$, *ns*) was a significant predictor of motivational strength. Importantly, and as predicted, ideological motives were a significant predictor of motivational strength (R^2 change $= .27, p < .001$).

Concerning the analysis for the power-oriented protest, results showed that age was a significant predictor of motivational strength; the older the participants, the more motivated they were. It can be argued that this is not surprising in light of the goal of the demonstration (i.e., early retirement rights). As predicted, results showed that both instrumental motives ($\beta = .12, p < .10$) and efficacy ($\beta = .15, p < .05$) were significant predictors of motivational strength. Unexpectedly, results showed that ideology motives were also significant predictors of motivational strength ($\beta = .26, p < .001$).

We hypothesized that the relationship between motivational strength and instrumental/ideology motives would be contingent upon social movement context. In the above-mentioned analyses, context was not taken into account as a variable, although the effect of context was inferred from the difference between the power- and the value-oriented protest. To test our hypothesis concerning the moderator model of social movement context more precisely, we combined the two samples and regressed motivational strength on the interaction terms from mobilizing context (0 = *alliance*, 1 = *union*) X instrumental motives, mobilizing context X efficacy, and mobilizing context X ideology.

Important for our argument all three two-way interactions were significant: Ideology motive X Context: $F(1, 440) = 15.33, p < .001, \beta = .18, p < .001$; Instrumental motive X Context: $F(1, 430) = 5.59, p = .02, \beta = 12, p = .02$, Efficacy X Context: $F(1, 439) = 4.85, p = .03, \beta = 11, p = .03$, indicating that the relationship between instrumental and ideology motives and efficacy on the one hand and motivational strength on the other varied across mobilizing context.

To interpret these significant interactions, we plotted the relationship between motivational strength and low and high levels of instrumental and ideology motives and efficacy for power- and value-oriented protest separately. First, each predictor was standardized. Subsequently motivational strength was regressed on the interaction effects from the standardized regression equations. Predicted values were computed using scores that were one standard deviation below and above the mean of instrumental and ideology motives and efficacy (for value- and power-oriented protest, respectively). The influence of ideology motives, instrumental motives, and efficacy on motivational strength in power- and value-oriented protest are shown in Figure 1a–c, respectively.

Figure 1a reflects the finding that the motivational strength of participants in the context of value-oriented protest strongly increased as the strength of their ideological motives increases (simple slope $\beta = .41, p < .001$), whereas the motivational strength of participants in the context of power-oriented protest remained invariably high (simple slope $\beta = .12$, *ns*), irrespective of the level of ideology motives. As predicted, the motivational strength of protesters in the value-oriented protest increased as their ideology motives increased, whereas the level of ideology motives did not influence the motivational strength of participants in the power-oriented protest. The influence of ideology motives on motivational strength of participants in the power-oriented context was invariantly high. We will return to this unexpected finding in our discussion section.

Figure 1b reflects the finding that the motivational strength of participants in the context of value-oriented protest increased as the strength of their instrumental motives increased (simple slope $\beta = .19, p = .05$), whereas the motivational strength of participants in the context of power-oriented protest remained invariably high (simple slope $\beta = .09$, *ns*), irrespective of the level of instrumental motives. This implies that irrespective of the level of instrumental motives, instrumental motives had a stronger impact on motivational strength in the context of power- rather than value-oriented protest.

Figure 1c reflects the finding that efficacy was a significant predictor of motivational strength in the power-oriented protest (simple slope $\beta = .25, p <$

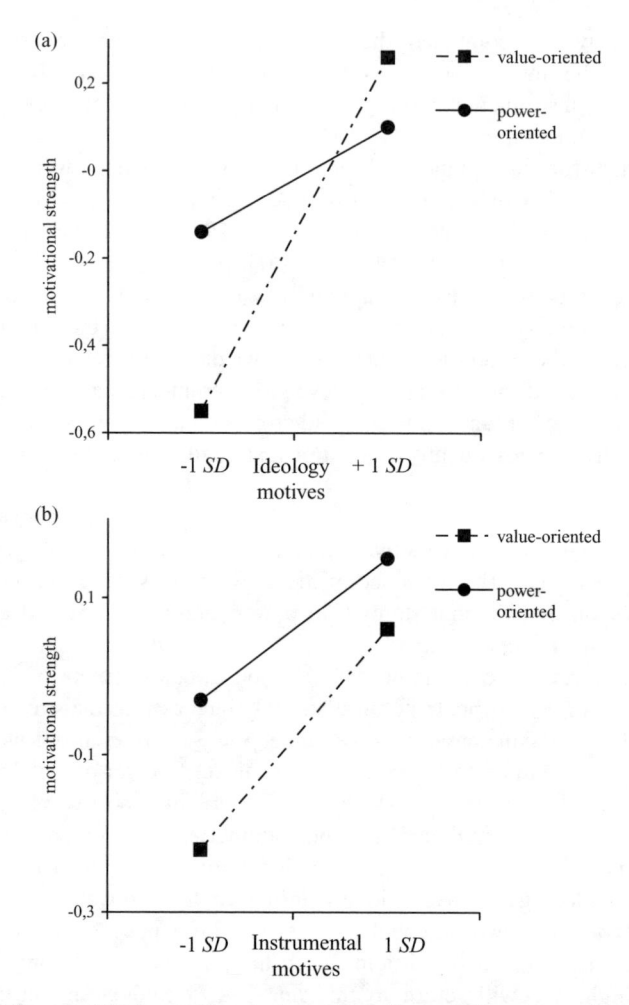

Fig. 1. The influence of ideology motives, instrumental motives and efficacy on motivational strength in power- and value-oriented protest. (a) Ideology motives, (b) instrumental motives and (c) efficacy.

.03), whereas the motivational strength of value-oriented protest was unaffectedly low (simple slope $\beta = .06$, *ns*). Hence, for efficacy the opposite pattern as for ideology motives was observed. Efficacy strongly influenced motivational strength in power-oriented protest and this influence was invariantly low in value-oriented protest, whereas ideology motives strongly influence motivational strength in value-oriented protest and this influence was invariantly high in power-oriented protest.

(c)

[Figure: graph showing motivational strength vs Efficacy (-1 SD to +1 SD) for value-oriented and power-oriented conditions]

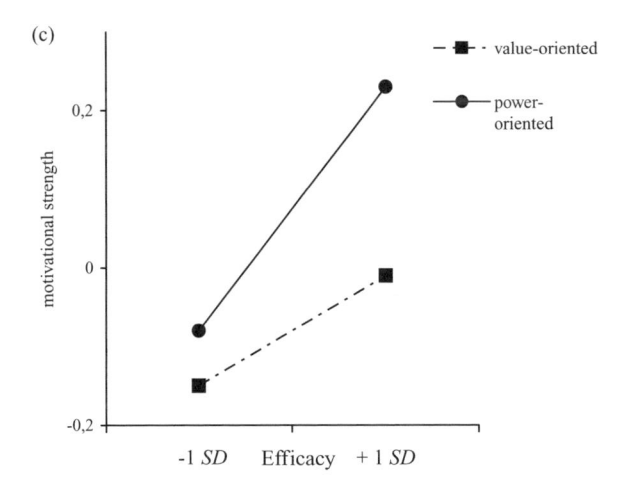

Fig. 1. Continued.

The Mediating Role of Efficacy

Taking mobilizing context into account may bring us in the position to finetune the findings of Simon et al. (1998) and van Zomeren et al. (2004). These authors showed that efficacy mediates on instrumental motives and motivational strength. Although we wholeheartedly agree that efficacy plays a mediating role in the instrumental path, we believe that such an effect will only emerge in the context of power-oriented protest. After all, specifically power-oriented actions (rather than value- or participation-oriented action) are appealing to feelings of efficacy (Klandermans, 1993). To test whether efficacy mediates instrumental motives conditionally on the mobilizing context we conducted two mediation analyses.

In the context of power-oriented protest the indirect relation in the instrumental path—that of instrumental motives via efficacy—was significant (Sobel's Z-value = 2.40, $p < .02$). Mediation analysis revealed that the regression coefficient of instrumental motives reduced from $\beta = .12$ ($p = .09$) to $\beta = .06$ ($p = .36$) when efficacy was entered in the equation. This suggests full mediation. Thus, in power-oriented protest the relation between instrumental motives and motivational strength can be completely explained by feelings of efficacy.

In the context of value-oriented protest the indirect relation in the instrumental path—that of instrumental motives via efficacy—was not significant (Sobel's Z-value = .44, $p = .66$). Just like in the power-oriented context, stronger instrumental motives were marginally accompanied by increasing motivational strength ($\beta = .12, p = .09$). However, adding efficacy did not reduce the strength of the

Fig. 2. Mediational model of efficacy on instrumental motives and motivational strength for power- and value-oriented protest.

Power-oriented protest: Instrumental motives → Motivational strength: .06 (.12°); Instrumental motives → Efficacy: .27***; Efficacy → Motivational strength: .19***

Value-oriented protest: Instrumental motives → Motivational strength: .12° (.12°); Instrumental motives → Efficacy: .20***; Efficacy → Motivational strength: .03

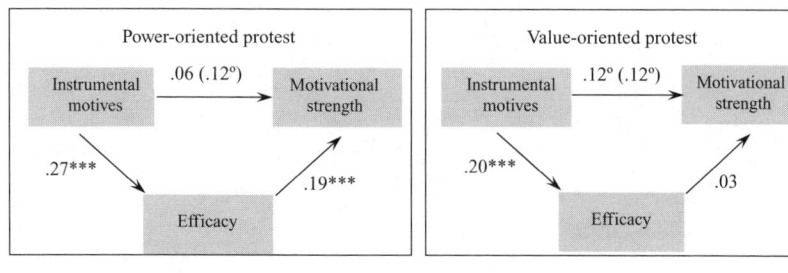

° $p < .10$, * $p < .05$, ** $p < .01$, *** $p < .001$,

relation between instrumental motives and motivational strength. This was probably because efficacy was not related to motivational strength ($\beta = .03, p = .65$). The observed mediation models of the instrumental path in power- and value-oriented protest events are presented in Figure 2. As can be seen, instrumental motives were completely translated into efficacy (cf. Simon et al., 1998; van Zomeren et al., 2004) but only so in the context of power-oriented collective action. Thus, in a mobilizing context in which movements disseminate messages of its effectiveness and its ability to exert influence, efficacy plays a key role in the motivational dynamics of participants and not in a value-oriented collective action. This confirmed our hypothesis regarding efficacy-as-mediator as a function of mobilizing context.

Discussion

In the present research we examined whether different mobilizing contexts appeal to distinct motivational dynamics. We argued that a value-oriented mobilizing context would appeal more to ideological motives, whereas a power-oriented mobilizing context would appeal more to instrumental motives. To test these ideas we conducted a field study during two demonstrations against the same governmental policy organized by two different movements. Thus we were able to set up a natural experiment to test whether differences in the mobilizing context appeal to different motivational dynamics. We found that ideological motives were important in the context of value-oriented action, whereas both instrumental and ideological motives played a role in the context of power-oriented action. Moreover, taking mobilizing context into account made it possible for us to fine-tune the repeatedly reported effect of efficacy on collective action participation. Indeed, instrumental motives were fully translated into efficacy (cf. Simon et al., 1998; van Zomeren et al., 2004), but only so in the context of power-oriented protest.

Individual Motivational Dynamics

Our results suggest that it is relevant to conceive of an ideology path next to an instrumental path. Indeed, our study demonstrated that the wish to express one's view when one's values have been violated influences someone's motivation to take part in protest (see for a similar argument, Hornsey et al., 2006). In the context of value-oriented protest the ideology motive added 27% to the variance explained by instrumental motives and even in the context of the power-oriented protest, ideology motives added 7% to the variance explained. This suggests that motivation to take part in protest is strongly influenced by the desire to express one's view when one's values are violated, net of perceiving protesting as an effective strategy to defend imperiled interests. By introducing an ideology path next to the instrumental path we hope to show that people do take part in protest even if the perceived likelihood of success is relatively low. They do so, not because they assume that participation will be effective in defending imperiled interest, but because protest participation is seen as a means to express their indignation when their values have been violated.

The rational choice perspective focused attention on goals and efficacy as important explanations of collective action participation. According to this perspective "rational individuals [will] attempt to achieve collective goods through political participation but only when the collective chances of success and their own personal influence are high" (Finkel & Muller, 1998, p. 39). In a world where the norm of self-interest is pervasive (Miller, 1999) it seems "natural" to participate in protest in the pursuit of one's own material interests, but in the skeptical modern world the pursuit of distant ideals needs explanation (Jasper, 2007). Consequently, in earlier studies of collective action participation much attention was given to efficacy, but less attention has been paid to expressing one's view after violated values as explanation of action participation. Our research, however, suggests that reducing protest participation to rational, structural and organizational processes neglects important reasons why people take part in such actions. Indeed, a narrow focus on instrumentality may fail to disclose other motivations, such as strengthening solidarity, influencing third parties (Simon & Klandermans, 2001), and the urge to express one's values (Hornsey et al., 2006; van Stekelenburg & Klandermans, 2007; van Stekelenburg et al., 2008; van Zomeren & Spears, 2009).

By introducing an ideological path to protest we have attempted to contribute to the newly emerging interest in "expressive" motivations contrary to instrumental motivations within collective action studies. We do not want to leave the impression that instrumentally based participation is rational, whereas ideologically based participation is irrational. We want to emphasize that taking the ideological path to action can be as rational or irrational as taking the instrumental path to action. Hence, instrumentally based participation is seen as purposeful in solving a social or political problem whereas ideologically based participation is seen as purposeful in maintaining moral integrity by voicing one's indignation.

Social Movement Context

Our results suggest that campaigns of different social movements appeal to distinct individual participation motives; thus context seems to matter. Indeed, probably the most important finding of our study is the importance of context effects. As expected, in the context of value-oriented protest only the ideology path influenced the motivation to participate, whereas the instrumental and, unexpectedly, the ideology path prevailed in the context of power-oriented protest. Moreover, taking context into account also specified the effects of efficacy: efficacy is a key variable in the instrumental path to protest, but only in the context of power-oriented protest. The present study connects the microlevel of cognitions, feelings, and behaviors of individual protesters with the mesolevel of social movement characteristics. As such, it speaks to the theoretical debate about structural-level explanations of collective action participation versus individual-level explanations. Few collective action scholars have actually linked characteristics of the mobilizing context to the motivational configuration of individual protesters (for an exception see Klandermans, 1993). Our results suggest that it is worthwhile to study the reasons why people take part in protest as a function of various movement characteristics (e.g., type of action orientation). Such variation is easily overlooked. Had we aggregated the data and neglected the variation in context, we would not have discerned the diverging motivational patterns in response to the differences in context. Indeed, without comparative studies of different campaigns, we would never be able to sort out these individual sources of variation (Klandermans, 1993).

Moreover, aggregation of the data would not have revealed the interesting, but unexpected, finding of an ideology path in the context of power-oriented protest. On further consideration, the ideology path was not so unexpected in the context of trade unions. Various studies have found support for both an instrumental and an ideological route to union commitment and support, including studies examining motives for joining a union (de Witte, 1995), union commitment (Sverke & Sjöberg, 1997), and trade union participation (Sverke, 1996). Indeed, "there is now general support for there being two main routes for union commitment and union support, the instrumental route and the ideological route" (Blackwood, Lafferty, Duck, & Terry, 2003, p. 488). This has (at least) two potential implications for the results of our studies. It may indicate that, even in the context of power-oriented protest, ideological considerations influence the motivation to participate, or it may suggest that the action orientation of the trade union federations was not "purely" power oriented. The latter reasoning corroborates Turner and Killian's (1987) view that all three orientations play a role in every mobilization campaign.

Future research might investigate whether the findings about instrumentality and ideology are related to this specific event or are a more general effect due to the combination of the two motives into a single model.

Recently, it has been widely acknowledged that the dynamics of protest participation are created and limited by characteristics of the societies people are embedded in (see Koopmans, Statham, Giugni, & Passy, 2005). As social psychologists, however, we are never tired of asserting that people live in a perceived world. They respond to the world as they perceive and interpret it, and if we want to understand their cognitions, motivations, and emotions we need to know their perceptions and interpretations. Hence, people perceive the macro- and mesopolitical, socioeconomic, cultural, and mobilizing contexts that influence and shape a mental model about what the social world looks like and what it ideally should look like. Indeed, these collective mental models may create and limit goals, aims, objective opportunities of both individuals and organizations, and therefore may shape the reasons why people participate in protest. Therefore we argue that, while context matters, perceptions of the context matter even more. Yet, little is known about the relation between sociopolitical context and motivational dynamics of protest, let alone about how perceptions of the sociopolitical environment relate to motivational dynamics. Future research could investigate this issue.

Broader Applications

What are possible broader implications for the current study? First of all, organizers of protest should be aware of the fact that potential participants can have different motives to take part in the actions they organize. It suggests that organizers of protest might benefit from tailoring their campaigns to the motivational make-up of their potential participants. They should realize that persuasive messages are not only about consensus formation (i.e., raising consciousness) and consensus mobilization, but should preferably provide reasons to participate that fit the motives of potential participants. A related issue is the link between the choice of the means of action and the motives they appeal to. Hence, power-, participation-, and value-oriented actions appeal to different motives and organizers may increase the level and intensity of participation and decrease the level of disengagement if they are able to create a fit between the individual participation motives and the right choice of means of action.

Methodological Considerations

Prior to discussing possible limitations of our study and some future directions, we want to devote a few words to the method we employed. Collecting valid and reliable data on protest behavior is a complicated matter. Therefore researchers tend to focus on investigating past protest participation (e.g., World

Value Survey) or intentions to participate in future protest. However, both methods hamper a thorough investigation of protest participation: the former because the survey questions relate to protest in general and the latter because intentions to participate are weak predictors of actual participation (Klandermans & Oegema, 1987). A third option is the one employed in the current research, namely, approach participants in the act of protesting. Very few empirical studies are available in the literature on actual participants. Obviously, field research investigating people's motives in the act of protesting calls for completely different research methods to get reliable data. The two strategies developed by Walgrave and colleagues (van Aelst & Walgrave, 2001) seem appropriate to do so. Area sampling helps to ensure that every protester has a relatively equal chance of being selected, and comparing face-to face interviews with returned questionnaires provides a check for response bias. In our view, this method should be applicable, with appropriate modifications due to local circumstances, to static and moving demonstrations (e.g., marches, parades, etc.). The method is particularly designed to obtain data on attitudes, motivations, emotions, sociodemographics, mobilization channels, and recently it has also been used to collect data on organizational networks tying organizers to their constituencies (Diani, in press). All in all, we believe that it is an appropriate method to get reliable data on (social) psychological motivational dynamics of the people who are actually taking part in political protest.

Possible Limitations and Future Directions

Before we discuss implications of our study for future research, we will make a few remarks on possible limitations. First, in our present research, we only studied people in the act of protesting. Hence, we are not able to predict why some do participate, while others do not. Despite the fact that our dependent variable—motivational strength—showed enough variability to enable us to study the variance of the motivational concepts as a function of variability in motivational strength, it begs the question whether the findings can be generalized to predict why some do participate, while others do not. The elements we have integrated into our model originate from studies that were designed to test hypotheses regarding participation and nonparticipation; hence, we presume that our model will also work in those settings. However, future research is needed to test this assumption.

In terms of future directions, we would like to raise the question of whether being a member of a disadvantaged or advantaged group influences participation motives. Is it self-interest or solidarity and how does that relate to instrumental and ideology motives? A formal theoretical version of this distinction is made by the sociologists McCarthy and Zald (1976), who propose that participants in social movements may be classified as conscience constituents or potential beneficiaries. The first type includes people who support a movement even though they do not stand to benefit directly from its success in goal accomplishment—in other words "they believe in the cause" (Turner & Killian, 1987, p. 32). Potential beneficiaries are those who would benefit directly and personally from accomplishment of the movement's goals. Little is known about group status and motives to take part in collective action. It would be worthwhile to elaborate on the moderating effects of context on the relative weight of the various motives as a function of group status.

Future research might theorize on the relationship between the structural location of social actors and their individual preferences and show how this leads them to participate in collective action. For instance, currently we are working on group identification as a mechanism that might link the individual level with the meso- or macrolevel. Group identification has pervasive effects on what people feel, think, and do (Terry & Hogg, 1996). Therefore we assume that the stronger the identification with a collective the more "the group is in me," the more group-based grievances are incorporated. As such group identification might function as a link between meso and macro collectives and individuals.

Finally, in terms of the direction future research could take, we would like to focus on the process rather than the act of protest participation. When an individual participates in collective political action staged by a social movement organization, this is the result of a sometimes lengthy process of mobilization. Successful mobilization gradually brings what Klandermans (2004) calls "demand" and "supply" together. Our theoretical framework is a first cautious step in studying the complex relation between demand and supply; this may make it a fruitful bridge builder between the micro-, meso-, and macrolevels of protest. But the present study also leaves unanswered a lot of questions regarding the process by which societies generate demand for participation and the transformation of demand into actual participation by appealing supply factors (Diani & McAdam, 2003; Klandermans, 2004). For instance, why is it that the one grievance translates into action while others do not? Or why is it that the same problem in the one society leads to mobilization whereas it remains quiet in the other? Indeed, a more dynamic approach could explore the question of whether social movements appeal to motives already prominent in someone's mind or raise to prominence in someone's mind the motives they appeal to.

References

Benford, R. D., & Snow, D. A. (2000). Framing processes and social movements: An overview and assessment. *Annual Review of Sociology, 26*, 11–39.
Blackwood, L., Lafferty, G., Duck, J., & Terry, D. (2003). Putting the group back into the unions: A social psychological contribution to understanding union support. *The Journal of Industrial Relations, 45*(4), 485–504.
De Witte, H. (1995). Worden vakbondsleden (nog) bewogen door ideologie? *Tijdschrift voor Arbeidsvraagstukken, 11*(3), 261–279.
Diani, M. (in press). Promoting February 15. The organizational embeddedness of the demonstrators. In S. Walgrave & D. Rucht (Eds.) *Protest politics. demonstrations against the war on Iraq in the US and Western Europe*. Minneapolis: University of Minnesota Press.

Diani, M., & McAdam, D. (Eds.) (2003). *Social movements and network. relational approaches to collective action*. Oxford: Oxford University Press.
Feather, N. T., & Newton, J. W. (1982). Values, expectations, and the prediction of social action: An expectancy-valence analysis. *Motivation and Emotion, 6*, 217–244.
Finkel, S. E., & Muller, E. N. (1998). Rational choice and the dynamics of collective political action: Evaluating alternative models with panel data. *The American Political Science Review, 92*(1), 37–49.
Hornsey, M. J., Blackwood, L., Louis, W., Fielding, K., Mavor, K., Morton, T., et al. (2006). Why do people engage in collective action? Revisiting the role of perceived effectiveness. *Journal of Applied Social Psychology, 36*(7), 1701–1722.
Jasper, J. (2007). Cultural approaches. In B. Klandermans & C. M. Roggeband (Eds.), *Handbook of social movements* (pp. 59–100). New York: Springer.
Klandermans, B. (1984). Mobilization and participation: Social-psychological expansions of resource mobilization theory. *American Sociological Review, 49*(5), 583–600.
Klandermans, B. (1993). A theoretical framework for comparisons of social movement participation. *Sociological Forum, 8*, 383–402.
Klandermans, B. (1997). *The social psychology of protest*. Oxford: Blackwell Publishers.
Klandermans, B. (2004). The demand and supply of participation: Social-psychological correlates of participation in social movements. In D. A. Snow, S. A. Soule, & H. Kriesi (Eds.), *The Blackwell companion to social movements* (pp. 360–379). Oxford: Blackwell Publishing.
Klandermans, B., & Goslinga, S. (1996). Media discourse, movement publicity, and thegeneration of collective action frames: Theoretical and empirical exercises in meaning construction in comparative perspectives on social movements. In D. McAdam, J. D. McCarthy, & M. N. Zald (Eds.), *Political opportunities, mobilizing structures, and cultural framings* (pp. 312–337). New York: Cambridge University Press.
Klandermans, B., & Oegema, D. (1987). Potentials, networks, motivations, and barriers: Steps toward participation in social movements. *American Sociological Review, 52*, 519–531.
Koopmans, R., Statham, P., Giugni, M., & Passy, F. (2005). *Contested citizenship: Immigration and cultural diversity in Europe*. Minneapolis: University of Minnesota Press.
Lazarus, R. S. (1991). *Emotion and adaptation*. New York: Oxford University Press.
Marwell, G., & Oliver, P. (1993). *The critical mass in collective action: A micro-social theory*. Cambridge: Cambridge University Press.
McAdam, D. (1982). *Political process and the development of black insurgency, 1930–1970*. Chicago: The University of Chicago Press.
McCarthy, J. D., & Zald, M. N. (1976). Resource mobilization and social movements: A partial theory. *American Journal of Sociology, 82*, 1212–1241.
Miller, D. T. (1999). The norm of self-interest. *American Psychologist, 54*(12), 1053–1060.
Przeworski, A., & Teune, H. (1970). *The logic of comparative social inquiry*. New York: Wiley.
Rokeach, M. (1973). *The nature of human values*. New York: Free Press.
Schwartz, S. H. (1992). Universals in the content and structure of values: Theoretical advances and empirical tests in 20 countries. In M. P. Zanna (Ed.), *Advances in Experimental Social Psychology* (pp. 1–65). San Diego: Academic Press.
Simon, B., & Klandermans, B. (2001). Politicized collective identity. *American Psychologist, 56*(4), 319–331.
Simon, B., Loewy, M., Sturmer, S., Weber, U., Freytag, P., Habig, C., et al. (1998). Collective identification and social movement participation. *Journal of Personality and Social Psychology, 74*(3), 646–658.
Social and Cultural Planning Office. (2004). *Summary of the social state of The Netherlands* (SCP working paper 107, English edition). The Hague: Social and Cultural Planning Office.
Sverke, M. (1996). The importance of ideology in trade union participation in Sweden: Asocial-psychological model. In P. Pasture, J. Verberckmoes, & H. De Witte (Eds.), *The lost perspective: Trade unions between ideology and social action in the new Europe* (pp. 353–376). Aldershot: Avebury.

Sverke, M., & Sjöberg, A. (1997). Ideological and instrumental union commitment. In M. Sverke (Ed.), *The future of trade unionism: International perspectives on emerging union structures* (pp. 277–293). Aldershot: Ashgate.

Terry, D. J., & Hogg, M. A. (1996). Group norms and the attitude-behavior relationship: A role for group identification. *Personality and Social Psychology Bulletin, 22,* 776–793.

Turner, R. H., & Killian, L. M. (1987). *Collective behavior* (3rd ed.). Englewood Cliffs, NJ: Prentice Hall.

van Aelst, P., & Walgrave, S. (2001). Who is that (wo)man in the street? From the normalisation of protest to the normalisation of the protester. *European Journal of Political Research, 39,* 461–486.

van Leeuwen, J. (2004, October 12). Arrogant. *Volkskrant,* p. 6.

van Stekelenburg, J., & Klandermans, B. (2007). Individuals in movements: A social psychology of contention. In B. Klandermans & C. M. Roggeband (Eds.), *The handbook of social movements across disciplines* (pp. 157–204). New York: Springer.

van Stekelenburg, J., Klandermans, B., & van Dijk, W. W. (2008). *A comprehensive model accounting for collective action participation: Integration of relative deprivation, motivations and emotion.* Unpublished manuscript.

van Zomeren, M., & Spears, R. (2009). Metaphors of protest: A classification of motivations for collective action. *Journal of Social Issues, 65,* 661–679.

van Zomeren, M., Spears, R., Fischer, A. H., & Leach, C. W. (2004). Put your money where your mouth is! Explaining collective action tendencies through group-based anger and group efficacy. *Journal of Personality and Social Psychology, 87*(5), 649–664.

Wright, S. C., Taylor, D. M., & Moghaddam, F. M. (1990). Responding to membership in a disadvantaged group: From acceptance to collective protest. *Journal of Personality and Social Psychology, 58,* 994–1003.

JACQUELIEN VAN STEKELENBURG is a post-doc researcher at the Sociology department of the VU-University Amsterdam, The Netherlands. She studies the social psychological dynamics of moderate and radical protest participation with a special interest in group identification, emotions, and ideologies as motivators for action. She is recently graduated (*cum laude*) on the thesis: *Promoting or Preventing Social Change. Instrumentality, Identity, Ideology and Groups-Based Anger as Motives of Protest Participation* supervised by Prof. Dr. B. Klandermans and Dr. W. W. van Dijk. She is co-author (with B. Klandermans) of "Individuals in Movements: A Social Psychology of Contention" (In *The Handbook of Social Movements across Disciplines*, Springer, 2007). She is also co-author of "Embeddedness and Grievances: Collective Action Participation Among Immigrants" (In *American Sociological Review*, 2008, together with B. Klandermans and J. van der Toorn).

BERT KLANDERMANS is Professor of Applied Social Psychology and Dean of Social Sciences at the VU-University, Amsterdam, The Netherlands. The emphasis in his work is on the social psychological consequences of social, economical, and political change. He has published extensively on the social psychology of participation in social movements and labor unions. He is the editor of *Social Movements, Protest, and Contention*, the prestigious book series of the University of Minnesota Press. His *Social Psychology of Protest* appeared with Blackwell in

1997. He is the editor and co-author (with S. Staggenborg) of *Methods of Social Movement Research* (University of Minnesota Press, 2002) and (with N. Mayer) of *Extreme Right Activists in Europe* (Routledge, 2006). With C. Roggeband he edited *The Handbook of Social Movements across Disciplines* (Springer, 2007).

WILCO W. VAN DIJK is an Associate Professor of Social Psychology at the department of Social Psychology at the VU-University Amsterdam, The Netherlands. His work concentrates on feelings and emotions. Some of his recent key publications are: "A Bumpy Train Ride: A Field Experiment on Insult, Culture of Honor, and Emotional Reactions" (In *Emotion*, 2007, with H. IJzerman, & M. Gallucci), "When People Fall from Grace: Reconsidering the Role of Envy in *Schadenfreude*" (In *Emotion*, 2006, with J. W. Ouwerkerk, S. Goslinga, M. Nieweg, & M. Gallucci) and "Deservingness and *Schadenfreude*," *Cognition and Emotion*, 2005, with J. W. Ouwerkerk, S. Goslinga, & M. Nieweg).

Collective Action as the Material Expression of Opinion-Based Group Membership

Craig McGarty*
Murdoch University

Ana-Maria Bliuc
The University of Sydney

Emma F. Thomas
The Australian National University

Renata Bongiorno
Murdoch University

In this article, we argue that progress in the study of collective action rests on an increasingly sophisticated application of the social identity approach. We develop the view, however, that the application of this theoretical perspective has been limited by theoretical and empirical difficulties in distinguishing between social categories and psychological groups. These problems have undermined the ability of researchers to correctly specify the collective identities that actually underpin many instances of collective action. As a partial solution to this problem we focus on collective identities based on shared opinion (opinion-based groups). We develop the proposition that much collective action reflects the crystallization or instantiation of opinion-based groups. We also outline an intervention aimed at stimulating commitment to collective action through group-based interaction involving opinion-based group members. We conclude by emphasizing that opinion-based groups tend to be most successful when they present themselves as

---

*Correspondence concerning this article should be addressed to Craig McGarty, Murdoch University, South Street, Murdoch, Western Australia 6150, Australia [e-mail: c.mcgarty@murdoch.edu.au].

This research was supported under Australian Research Council's Discovery Projects funding scheme (projects DP0343941 and DP0770731). The views expressed herein are those of the authors and are not necessarily those of the Australian Research Council.

being representative or aligned with dominant, positively valued social categories such as nations.

> First, individuals must have internalized their group membership as an aspect of their self-concept: they must be selectively identified with the relevant in-group. It is not enough that others define them as a group, although consensual definitions by others can become, in the long run, one of the powerful causal factors for a group's self-definition
> (Tajfel & Turner, 1979, p. 41).

> (...) I am a feminist first, not a woman, and a socialist first, not a Scot.... unite with people who share your ideas not your accent [or] your genitals (Harpies & Quines, quoted by Hopkins, Kahani-Hopkins, & Reicher, 2006).

In this article, we focus on the potential of the social identity perspective developed by Tajfel, Turner, and their colleagues to provide a unique standpoint to the study of collective action. We suggest that this theoretical tradition has already made great progress in providing a more complete understanding of the nature of the collectives that take collective action and that this contribution has already been deep and significant.

We also argue, however, that some of the theoretical potential of the social identity perspective has been compromised by the operational inability of social identity researchers to pursue the theoretical distinction between social categories and groups. This is a widespread problem, but there is possibly no domain where it is more limiting than in the study of collective action. The reason for this is deceptively simple. If we fail to understand the nature of the collectives in collective action we will inevitably fail to understand collective action. We suggest that the social identity perspective can avoid these problems by recognizing that much collective action is not so much *by* social categories but about or on behalf of social categories. In this article, we also seek to clarify the nature of the collectives involved in taking collective action through our focus on opinion-based groups. Indeed the quote above passed on through the work of Hopkins et al. (2006) anticipates our argument very neatly. We argue that people form common cause with others by forming groups based on shared opinions, despite expectations that they should organize around social categories.

In developing these points we follow the lead of Hopkins and Reicher (1997) that collective action stems from category definition. In doing so we believe we are contributing to filling a gap that has been identified by Reicher, Cassidy, Wolpert, Hopkins, and Levine (2006):

> In the case of helping, then, we might expect that those who wish to create social movements in favour of intervention might do so, firstly, by constructing social categories in such a way that victims and potential helpers form a single ingroup and/or, secondly by constructing norms in such a way that humanitarian action is a central tenant of the group... The implication is that... helping is something that can be actively created through argument. It is something that can be publicly mobilized. (p. 53)

The first of the alternatives raised by Reicher et al. has received considerable attention through work on common in-group identity (e.g., Dovidio et al., 1997; Gaertner & Dovidio, 2000, 2005). The idea that cooperation stems from inclusive category membership can be considered as social psychology's long-standing solution to this problem (McGarty, 2006; though it is important to note the burgeoning array of dual-identity alternatives to the superordinate approach; e.g., Eggins, Haslam, & Reynolds, 2002; Hornsey & Hogg, 2000; Mummendey & Wenzel, 1999). A key thrust of our article is to develop our own take on Reicher et al.'s second option of understanding how constructing norms makes action a central tenet of the group.

From our discussions we are aware that many researchers who adopt the social identity perspective have an excellent understanding of the distinction between social categories and groups that we are going to labor in this article. We would concede that the problem that we address here is not one that has been created by scholars working in the field of collective action but one that has been imported from other fields of the social psychology of intergroup relations. We are concerned, however, that the imprecision that we want to address has starker negative consequences in the field of collective action than it does in some other areas. The most positive construction that can be placed on our contribution is that we are encouraging researchers to go further in a direction in which they have already made great progress.

Distinguishing between Groups and Social Categories

To pursue our first point we need to enter a very old debate that may seem somewhat abstract but nevertheless promises some general practical benefits. Researchers have long entertained a distinction between in-groups and out-groups, and the conventional wisdom for most of social psychology's history has been that in-groups reflect categories that the perceiver belongs to and out-groups represent categories to which they do not.

In our view this categorical definition of in-groups, derived from Summer (1906) lies at the heart of the problem. Social identity researchers have adopted a contemporary theory that incorporates a subjective and dynamic definition of the group, but they too often uncritically accept a definition of the in-group that is based on objective and static social categories.

Most treatments assume that nominal social category memberships and subjective group memberships are one and the same. That is, it is assumed that a person's in-groups are identical to the social category memberships regardless of their subjective identification. Thus men might be said to represent an out-group for women and women are an out-group for men. The same might be said about Blacks and Whites or Muslims and Jews.

It is easy to see the appeal of this simple equation but the problem with it becomes obvious when we consider Turner's (1982) definition of a social group: "a social group can be defined as two or more individuals who share a common social identification of themselves or, which is nearly the same thing, *perceive themselves to be members of the same social category*" (p. 15, emphasis added).

This is the definition that seems to be accepted by most social identity researchers. This definition laid the foundations for self-categorization theory with its emphasis on variable, flexible, and context-dependent self-perception. Contrary to the view imported from Summer (1906) a social category cannot be an in-group until the perceiver recognizes that that category is an aspect of self at that particular time. It makes no sense under this definition for other people to specify your group memberships.

Turner's definition is thus completely incompatible with an approach that assumes that group memberships are invariant aspects of social structure. The incompatibility emerges most starkly in the analysis of collective action where we are forced to consider the nature of the collectives that act and to consider the ways in which common causes come to exist between people with different social category memberships.

However, Turner, Hogg, Oakes, Reicher, and Wetherell's (1987) self-categorization theory articulates the conceptual tools they intended to solve the problems raised here and should have overcome that confusion. Hypothesis 4 of self-categorization theory is "That psychological group formation takes place to the degree that two or more people come to perceive and define themselves in terms of some shared ingroup-outgroup categorization" (Turner et al., 1987, p. 51).

Thus, according to self-categorization theory, group membership is intensely subjective. People do not become part of a group until they feel they are part of that group. Mere membership of a social category cannot constitute an in-group membership unless the perceiver is subjectively identified with that category. The theory expands on this requirement by specifying that those social identifications must also be shared with others.

Self-categorization theory is a theory of dynamic self-perception that seeks to explain how people can act as individuals at some times and in terms of any one of an endless number of different group memberships at other times. The theory explains these variations in perspective in terms of the construct of category salience. As particular (social) categories become salient (i.e., switched on or activated) people are expected to act in terms of the social identities associated with those categories.

Before going further we need to note some caveats. A number of scholars, especially Spears, Ellemers, and Doosje (e.g., Doosje, Spears, & Ellemers, 2002; Ellemers, Spears, & Doosje, 1997) have very seriously followed the argument by Tajfel and Turner (1979) that intergroup differentiation (and related phenomena) will be qualified by subjective group membership identification. Predictably, given the view we have presented so far, we endorse this concern. However we would also caution that social identification or commitment to a group membership does not fully capture the degree to which self-categorization qualifies action. As we will argue below, we think the problem is not only that there is variation in social identification across members of a social category, but also that we do not always measure identification with the relevant category. In the tradition of research on collective action, the point that commitment to a cause is a critical determinant of support for action is also strongly evident in the work of Klandermans and colleagues (de Weerd & Klandermans, 1999; Klandermans, 2000; Klandermans, Sabucedo, & Rodriguez, 2002) on the social identification route to collective action, in Simon and colleagues' (Simon et al., 1998; Simon, Stürmer, & Steffens, 2000; Stürmer & Simon, 2004) work on activist identity and in their joint work (Simon & Klandermans, 2001) on politicized collective identity.

The other key caveat is that we fully accept that social categories, where they represent aspects of social structural relations, are likely to continue to be psychologically consequential, even where they do not form the basis for the salient group membership. Indeed work by Bongiorno and David (2008) suggests that there are excellent reasons why certain social categories (such as gender) function as categories rather than group memberships in a range of situations. Thus, an unintended benefit of the category-group confusion is that by ignoring the subjective aspects of group memberships, many social psychologists have incorporated social structural variables such as gender, ethnicity, class, and nationality into their analyses.

Those points notwithstanding, the problem of equating social categories and group memberships remains particularly marked when we consider collective action. We think this is because collective action frequently involves action that is about relations between social categories, is taken by members who span those categories, and perhaps most importantly, often takes place under circumstances where there is intense contestation within those categories.

It is useful to illustrate these points with two examples. Very widespread collective action was taken by opponents of the U.S.-led invasion of Iraq in 2003. Focus for a moment on participants in this protest action drawn from the United States, Britain, and Australia (the Western democracies that took part in the initial invasion). There is no political, institutional, religious, ethnic, or social category that binds these people together. One thing that the protesters may have had in common was a national sense of responsibility (e.g., that it was wrong for their nation to invade another country without the full authorization of the United Nations), but even the most casual observers would have noted that ownership of the national identity was hotly contested in this context (in very much the way that Reicher et al., 2006, have argued). Opponents of the invasion were derided by people with opposite views as being disloyal to their own nation and as lending comfort to the regime of Saddam Hussein. We need other collective identities to explain these contested movements and evidence of mechanisms for contestation within the movement whereby different emotions lead to different action strategies (see Iyer, Schmadel, & Lickel, 2007).

Industrial action shows similar levels of contestation. It might be convenient to understand the identity dynamics in that domain as involving conflicts between workers and bosses or union and management, but real-life contexts are more subtle. Industrial action is taken by workers (sometimes including people who are not members of a union) because they support a cause and industrial action can be vociferously opposed by union members and other workers (see Taylor & McGarty, 2001).

Identity Alternatives for Explaining Collective Action

What are the current options for explaining collective action in social identity terms? Put another way, if collective action is genuinely collective, then what are the collective identities involved?

A dominant account that has been widely deployed relies on social category and institutional identities. In an excellent exposition of the social identity approach to social movement participation, Stürmer and Simon (2004) observe that:

> Social movements often, if not typically, build on pre-existing collective identities. These derive from membership in a disadvantaged group (e.g., collective identity as labourer, woman, member of a particular ethnic or religious identity, as a gay man or a lesbian woman) or from membership in more exclusive political groups and organizations actively promoting social change on behalf of the disadvantaged in-group (e.g., collective identity as a trade unionist, a feminist, or a minority rights advocate). (p. 68)

A good example of the general approach described by Stürmer and Simon is the paper by de Weerd and Klandermans (1999). These authors explored the social identification and collective action intentions of Dutch farmers (in their terms a disadvantaged "group" but what we would prefer to call a social category). Their most important finding for our purposes was that the correlation between identification with the social category and the degree to which the farmers intended to take part in protest action to support their cause was weak. Kelly and Breinlinger (1995) obtained similar findings for gender categories in earlier research. The extent to which women identified with the category "women" was a weak predictor of intentions to take protest action. Most compellingly, Simon et al. (1998) found in a range of contexts, that identification with social category memberships (gay people, older people, and overweight people) was weakly correlated with intentions to take action.

These findings are important in relation to our argument as they suggest that, in order to better understand collective action, it is necessary to explore identification with more specific categories which are relevant in the context of action, rather than broader social categories. Activist identities seems to get closer to the core of the issue of collective action, by offering a more direct route to predicting intentions to take or become involved in collective action. Indeed both Kelly and Breinlinger (1995) and Simon and colleagues (1998) found that the correlations were stronger when identification with broader categories was replaced by identification with an activist identity.

However we believe that activist identities are profoundly limited by their subjective applicability. Activists are rare and mass movements (by definition) involve large numbers of people who mostly do not fall into the activist category. The problem here is not so much that most movement participants are weakly identified as activists but that the vast majority of participants would avidly reject such a label. That is, the participants are not so much activists as supporters of that cause.

Simon and colleagues have developed two solutions to this problem building on the work of Klandermans (1997). The first, as articulated in the work of Stürmer and Simon (2004), is to focus on identification with a movement. We agree that this is a positive development, but it is also limited. Many of the collective forces in society are conservative, and with the exception of explicitly reactionary ones, they are not movements because they are not going anywhere. Given Stürmer and Simon's focus on collective action (rather than inaction) this omission is fair for tactical reasons; but, in our view, it risks missing some of the bigger picture. A related positive contribution is the idea of politicized collective identity (Simon & Klandermans, 2001). We agree that to the extent that people become aware of shared grievances, and understand that these grievances can be addressed by influencing other members of society, they will come to develop a form of identity that incorporates explicit motivations to engage in a struggle for power. Our concern here is that we agree that politicization may be sufficient to promote collective action but it may not be necessary.

This point needs some elaboration. We argue that much collective action does indeed stem from well-developed political identities based on ideological engagement and contestation, but there are other domains where collective action is relatively spontaneous and involves group formation around causes that are political only in a minimal sense. The members of a group of residents who protest over the closure of a local library, or a group of students who protest over a change of examination format, may have developed a politicized collective identity but this seems hard to justify when we consider the rapidity with which such protests can emerge and the fact that such protests can emerge within tiny pockets of a community (e.g., within a particular street or a particular classroom). It seems difficult to claim that such local activists have developed a consciousness (as a resident or student) based on shared grievances before they take action (though again we stress that we have no doubt that such a consciousness will positively contribute to the commitment to change).

Some might be tempted to dismiss such everyday instances of dissent and protest as being trivial. This is a judgment of degrees, but in our view it would be a mistake to fail to see these phenomena as resting on collective processes. Thus we see great merit in the ideas of identification with social movements and of politicized collective identity. We believe both concepts are phenomenologically and subjectively valid, but we argue that both concepts are limited by the same constraint. They do not easily allow us to consider cases where members from different social categories (or what Simon & Klandermans, 2001, term "real-life social groups") come together to form common cause, and in particular where members of high-status "groups" work to overcome the disadvantage of others. As Duncan and Stewart (2007) observe in relationship to activism for gay rights and against racism: "individuals develop collective identities based not solely on their position in the social structure (as straight or white), but based on their analysis of the damage done by that social structure." Perhaps more importantly, previous approaches also fail, in our view, to capture the dynamics of deep division within disadvantaged or otherwise aggrieved social categories that provides a backdrop for collective action.

To return to the domain studied by Kelly and Breinlinger (1995) we would argue that identification with women is a weak predictor of action intentions to advance the cause of women because of political contestation within that category. Feminists may very well have developed a politicized collective identity whereas "traditional" women may reject this. Again the issue is not that the antifeminists are weak female identifiers, or that they have somehow failed to develop a politicized gender identity (a factor that Duncan & Stewart, 2007, show to be an excellent predictor of political participation). On the contrary, such antifeminists may even be highly identified with a cause that has the aim of defeating feminism.

For these reasons and others we believe that there is space to pursue alternatives to complement these ideas. We now turn to our preferred alternative.

The Opinion-Based Group Alternative

Opinion-based groups are psychological groups in the sense used by Turner (1982) but have a social identity defined by a shared opinion (see Bliuc, McGarty, Reynolds, & Muntele, 2007). Merely holding the same opinion as others is not sufficient for such a group to be said to exist, rather the shared opinion needs to become part of that social identity. In this way, people can come to perceive and define themselves in terms of their opinion group membership in the same way as they would with any other psychologically meaningful social category or group. Where the opinion-based group membership becomes switched on, group members should behave in line with the norms of that group.

Opinion-based groups are particularly relevant for understanding collective action for a number of reasons. Firstly, they often form around controversial issues, and oppositionally defined opinion-based groups tend to champion opposing perspectives on key issues. In other words, there are opinion-based groups that aim to change the social world in some way and, on the contrary, groups which aim to preserve the status quo.

Opinion-based groups can be readily distinguished from social categories and action groups. Opinion-based groups can often be formed within a broader social category (or be more broad than a social category). One important idea in relation to opinion-based groups is that they are often formed about the relations between social categories or groups, or on behalf of those social categories or groups. This is the case with feminist and antifeminist opinion-based groups, which are groups formed around ideologies about relations between social categories based on gender. In this way, opinion-based groups can also help to restructure problematic intercategory boundaries. It is easier for women and men to work together to promote gender equality, or for people of different races to work to promote tolerance and acceptance, if members of both categories share a relevant opinion-based group membership.

Opinion-based groups can also be distinguished from action groups. Most action groups are in fact based on shared opinions and opinion-based groups can be seen as incipient action groups. Specifically, activist groups can be considered as emerging from opinion-based groups. The "single-issue pressure groups" studied by Kelly and Breinlinger (1995) and the activist groups such as Gray Panthers, gay movement, AIDS volunteer service organization, and fat acceptance movement investigated by Simon et al. (1998, 2000) and Stürmer, Simon, Loewy, and Jörger (2003), can be regarded as directly emerging from opinion-based groups. They all represent the active, strongly committed, and organized faction of a broader opinion-based group. All members of an opinion-based group may have the potential to take spontaneous collective action in specific circumstances, but only a small fraction of the membership will be involved in organizing it.

In other ways, the idea of opinion-based groups involves a return to themes developed earlier by Klandermans and Oegema (1987) and Oegema and Klandermans (1994). These authors suggested that action mobilization involves four phases (1) becoming sympathetic to a cause (or part of the mobilization potential for a cause), (2) becoming a target for mobilization attempts, (3) becoming motivated to participate, and (4) overcoming barriers to participation. Arguably, opinion-based groups capture a similar idea to Klandermans and Oegema's (1987) concept of mobilization potential (the first stage of the model). These authors define mobilization potential as "those who take a positive stand towards a social movement" which they then equate with Kriesi's concept of *manifest political potential*, which they describe as "a group of people with a common identity and a set of common goals." As social movement formation proceeds down the steps identified by Klandermans and Oegema, it seems plausible that politicized collective identity as described by Simon and Klandermans (2001) will become increasingly relevant but we would argue that to understand the political cleavages at the incipient stage of action, then other identities that recall Kriesi's ideas seem highly relevant.

Opinion-based groups, when compared to groups based on social categories, do tend to be easy to connect to group normative behaviors. This is because opinion-based group membership hinges on consensus between members that imply certain courses of action and rules out other alternative actions. As Kelly and Breinlinger (1995) showed, being a woman does not imply a particular stance on gender equality, but we would argue that membership of a feminist opinion-based group will tend to imply much clearer stances and courses of action.

Our research (e.g., Bliuc et al., 2007) conducted in Australia and Romania shows that identification with a political opinion-based group is an excellent predictor of intentions to take politically relevant behavior. Our strongest claim is that to talk of collective action is to talk of opinion-based groups in action. In other words, collective action is the material crystallization or expression of the existence of salient opinion-based group memberships. Work by Musgrove and McGarty (2008) also suggests that opinion-based group memberships about the war on terror are excellent predictors of contrasting group-based emotions and actions (cf. McGarty et al., 2005, who found weak evidence for such relationships with national identification; see also McGarty & Bliuc, 2004).

Collective action is strongly linked to opinion-based group identity for a number of reasons. First, opinion-based groups are formed primarily to convert broad ideologies or affinities into collective action. Unified social action is aimed either to create social change or to preserve the status quo. Building on social identity (Tajfel & Turner, 1979) and Klandermans' (2000) ideas, such action is taken by people who share an opinion about achieving or rejecting social change. Depending on the opinion they hold, they can be considered to be members of one opinion-based group or another (e.g., pro- or antichange of the status quo).

As intimated earlier, activist groups can be seen as organized subcategories of larger opinion-based groups or as factions organized to act in terms of a certain subjective opinion-based group membership. Thus, in terms of relevance to action, broad social categories should be the least relevant, with opinion-based group representing the missing link between them and activist groups. In order to understand the mechanisms and links between collective identities and action, it is essential to look at the underlying nature of collective action and of the groups participating in collective action.

Thus, activist identities can be considered to be opinion-based group identities that are aligned with organizations constituted on the basis of opinion-based group membership, with rules and a structure designed to promote a certain stance or view of the world. In other words, activist identities are opinion-based group identities which have achieved a more objective consistency and which take responsibility for more organized forms of collective action. In the case of spontaneous collective action, opinion-based groups may appear in a raw, less structured form. Participants in action need not be attached to specific activist groups but simply share a common understanding and stance on a certain issue and hence come to share an opinion-based group membership. In the next section we explore how these understandings and stances can come to be shared and intensified.

Sharpening Opinion-Based Group Memberships through Group-Based Interaction

In a very perceptive chapter, Wright and Lubensky (2008) observe that prejudice reduction interventions have the potential to demobilize collective action. This is a subtle point. Blurring or invalidating category boundaries (e.g., "color blindness") can undermine efforts by members of disadvantaged groups to work together to overcome injustice. Indeed affirmative action policies are often challenged by White Power advocates (and others) on the grounds that they involve racial discrimination (against whites).

Motivated in part by Wright and Lubensky's concerns, we have adopted a new approach to the problems of reducing prejudice and promoting commitment to positive social change. In doing so, we also acknowledge that previous interventions may have had limited success because they are attempts to achieve an extremely difficult goal. It may be unproductive to attempt to change the opinions of people who already have hostile or negative attitudes toward disadvantaged or stigmatized groups. Our work instead explores the possibility of boosting commitment to oppose prejudice among people who are already, at least nominally, opposed to it. Our reasoning is that such bolstering of commitment amongst otherwise mildly committed people can serve to empower them on the path toward active opposition to prejudice. Where ordinary people become increasingly committed to talking and acting in line with antiprejudiced norms, they should also be more likely to confront racism when they encounter it.

Indeed, by using the concept of the opinion-based group, we have designed an opinion-based group interaction method that our ongoing research suggests provides us with an effective way to energize and sharpen peoples' commitment to engage in collective action. Our intervention, which is inspired by work on group decision making and polarization (in particular Lewin, 1947; Postmes, Spears, Lee, & Novak, 2005) involves recruiting participants for a study to discuss a certain issue (say attitudes to Reconciliation between Indigenous and non-Indigenous Australians). Privately, participants are asked to specify a relevant opinion-based group membership, for example, whether or not they consider themselves to be supporters of efforts to promote Reconciliation.

Participants assigned to experimental conditions are then asked to take part in a group discussion with other nominal supporters. The discussion takes the form of a planning session where participants are asked to reach agreement on ways to achieve the goals of this movement. They are told that their written deliberations will be included in (variously) a web site to be hosted by the School of Psychology, a letter to a responsible authority, or an article to be submitted to a campus or community newspaper. The groups are given around 30 minutes to complete the discussion and to note down their agreed positions. They are then measured on a series of items capturing relevant beliefs, emotional and action intentions, and measures of social identification. Responses are compared with participants who have been randomly assigned to a (no interaction) control condition.

The method is designed to energize action by giving participants the opportunity to articulate norms of action in a way that is validated both through the development of consensus within the group and because it is considered to be part of real and legitimate efforts to create that social change. The method also adds to the tool kit of social psychological research in that, through group-based interaction, we are able to observe processes of consensus and dissensus which are likely to be highly analogous to what would occur in everyday settings when people talk to others about a particular issue and become galvanized to engage in collective action. Indeed, the group-based interaction technique has been effective in improving attitudes to people with mental disorders and Australian Aborigines (Blink, 2005, unpublished data; Gee, Khalaf, & McGarty, 2007) and bolstering commitment to combat poverty in developing countries (Thomas & McGarty, 2009) and more recently in promoting commitment to combat climate change (Bongiorno, McGarty & Kurz, 2009, unpublished data).

Importantly, we are not suggesting that merely bringing people into a room to discuss an issue of mutual interest or importance will change their attitudes in positive and lasting ways. We have observed that introducing such discussion as part of a routine class activity has no effect of itself. This was further borne out in research by McGarty et al. (2008, Study 1) who showed that in conditions where the experimenter presented herself as someone who was uncommitted to the aims of the movement and more interested in gathering data for a research project, the positive effects of the interaction were negated.

Our general impression of the method is that it tends to be successful in promoting change when the groups agree about the overall direction that the cause needs to take, perceive the process as a legitimate activity for the opinion-based group, and find the experience of the group-based interaction to be validating and positive. We think that the overlap with Klandermans and Oegema's (1987) first three steps in action mobilization process is because we have created an analogue of processes that frequently occur in community centers, church halls, bars, and other locations.

While results have suggested that there are some elements which will undermine and "switch off" the opinion-based group interaction, we have also identified some key processes which we believe work to enhance the opinion-based group interaction. We draw on work by van Zomeren, Spears, Leach, and Fischer (2004), who identified two potentially important variables in motivating collective action. Their dual-pathway model suggests that people will take action when they feel a relevant group-based emotion (such as anger or outrage at a perceived injustice) and/or when they believe that their actions will be effective (collective efficacy, following Bandura, 2000). In the context of opinion-based groups and collective action more generally, it is clear that where groups experience feelings of pity for the disadvantaged, or do not believe that their actions will make any difference to their cause, these groups are unlikely to be galvanized to act (or, at least, not in a way designed to bring about positive social change).

We investigated the interplay of emotion (particularly outrage), efficacy, and opinion-based group identities in the context of the group-based interaction, reasoning that both emotion and efficacy processes were likely to be implicated in the group-based interaction, in different ways. Emotions, and expressions of emotion, may play a particularly important role in collective action, because of the ease with which they are communicated, and the strong motivational base they can provide (Leach & Tiedens, 2004). The statement that, for example, "the situation makes me angry" conveys a large amount of information about how a person feels about the situation, his or her attributions for responsibility, and even the physiological sensations that accompany the experience. As such, shared emotion might play a useful coordinating role in the context of the opinion-based group interaction, in so much as it implies a shared understanding of the world.

Consistent with this argument we find that when groups are given a specific emotion norm (in this case outrage) to incorporate in their planning session and to consensualize around, this boosts mean levels of commitment to action, outrage and identification with the opinion-based group, over and above the standard effects of the opinion-based group interaction method (Thomas & McGarty, 2009). This suggests that where outrage is taken on, as a shared, meaningful norm for that particular opinion-based group, it is able to energize action, perhaps because this outrage norm effectively replaces potentially demotivating emotion. For example, it becomes antinormative for a member of this opinion-based group to feel pity as it becomes normative for them to feel outraged at the situation.

Similarly, we would expect efficacy processes to be implicated in the opinion-based group interaction, just as they would seem to be in real-life opinion-based groups contemplating collective action. Given that the nature of the task is to discuss practical solutions for overcoming the disadvantage, we would expect this process to boost efficacy beliefs. And indeed, we do find evidence that where groups are able to work effectively and come up with strategies to work to overcome the disadvantage, this does boost efficacy beliefs. Conversely, as indicated above, where efficacy is undermined, or groups consensualize around a demotivating emotion norm, the effects of the intervention seem likely to be undermined.

Thus we find that the group-based interaction leads to significant boosts in commitment to take action to overcome disadvantage under conditions where participants (1) endorse, and consensualize around a shared understanding that it is appropriate to feel outraged at the situation and (2) are effectively able to come up with strategies to do something about it, which boosts efficacy beliefs. While this seems to be the case in the context of the opinion-based group interaction, it is worth noting the intriguing possibility that there may be other ways to align opinion-based group identification, emotion, and efficacy to produce shifts in commitment to take action.

The opinion-based group concept, in conjunction with the group interaction method, is a very useful tool for studying the processes by which real-life opinion-based groups come to take action or refuse to do so. We do caution though that while our research has concentrated on the promise of the method for understanding and promoting positive social change, it is likely that similar processes operate in more sinister instantiations of negative and destructive collective action (Smith & Postmes, 2009).

Problems with and Prospects for the Opinion-Based Group Formulation

Before concluding this article, we wish to address some of the problems and prospects of the opinion-based group formulation. We believe that the approach has some distinctive virtues. We have argued in some detail that the idea of opinion-based group membership can complement the progression that is evident in the field of collective action toward a clearer specification of identity dynamics. The opinion-based group formulation allows a theoretical solution to the problem of common cause.

The question arises as to what role the broad social categories serve in collective action. These are by no means irrelevant, and indeed our motivation for seeking to differentiate them from subjectively functioning group memberships is precisely because they are important. Let us be clear then that we are certain that social and institutional categories such as ethnicity, gender, class, nation, region, religion, and organizational membership can provide platforms for collective action, but that these memberships tend to be poorly served for taking action. Nevertheless as visible aspects of the self there is every reason to believe that these categories will be deployed, but in ways that are less likely to take the form of collective action unless they are accompanied by opinion-based group formation.

Nevertheless we believe that social categories will have tangible political consequences to the extent that opinion-based groups are able to align themselves with social categories. Indeed we go so far as to develop the argument elsewhere (Bliuc, McGarty, Hartley, & Muntele, 2008; Hartley, McGarty, & Donaghue, 2008) that the political success of an opinion-based group rests largely on the degree to which that group is able to align itself with some positively valued social category, that is, to the extent that membership of the opinion-based group comes to stand for or represent the broad social category (see Mummendey & Wenzel, 1999). Perhaps the clearest examples are provided by political parties that successfully align themselves with a national or regional identity so that their opinions are attributed broadly to virtually all members of a category. In this way, the social category may be reunited with the group in a way that is compatible with Simon and Klandermans' (2001) analysis.

To be sure social categories have powerful consequences even when they are not engaged as group memberships. They reflect social structure and relations and provide alternative categorizations. There are inevitable sensitivities and limits on members of advantaged social categories who seek to engage in collective action alongside members of disadvantaged social categories. What does it mean to be a male feminist or a white civil rights activist? These are not unproblematic or uncontested identities but our point is that they are possible identities and when salient they can have consequences that need to be understood.

There is also the question of why the opinion-based group idea is superior to the strategy of stressing superordinate group membership. This is a matter that one of us has addressed in some detail elsewhere (McGarty, 1999, 2006). McGarty argues that, contrary to self-categorization theory, there is limited evidence that the self (or for that matter other systems of categories) is hierarchically organized (as a tree structure) and that people do not use hierarchies for reasoning, even when they are presented with hierarchically organized categories. The problem becomes more acute for social categories given the inevitable containment and overlap relations. Are categories such as male and female subordinate to national categories such as Australian and American? Is not the opposite equally plausible?

This technical argument aside, we believe that opinion-based group memberships are not reducible to superordinate category memberships. Opinion-based groups can be more or less abstract or inclusive than other categories and therefore they cannot be equated with superordinate categories. Furthermore, to the extent to which superordinate categories are subjectively valid at some point of time (and we do not dispute that they can be) the content of those categories will be constrained to some degree by the relatively invariant features of social reality. As Wright and Lubensky (2008) explain in some detail, identification with superordinate categorizations may serve to reinforce the inferior status of disadvantaged group members. Opinion-based group membership can, but need not, fall victim to the same trap.

Conclusion

Our justification of our approach has necessarily been critical of the work of many scholars whose work we greatly admire. We do not seek to back away from that criticism in our conclusion except to say that we see the concept of the opinion-based group as complementing and extending the work that has established the value of the social identity approach. In particular, we believe that our approach carries to the next logical step a process that is inevitably set in motion by the work of Simon and Klandermans (2001), of Wright (2001), and of Hopkins and Reicher (1997).

If this logical thread can be expressed in a single sentence then it is the idea that collective action must be connected to ideas, and that political action must be connected to ideology, and all of these things, action, ideas, and ideology must be tied to collective identity. In recent years, social psychology has struggled to grapple with ideology in a way that is compatible with collective identity (many preferring to consider it as an expression of individual orientations): opinion-based groups represent one way in which the ideological aspects of society can be understood in collective terms.

References

Bandura, A. (2000). Exercise of human agency through collective efficacy. *Current Directions in Psychological Science, 9*, 75–78.

Bliuc, A.-M., McGarty, C., Reynolds, K., & Muntele, D. (2007). Opinion-based group membership as a predictor to commitment to political action. *European Journal of Social Psychology, 37*, 19–32.

Bliuc, A.-M., McGarty, C., Hartley, L., & Muntele, D. (2008). *Conservative opinion-based groups and collective action*. Unpublished manuscript, The University of Sydney.

Bongiorno, R., & David, B. (2008). *The status of gender in psychology: Basic primary category, variable self-category, or something in between?* Unpublished manuscript, The Australian National University.

de Weerd, M., & Klandermans, B. (1999). Group identification and social protest: Farmer's protest in the Netherlands. *European Journal of Social Psychology, 29*, 1073–1095.

Doosje, B., Spears, R., & Ellemers, N. (2002). Social identity as both cause and effect: The development of group identification in response to anticipated and actual changes in the intergroup status hierarchy. *British Journal of Social Psychology, 41*, 57–76.

Dovidio, J. F., Gaertner, S. L., Validzic, A., Matoka, K., Johnson, B., & Frazier, S. (1997). Extending the benefits of recategorization: Evaluations, self-disclosure and helping. *Journal of Experimental Social Psychology, 33*, 401–420.

Duncan, L. E., & Stewart, A. J. (2007). Personal political salience: The role of personality in collective action and identity. *Political Psychology, 28*, 143–164.

Eggins, R. A., Haslam, S. A., & Reynolds, K. J. (2002). Social identity and negotiation: Subgroup representation and superordinate consensus. *Personality and Social Psychology Bulletin, 28*, 887–899.

Ellemers, N., Spears, R., & Doosje, B. (1997). Sticking together or falling apart: In-group identification as a psychological determinant of group commitment versus individual mobility. *Journal of Personality and Social Psychology, 72*, 617–626.

Gaertner, S. L., & Dovidio, J. F. (2000). *Reducing intergroup bias: The common ingroup identity model*. New York: Psychology Press.

Gaertner, S. L., & Dovidio, J. F. (2005). Understanding and addressing contemporary racism: From aversive racism to the common ingroup identity model. *Journal of Social Issues, 61*, 615–639.

Gee, A., Khalaf, A., & McGarty, C. (2007). Using group-based interaction to change stereotypes about people with mental disorders. *Australian Psychologist, 42*, 98–105.

Hartley, L., McGarty, C., & Donaghue, N. (2008). *What to do after saying sorry? Understanding the enabling conditions for commitment to political action about reconciliation in Australia*. Unpublished manuscript, Murdoch University.

Hopkins, N., & Reicher, S. (1997). Social movement rhetoric and the social psychology of collective action: A case study of anti-abortion mobilization. *Human Relations, 50,* 261–286.
Hopkins, N., Kahani-Hopkins, V., & Reicher, S. D. (2006). Identity and social change: Contextualizing agency. *Feminism and Psychology, 16*(1), 52–57.
Hornsey, M. J., & Hogg, M. A. (2000). Assimilation and diversity: An integrative model of subgroup relations. *Personality and Social Psychology Review, 4,* 143–156.
Iyer, A., Schmader, T., & Lickel, B. (2007). Why individuals protest the perceived transgressions of their country: The role of anger, shame and guilt. *Personality and Social Psychology Bulletin, 33,* 572–587.
Kelly, C., & Breinlinger, S. (1995). Identity and injustice: Exploring women's participation in collective action. *Journal of Community and Applied Psychology, 5,* 41–57.
Klandermans, B. (1997). *The social psychology of protest.* Oxford: Basil Blackwell.
Klandermans, B. (2000). Identity and protest: How group identification helps to overcome collective action dilemmas. In M. Van Vugt, M. Snyder, T. Tyler, & A. Biel (Eds.), *Cooperation in modern society: Promoting the welfare of communities, states and organizations* (pp. 162–183). London: Routledge.
Klandermans, B., & Oegema, D. (1987). Potentials, networks, motivations and barriers: Steps towards participation in social movements. *American Sociological Review, 52,* 519–531.
Klandermans, P. G., Sabucedo, J. M., & Rodriguez, M. (2002). Identity processes in collective action participation: Farmer's identity and farmer's protest in the Netherlands and Spain. *Political Psychology, 23,* 235–251.
Leach, C. W, & Tiedens, L. Z. (2004). Introduction: A world of emotion. In L. Z. Tiedens & C. W. Leach (Eds.), *The social life of emotions* (pp. 1–16). Cambridge: Cambridge University Press.
Lewin, K. (1947). *Group decision and social change.* New York: Holt, Rinehart & Winston.
McGarty, C. (1999). *Categorization in social psychology.* London: Sage.
McGarty, C. (2006). Hierarchies and groups: The roles of salience, overlap, and background knowledge in selecting meaningful social categorizations from multiple alternatives. In R. J. Crisp & M. Hewstone (Eds.), *Multiple social categorization: Processes, models and applications* (pp. 25–49). Hove, UK: Psychology Press.
McGarty, C., & Bliuc, A.-M. (2004). Collective guilt in Australia. In B. Doosje & N. R. Branscombe (Eds.), *Collective Guilt: Antecedents, correlates and consequences* (pp. 112–129). Cambridge: Cambridge University Press.
McGarty, C., Pedersen, A., Leach, C. W., Mansell, T., Waller, J., & Bliuc, A.-M. (2005). Group-based guilt as a predictor of commitment to apology. *British Journal of Social Psychology, 44,* 659–680.
McGarty, C., Bongiorno, R., Blink, C., Thomas, E. F., & Kurz, T. (2008). *Opinion-based group interaction: An experimental model for exploring social change.* Unpublished manuscript, Murdoch University.
Mummendey, A., & Wenzel, M. (1999). Social discrimination and tolerance in intergroup relations: Reactions to intergroup difference. *Personality and Social Psychology Review, 3,* 158–174.
Musgrove, L., & McGarty, C. A. (2008). Opinion-based group membership as a predictor of collective emotional responses and support for pro- and anti-war action. *Social Psychology, 39,* 37–47.
Postmes, T., Spears, R., Lee, A. T., & Novak, R. J. (2005). Individuality and social influence in groups: Inductive and deductive routes to group identity. *Journal of Personality and Social Psychology, 89,* 747–763.
Oegema, D., & Klandermans, B. (1994). Why social movement sympathizers don't participate: Erosion and nonconversion of support. *American Sociological Review, 59,* 703–722.
Reicher, S., Cassidy, C., Wolpert, I., Hopkins, N., & Levine, M. (2006). Saving Bulgaria's Jews: An analysis of social identity and the mobilisation of social solidarity. *European Journal of Social Psychology, 36,* 49–72.
Simon, B., & Klandermans, B. (2001). Politicized collective identity: A social psychological analysis. *American Psychologist, 56,* 319–331.
Simon, B., Loewy, M., Stürmer, S., Weber, U., Freytag, P., Habig, C., et al. (1998). Collective identification and social movement participation. *Journal of Personality and Social Psychology, 74,* 646–658.

Simon, B., Stürmer, S., & Steffens, K. (2000). Helping individuals or group members? The role of individual and collective identification in AIDS volunteerism. *Personality and Social Psychology Bulletin, 26*, 497–506.
Smith, L. G. E., & Postmes, T. (2009). Intra-group interaction and the development of norms which promote inter-group hostility. *European Journal of Social Psychology, 39*, 130–144.
Stürmer, S., & Simon, B. (2004). Collective action: Towards a dual-pathway model. *European Review of Social Psychology, 15*(1), 59–99.
Stürmer, S., Simon, B., Loewy, M., & Jörger, H. (2003). The dual-path model of social movement participation: The case of fat acceptance movement. *Social Psychology Quarterly, 66*, 71–82.
Summer, W. (1906). *Folkways*. New York: Ginn.
Tajfel, H., & Turner, J. C. (1979). An integrative theory of intergroup conflict. In S. Worchel & W. G. Austin (Eds.), *The social psychology of intergroup relations* (pp. 33–47). Chicago: Nelson-Hall.
Taylor, N., & McGarty, C. (2001). The role of subjective group memberships and perceptions of power in industrial conflict. *Journal of Community & Applied Social Psychology, 11*, 389–393.
Thomas, E. F., & McGarty, C. (2009). The role of efficacy and moral outrage norms in creating the potential for international development activism through group-based interaction. *British Journal of Social Psychology, 48*, 115–134.
Turner, J. C. (1982). Towards a cognitive redefinition of the group. In H. Tajfel (Ed.), *Social identity and intergroup relations* (pp. 15–40). Cambridge: Cambridge University Press.
Turner, J. C., Hogg, M. A., Oakes, P., Reicher, S. D., & Wetherell, M. S. (1987). *Rediscovering the social group: A self-categorization theory*. Oxford: Basil Blackwell.
van Zomeren, M., Spears, R., Leach, C. W., & Fischer, A. H. (2004). Put your money where your mouth is! Explaining collective action tendencies through group-based anger and group efficacy. *Journal of Personality and Social Psychology, 87*, 649–664.
Wright, S. C. (2001). Strategic collective action: Social psychology and social change. In R. Brown and S. Gaertner (Eds.), *Intergroup processes: Blackwell handbook of social psychology* (Vol. 4, pp. 409–430). Malden, MA: Blackwell Press.
Wright, S. C., & Lubensky, I. (2008). The struggle for social equality: Collective action versus prejudice reduction. In S. Demoulin, J. P. Leyens, & J. F. Dovidio (Eds.), *Intergroup misunderstandings: Impact of divergent social realities* (pp. 291–310). New York: Psychology Press.

CRAIG MCGARTY is Professor of Psychology and the Director of the Social Research Institute at Murdoch University in Western Australia. He was previously Head of the School of Psychology at The Australian National University. He is the author of *Categorization in Social Psychology* (Sage, 1999) and editor of *The Message of Social Psychology* (Blackwell, 1997, with A. Haslam) and *Stereotypes as Explanations* (Cambridge, 2002, with V. Yzerbyt and R. Spears).

ANA-MARIA BLIUC is a post-doctoral researcher at the University of Sydney (Institute for Teaching and Learning). Her PhD in social psychology from The Australian National University explores the role of identification with opinion-based groups in predicting political involvement in non-activist people in several countries including Australia, Romania, and the Netherlands. Her current central interest is in opinion-based groups, more specifically, in the role played by opinion-based groups in spontaneous collective action and political participation, opinion-based group formation, the use of rhetoric by opinion-based groups' members, and strategies used by these groups to achieve political success.

EMMA F. THOMAS is completing her PhD at The Australian National University under the supervision of Craig McGarty and Ken Mavor. Her research focuses on ways to promote action to end poverty and preventable disease in developing countries, in particular by making prochange beliefs and emotional reactions normative for social groups.

RENATA BONGIORNO recently submitted her PhD (through the Australian National University). She moved to Murdoch University in 2007 to take up a position as a Research Associate on the Australian Research Council project, Bolstering Commitment to Positive Social Change through Group-Based Interaction, where she focuses in particular on ways of bolstering commitment to environmental sustainability. Her other major research interest is the persistence of gender discrimination in society and the ways that women can be marginalized through the pervasiveness of gender categorization.

The Next Generation of Collective Action Research

Stephen C. Wright*
Simon Fraser University

The articles presented in this volume describe part of a new generation of interest and vigor in the social psychological study of collective action. This new wave builds nicely on the foundation set by social identity, self-categorization, and relative deprivation theories but also introduces a number of important innovative perspectives and variables. In this commentary, I review some of these expansions and additions, raise a number of conceptual concerns that arise out of these new directions, and discuss more generally some novel and important directions that emerge from the work presented in the volume and in other recent work on collective action.

Improving intergroup relations has been a central focus of social psychology and of Society for the Psychological Study of Social Issues (SPSSI). A dominant strategy for achieving this goal has been prejudice reduction—reducing negative attitudes toward out-groups. Hundreds of studies have investigated the nature, causes, and consequences of prejudice (see Fiske, 1998; Wright & Taylor, 2003, for reviews). However, reducing the negative thoughts (stereotypes), attitudes (prejudice), and actions (discrimination) of individuals represents only one potential route to reduced group inequality and increasing social justice. A second approach focuses on collective action and social protest as a means of improving the status or treatment of disadvantaged groups.

Although both approaches explore intergroup injustice and both are plainly implicated in major intergroup relations theories (e.g., Turner, Hogg, Oakes, Reicher, & Wetherell, 1987), research on prejudice and collective action have developed quite independently (Wright & Lubensky, 2009), and collective action has received far less attention from social psychologists. Nonetheless, social psychology's focus on the mutual influences of the social context and individual psychological processes has provided important insights into the processes that

---

*Correspondence concerning this article should be addressed to Stephen C. Wright, Department of Psychology, Simon Fraser University, 8888 University Drive, Burnaby, British Columbia V5A 1S6, Canada [e-mail: scwright@sfu.ca].

fuel or undermine participation in collective action (see Reicher, 2004; Simon & Klandermans, 2001; van Zomeren, Postmes, & Spears, 2008; Wright, 2001, for reviews). The current volume's focus on recent and novel perspectives, as well as the implications of these ideas for policies and practices, adds nicely to this legacy. The articles provide a range of interesting investigations of the relationship between group-based inequality and/or injustice and efforts to produce (or in some cases prevent) social change. Collectively, they provide evidence of an exciting resurgence of interest in the study of collective action among social psychologists.

It would be impossible for a commentary such as this to do justice to the number of interesting issues and novel ideas raised in the pages that precede it. So, I will be unapologetically idiosyncratic about the issues I focus on. I will comment on what I see as interesting and important advances and will consider conceptual issues that could be important as we embark on this new wave of theorizing and research activity.

Sophistication and Precision: What is Collective Action?

As almost all of these articles show, the psychological study of collective action has been dominated by an interest in determining when and why individuals will (and will not) engage in collective action. One of the prominent contributions of this volume is that it brings attention to a broader array of antecedents, moderators, and mediators of collective action. I will expand on this general point later, but one inevitable consequence of this expansion will be a growth in healthy debate over the relative importance of these variables. The outcome of these debates should be more sophisticated models and perhaps greater confidence in suggestions made to practitioners and policy makers (another valuable goal of this issue). However, this expansion and the resulting debates make apparent another critical, although often ignored, issue—the issue of definition. Before we can argue about what produces (or prevents) collective action, we need to try to build some agreement about what collective action is. What do we mean when we say that an individual "participates in collective action" or is "motivated to take collective action"?

The issue of definition is not trivial. If different theoretical accounts begin with different conceptions of what collective action is, it is not surprising that they will predict (and find in empirical tests) different antecedents and mediators of collective action. Unfortunately, many discussions of collective action fail to provide a clear definition. However, numerous social psychological investigations have settled on a definition that locates collective action in the psychology of the individual. A group member engages in collective action any time she or he acts as a representative of the group and where the action is directed at improving the conditions of the group as a whole (Wright, Taylor, & Moghaddam, 1990a). Definitions consistent with this are provided or implied in many of the articles in this volume (Ellemers & Barreto; Louis; Postmes & Smith; van Stekelenburg et al.; van Zomeren & Iyer; van Zomeren & Spears).

This definition is consistent with the well-established recognition (Tajfel, 1982) that human behavior can be intergroup as well as interpersonal. Intergroup behavior emerges when the self and others are perceived in terms of the collective identities (in terms of their memberships in different groups), and when thoughts and actions are guided by group interests and in-group norms. In contrast, interpersonal behavior emerges when personal identities are the salient self/other-representation. Thus, by this definition collective action is a specific case of intergroup behavior that is strategic in its intent to improve the position of the in-group, and can be contrasted with individual action designed to improve one's personal position.

It's not about numbers. This conception of collective action is fundamentally psychological. It describes collective action as independent of the number of participants and of the specific content or eventual outcome of the action. Instead, whether an action is collective or individual depends on the actors' level of self-categorization and her/his intentions. This differs from a number of alternative perspectives that define collective action in terms of an observable group presence and group members acting in concert. For example, Stürmer and Simon appear to equate collective action with participation in social movement activities or group protests. Similarly, Drury and Reicher describe collective action as synonymous with crowd behavior, and McGarty, Bliuc, Thomas, and Bongiorno describe collective action as unified social action, both implying group members acting in concert. The psychological definition of *collective action*, as Louis points out, "does not require physical and temporal proximity of members" (p. 727). Collective action can be engaged in by a single individual acting alone.

Collective, not individual, action. The current definition also requires that group identity be the salient self-categorization and that group concerns motivate action. Thus, some joint actions by a large group would not qualify as collective action if the individual actors are motivated by personal self-interests. For example, Stürmer and Simon's dual-pathway model proposes one pathway to participation in "collective action" that is driven by three key motives. One of these motives involves the possibility of changing the in-group's status (the collective motive). However, the other two motives involve concerns about the possibility of personal admiration or ridicule by others (the normative motive), and concerns for personal costs or rewards, such as loss of time or money or getting hurt (the reward motive). Similarly, van Zomeren and Spears describe "individual-based collective action" in their discussion of the intuitive economists. Here collective identity and group interests appear irrelevant. The group is simply a tool to be used to acquire personal rewards or garner personal admiration from others. If collective action is defined as actions that involve collective identities and group-based concerns, action produced by personal self-interest would not qualify as collective action. What this example is intended to point out is that when we define the dependent variable (collective action) differently, it is not surprising that we find a different set of antecedents and mediators.

As an in-group member or on behalf of an out-group? Finally, the current definition, which links collective action to acting as a representative of an in-group, would not include actions taken by nonmembers designed to improve the status or treatment of subordinated out-group. For example, Iyer and Ryan consider men's willingness to engage in actions in support of women, and van Zomeren and Iyer identify the growing literature investigating when members of advantaged/high-status groups will join or perhaps even instigate protests or actively support policies designed to improve the status or treatment of a disadvantaged out-group (e.g., Iyer, Schmader, & Lickel, 2007; Mallett, Huntsinger, Sinclair, & Swim, 2008). Understanding the motives and intentions of those who are willing to act on behalf of a disadvantaged out-group is undoubtedly extremely important, and has until very recently been ignored and even downplayed in the social psychology literature. However, if the advantaged group members who are participating in these actions are truly acting on behalf of a group that they recognize to be an out-group, then they are not acting as a representative of that group. Thus, this would not fit the current definition of collective action. In addition, if the actors recognize that their behavior will serve to reduce group-based inequality then these actions may, in fact, be quite the opposite of collective action as their success will undermine the relative status or power of the actors' in-group.

One solution to this is provided by McGarty et al.'s concept of opinion-based groups whereby traditional in-group/out-group distinction can be rendered mute by the formation of a categorization that includes the advantaged group member and the disadvantaged group. For example, the group "supporters of racial justice" could include Whites as well as ethnic minority group members, or "feminists" could include men. In this case, the actions fit the definition of collective action. The advantaged group member is no longer acting on behalf of an out-group but rather is acting as a representative of a newly defined in-group.

Definitions evolve. My general point here is that a definition provides the boundary conditions for the concept of interest. Without some agreement about these boundary conditions it is unlikely that we will develop agreement about the nature of the phenomenon, let alone establish a clear understanding of the antecedents that produce it or barriers that prevent it. In order to build a sophisticated social psychology of collective action we need greater precision in our conceptualizations of what it is.

It is certain that the definition of collective action will continue to be contested, and this is a good thing. However, an important step is for people to be clear in providing their own working definition and establishing for their readers the boundary conditions of the concept they are calling *collective action*. For my own part, I propose that we take seriously the distinctions between more specific actions like participation in a social movement or support for a particular policy or practice versus the full range of group-serving actions that could be included within a broader psychological definition of *collective action* (like the one presented in the introduction to this volume). Participation in a particular event or movement (or set of activities) may be motivated by individualistic concerns or by an interest in helping a group that the participant recognizes is an out-group. It seems valuable to distinguish this from actions motivated by collective identities, collective interests, and in-group goals.

Similarly, I think it is valuable to be clear when we are focusing on behaviors that occur during a protest or when a crowd gathers. Using more specific terms like social protest and crowd behavior make it clear that what is being considered may or may not be collective action. Also, it seems valuable to distinguish collective action from the much larger concept of intergroup behavior. I believe that the concept of collective action is being stretched far too thin if it is to refer to all actions that are prescribed by the individual's understanding of intergroup norms.

Elaborating the Antecedents of Collective Action

Many of the articles in this volume find their theoretical roots in social identity theory (SIT) and self-categorization theory (SCT). Thus, it is not surprising that many consider the importance of in-group identification (Drury & Reicher; Iyer & Ryan; Louis; McGarty et al.; Stürmer & Simon; van Zomeren & Iyer; van Zomeren & Spears), perceptions of illegitimacy/injustice (Ellemers & Barreto; Drury & Reicher; Louis; Postmes & Smith; Iyer & Ryan; van Zomeren & Iyer; van Zomeren & Spears), perceived instability of the status relationships (Louis; Postmes & Smith; van Stekelenberg et al.; van Zomeren & Iyer; van Zomeren & Spears), and boundary impermeability (Louis; van Zomeren & Iyer; van Zomeren & Spears) in motivating collective action. In addition, instrumental concerns regarding potential costs and rewards also play prominently in several of the articles (Stekelenberg et al.; Stürmer & Simon; van Zomeren & Iyer). However, more interesting is that many articles expand on and extend these concepts and consider novel processes that moderate or mediate their impact on collective action participation.

In-group identification. The concept of in-group identification is elaborated in a number of interesting ways. Stürmer and Simon, for example, describe the particular potency of a politicized social identity as the kind of collective identity most likely to inspire participation (see also van Zomeren & Spears). Collective action is far more likely when the identity supporting it contains normative ideological components stressing the competitive nature of the intergroup relationship and the culpability of the out-group.

Drury and Reicher and McGarty et al. both discuss another welcome forward step in their theorizing about collective action. They both describe processes by which identification is constructed, altered, and reconstructed as groups form, enact their identity through collective action, and interact with relevant out-groups. This fluid and dynamic nature of collective identities, while consistent with early theorizing about social identity and self-categorization, has not been properly explored in the collective action literature until relatively recently. However, the value of this approach in describing not only when and why collective action occurs, but how different forms of collective actions will emerge and evolve over time, suggests that this approach should play an increasingly important role in our understanding of social change.

Instability. We also see some attention to the importance of perceived instability. Connecting the concept of stability to related ideas like collective efficacy and instrumental concerns (and more generally to resource mobilization theories) seems a highly productive approach (McGarty et al.; van Stekelenberg et al.; van Zomeren & Spears). However, it would be a mistake to conclude that the concept of stability can be reduced to collective efficacy. Elsewhere (Wright, 2001; in press), I have described the distinction between stability and efficacy in terms of perceived collective control. In order to believe that one's group has control one must believe: (1) that social change is contingent upon behavior (i.e., that the situation is modifiable) and (2) that my group in particular can execute the behaviors necessary to produce the desired change (see also, Mummendey, Kessler, Klink, & Mielke, 1999). The first judgment corresponds with perceived instability, and the second with collective efficacy. Thus, perceived collective control can be undermined by a belief that the system is unresponsive to actions (stability), or that the in-group lacks the resources or abilities necessary to effect change (lack of efficacy).

This distinction has several implications. Clearly, if the system is perceived as stable the question of efficacy becomes irrelevant. If the system cannot be changed, there is no basis for considering the in-group's capabilities. Thus, efforts to build collective action must first undermine the perceived inevitability of the current social order and build in the minds of potential participants what SIT refers to as *cognitive alternatives*; an imagined alternative social reality in which the in-group holds higher status. Although there is evidence of the importance of this kind of instability, there has been limited research on the conditions that lead people to see the current social order as malleable. One possibility is that groups are influenced by the successful collective action by other low-status groups (see Reicher, 2004). For example, successful liberation movements in Africa and India may have provided evidence that change is possible for organizers of the U.S. civil rights movement. Similarly, the success of that movement may have influenced growth in the anti-apartheid movement in South Africa and the women's movement in North America. The success of others provides evidence of instability.

However, group members must also believe that their in-group has the resources and capacities to influence a malleable system. Here, resource mobilization theories seem highly relevant (Drury & Reicher; Louis; van Stekelenburg et al.; van Zomeren & Iyer; van Zomeren & Spears). While early resource mobilization theorists focused exclusively on the objective presence of resources and had little interest in psychological variables, recent versions (e.g., Klandermans, 1997) focus on both objective availability of resources and subjective expectation that the in-group can effectively utilize them.

Emotions. A number of articles explore the role of emotions such as anger (e.g., Ellemers & Barreto; van Zomeren & Spears), sympathy (Iyer & Ryan) or outrage (e.g., McGarty et al.), describing these emotions as the result perceived illegitimacy or injustice. From this perspective emotions emerge as a result of perceptions of unjust disadvantage and inspire the confrontational action tendencies that produce collective action. Stürmer and Simon propose an interesting alternative in which emotions play their part at an earlier stage in the causal chain. They hold that negative emotions directed at the oppressor play a role in developing the potent politicized social identity, and that it is this identification that is the proximal inspiration for collective action participation. Together these two ideas make apparent that one important issue for subsequent research will be to clarify the multiple roles of emotions in inspiring collective action, and to illuminate the conditions that determine when these specific roles are played.

This recent and growing focus on emotions harkens back to work on relative deprivation theory that also made the distinction between feelings/emotions associated with experienced deprivation, and the colder more cognitive recognition of deprivation (see Smith & Ortiz, 2002). However, this new generation of emotion research offers a more sophisticated theoretical framework (some based on appraisal theories; e.g., Iyer & Ryan). Thus, this new focus on emotions is likely to lead to the erroneous interpretation that collective action participation can be reduced to a kind of LeBonian irrationality. Anger or exhilaration need not replace rationality in some "oil and water" sense. Emotions are intertwined with cognition in ways that make feelings an outcome of, as well as an influence over, rational thought. Drury and Reicher provide a very nice example of their complementarity by showing the connection between positive emotions and the process of empowerment.

Another positive direction has been to expand the array of emotions that are considered relevant to collective action. Although the usual suspects of anger, frustration, and resentment are of course relevant, it seems valuable to consider a broader range of emotions. Drury and Reicher's discussion of empowerment provides a strong case for considering positive emotions like exhilaration, and even joy. Smith, Cronin, and Kessler (2008) show that perceiving the in-group to be unjustly disadvantaged, and believing that things are likely to get worse, can be associated with feelings of sadness and fear. These emotions undermine collective action participation, leading instead to withdrawal and avoidance. In addition, recent consideration of the actions of advantaged group members has initiated a focus on emotions like sympathy and guilt (Iyer & Ryan).

It might be fruitful to widen the focus even further. For example, Drury and Reicher describe exhilaration as an outcome of successful expression of one's collective identity and achieving group goals. However, exhilaration might also be experienced when the in-group's actions cause what is seen to be well-deserved harm to the out-group or its members. The joyous collective celebrations following violent retribution against a perceived oppressor may result from successful expression of a collective identity, but also from positive emotions associated with extracting a measure of revenge for past wrongs. It is possible that the anticipation of these "positive" emotions may also facilitate collective action participation.

Similarly, while fear and anxiety are usually considered negative emotions, in some cases they can be experienced as highly positive. People climb sheer rock cliffs, jump out of airplanes, and drive exceedingly fast in order to experience the "adrenaline rush" associated with these risks. Apparently, some thrive on anxiety that is interpreted in this way. Having participated in several "high-risk" collective actions, it appears to me that at least some people participated for the same reasons that they might also mountaineer, skydive, or race a car. The fear that one could get caught and arrested (or worse) was part of the thrill of being there. Breaking the rules and facing the dangers associated with angering the oppressor can be fun! Especially when we are considering collective actions that involve real risks, I think we might be wise to consider risk taking and the associated positive side of fear as a motivator for at least some participants.

Conversely, hope is usually seen as a positive emotion, assisting one to cope with an existing negative situation, or as a basis for efficacy that one's group can change things. However, hope can also be a negative force (Wright, Taylor, & Moghaddam, 1990b). One can also be hopeful that things will simply get better; that the situation is changing, evolving and that we need only wait for the gears of change to grind on. This is a message often heard in reference to groups who have seen some positive change. "Things are so much better than they use to be." "Times are changing." Although these expressions should make group members feel better, they do not necessarily compel them to continue the fight. Rather this kind of hope can imply that continued change is inevitable and thus continued action is unnecessary.

In summary, the current more sophisticated look at emotions as antecedents to action (be it a proximal cause or as a contributor to politicizing identity) and as consequences of successful collective actions, seems extremely valuable. I believe the field will benefit from widening the focus, not only to consider the multiple roles played by emotion but also to consider a wider array of specific emotions that may inspire, accompany or emerge as a result of collective action.

Broadening the Array of Antecedents and Motivations

A number of the articles in this volume also explore motives and conditions less directly tied to the SIT tradition. I have already described one of these in my earlier discussion of the definition of *collective action*. If collective action is equated with participation in a joint social action, or with membership in a social movement, or with being part of a crowd, then personal self-interest may also be an important motivation (e.g., Stürmer & Simon; van Stekelenburg et al.; van Zomeren & Spears). Participation (or intention to participate) in joint action with other in-group members (e.g., social protest) might result because the individual is seeking personal approval from others, or the opportunity for personal rewards.

Intragroup concerns. In an interesting extension, Postmes and Smith point out another level of motives that, although primarily self-interested, also involve a salient collective identity. When one engages in actions directed at an out-group in order to enhance or solidify one's personal position within the in-group (intragroup concerns), collective identity is clearly relevant. Postmes and Smith focus on these intragroup concerns as the advantaged group members to discriminate against the disadvantaged group. However, they appear to dismiss the importance of this kind of self-interest for disadvantaged group members by describing the "negative interdependence between the interests of the individual and those of the collective" (p. 774). Clearly, this is often the case. Collective action can involve personal costs for participants that can, at times, be extremely high (e.g., economic losses, imprisonment, even death).

However, I would argue that dismissing intragroup concerns as a motivator for disadvantaged group action incorrectly equates direct personal costs with intragroup costs and benefits. Vigorous engagement in actions that are not endorsed by the advantaged out-group can result in substantial personal costs. However, when these actions are endorsed and supported by the disadvantaged in-group, those who suffer these personal costs may gain enormous esteem within the in-group. Thus, direct personal losses may be high while intragroup benefits are also high. The most extreme case of this is the martyr who suffers the ultimate personal cost but gains the highest level of intragroup acclaim. In a much less dramatic example, being the one who is arrested and jailed at an antiwar protest can be a source of considerable acknowledgement, even adoration, among other protestors.

The discomfort of a night in jail, the possibility of a criminal record that could undermine future opportunities, and even the bruises from the handcuffs can all be worn as "badges of honor" in later interactions with the in-group. Thus, when we distinguish between the personal costs and intragroup status concerns it would seem that intragroup concerns could quite easily play a critical role in collective action participation for disadvantaged group members as well as members of privileged groups.

The idea that participation in collective action may be inspired by interest in garnering the approval of others is also reflected in Stürmer and Simon's description of the normative motive (i.e., Klandermans' [1997] *social motive*). However, although the label "normative motive" implies intragroup concerns, the description seems more about concerns that are interpersonal in nature. It "derives from the expected reactions of significant others to one's participation in collective action (e.g., ridicule or admiration by friends or family)" (p. 682). This appears to imply that it is the approval or disapproval of others with whom one has a personal relationship, rather than the collective (normative) approval of one's in-group. Again, we see subtle, but nonetheless important, differences in the level of identity that is being described as relevant.

However, even though intragroup concerns represent an "intermediate" level between interpersonal and intergroup concerns, the primary motivational push at this level is not improving the in-group's status, but rather securing one's personal position within the in-group. Thus, similar to motivations based entirely on personal concerns, it is questionable if actions that result from intragroup concerns should be considered collective actions at all.

Ideology. One exciting trend in the new wave of interest in collective action involves the reintroduction of the concept of ideology. Van Zomeren and Spears and van Stekelenburg et al. describe ideological convictions and discontent about violation of cherished, even sacred, values as a key motivator of collective action. Like Hornsey and colleagues (2006), these articles describe participation in group action that is motivated by principle, contrasting this motivation with more economic self-interest and expectation of personal benefits. However, van Stekelenburg et al. focus on ideology as a "personal set of values" and describe the principles (values) that drive action as quite personal/individualistic. By this account, participation in group protests is motivated by a desire to publicly express one's personal values.

Van Zomeren and Spears, on the other hand, describe ideology in terms of a set of "sacred group values," values and beliefs that are shared (normative) among members of the in-group. Thus, it is not personal values that are expressed or defended by participation in the group action, but rather values that are understood by the participants to be important (even sacred) to all members of the in-group. Again, these two different analyses bring into focus the issue of level of identity.

Both describe group action as ideologically driven, but they differ in level of identity that is seen to be central, with van Stekelenburg et al. focusing on personal identity (individual values) and van Zomeren and Spears on collective identity (group values).

I (see Wright, in press) share with van Zomeren and Spears the view that Skitka and colleagues' concept of moral conviction provides a valuable analysis of the role of ideology in collective action. Moral convictions—the "strong and absolute belief that something is right or wrong, moral or immoral" (Skitka & Bauman, 2008, p. 31)—compel action more so than other strongly held beliefs, because they describe what one "ought" to do. When something carries the mark of immorality, no other explanation is needed for opposing it, considering alternative perspectives will be strongly resisted, and failing to oppose it in favor of other considerations (e.g., personal preferences, normative conventions, potential costs) will evoke regret, shame, or guilt. Thus, if the current in-group position or treatment can be framed as a moral violation or the outcome of an immoral act by the out-group, taking action to rectify the situation becomes a moral mandate, making other concerns (e.g., stability, efficacy, personal costs, etc.) less relevant.

McGarty et al. make perhaps the strongest case for ideology, describing opinions (shared ideological beliefs) as not only the motivator of collective action but as the basis for the shared collective identity around which the action is organized. In this case "the cause" not only motivates group members, but is the defining feature of the collective identity as well.

Affirming collective identity. Collective action provides an opportunity to demonstrate and instantiate a valued collective identity "as a living agent, a locus of possibility" (Drury & Reicher, 2005, p. 54). Collective action can affirm the existence and legitimacy of the relevant collective identity, and these affirmations can, in and of themselves, be enough to motivate action. Collective action can also serve to identify the in-group as a distinct entity and affirm its dissimilarity from the offending out-group who unjustly mistreats or oppresses the in-group. The general point is that collective action can raise the psychological meaning and the perceived status of the in-group by demonstrating that it is a viable agent, distinct from the oppressive out-group, even when these actions have no discernable impact on the actual status, resources or the physical realities of the group (see Drury & Reicher; Louis; Simon, Trötschel, & Dähne, 2008).

Psychological coping. Similarly, some forms of collective action may serve primarily as a means of coping with the psychological stress associated with being a member of an oppressed minority (e.g., Outten, Schmitt, Garcia, & Branscombe, 2009). Here I am reminded of an Ethiopian proverb; "When the great lord passes the wise peasant bows deeply and silently farts." We might not usually consider a "silent fart" to be collective action. However, this kind of small, even invisible, act may be an important form of resistance. In Klandermans' terms (see van Zomeren & Iyer), these acts position the person as part of the mobilization potential; that they recognize the illegitimacy of their current disadvantage. In addition, such minor acts of resistance may also be a tool to build stories of resistance that can be quietly shared with other members of the group. Finally, these acts can be a source of pride and psychological empowerment for the actor, as they represent a source of self- and in-group-affirmation. I suspect that a social psychological analysis of these "hidden" forms of collective resistance could be quite rich and valuable.

Influencing others: "Rallying the troops" and third parties. Hornsey and colleagues (2006) point out that some collective actions, while in service of the long-term goal of improving the status of the in-group, may have a specific short-term goal of inspiring in-group members to join or continue the fight. Actors may realize that the current action stands little chance of creating real change but nonetheless expect that it will inspire in-group members to become part (or to remain part) of the movement. This view that some collective actions are actually designed to inspire future larger collective actions is reminiscent of the concept of consciousness raising (e.g., Taylor & McKirnan, 1984) where the intention is to influence the beliefs and feelings, and thus future actions, of in-group members.

In addition to targeting the in-group (rallying the troops), some collective actions may be designed to influence the thoughts and feelings of the out-group in an attempt to persuade them to voluntarily reduce the intergroup inequality. Further, recognizing that social change often involves more than the two primary groups, Simon and Klandermans (2001) point out that some collective actions may be attempts to influence a currently uninvolved third party (e.g., the general public, the international community, etc.), who might then throw their weight behind efforts to force the out-group to give up some of its power and/or improve its treatment of the in-group. This idea is described in some detail in van Zomeren and Spears' description of political motives. The general idea that collective actions can, at times, represent strategic efforts to influence others is an important addition to the literature. In addition to explaining collective actions that occur when there is little chance that they will have any immediate impact on current group status difference, this analysis could also serve as an avenue for connecting theorizing about collective action to the broader (and larger) social psychological literature on social influence.

Intergroup competition versus conversionary collective action.[1] This idea that collective action can also be a social influence tool can be expanded even

---

[1] This idea was one of the topics of discussion in a seminar titled Dilemmas in Social Change at the Third International Graduate College Summer School in Luckenwalde, Germany June, 2004. I would like to acknowledge the contributions of all of the participants in that seminar for helping to elaborate this idea.

further to consider the possibility that collective actions might be divided into two major classes—competitive and conversionary. The dominant view of collective action in social psychology has been tied to Tajfel and Turner's (1979) idea of social competition. Put simply, when members of a group recognize their group's disadvantages, see group boundaries as impermeable (movement into a higher status group is impossible), and recognize the illegitimacy and instability of this situation, they will then be prepared to take direct competitive action to try and improve the status of their group relative to the more advantaged comparison outgroup. The idea here is that collective action is in service of a competitive goal of improving the relative status of the in-group.

This model of collective action works quite well to describe many examples, including the civil rights movement in the United States, or the women's movement, or the actions of First Nations groups in Canada or Aboriginal groups in Australia. In these cases, African Americans, women, First Nations, and Aboriginal peoples (and others supportive of the movement) engaged in collective actions to raise the group's status relative to White Americans, men, White Canadians, and White Australians. The success of these actions was determined by the degree to which they reduced intergroup inequality. This model also works well in describing some regional or international conflicts which involve people from one group acting to improve the relative status of their country/region/group relative to a neighboring country/region/group.

However, the representation of collective action as a struggle for relative group status does not fit quite so well for other large collective movements. For example, the collective actions of environmentalists are much harder to fit into this model. In this case, the broad goal is not to improve the status of the in-group relative to some out-group per se, but rather to convert as many nonmembers as possible to join the in-group and to take on the in-group's normative worldview. Of course, environmentalists at times identify out-groups (e.g., big industrial polluters, the oil industry, particular political parties, etc.) and some collective actions are directed at reducing the power or status of these out-groups. However, for the most part the general message put forward by the movement is that "everyone should be an environmentalist," and not that "environmentalists should be treated better."

One critical element of the difference between these two types of collective actions involves perceptions boundary permeability. Competitive collective action requires the perception that the boundaries between groups are impermeable. The concern is with out-migration; That group members who believe that they can move out of the disadvantaged in-group to join a more advantaged group will choose individual mobility over collective action. There is little concern in this model for the issue of in-migration, but we might assume that if group boundaries are impermeable, then they are impermeable in both directions. Thus, competitive collective action requires a clear boundary between us and them, where one of us cannot become one of them and assumedly one of them should not become one of us. Conversionary collective movements, on the other hand, are particularly focused on in-migration and are highly interested in (in fact, they are often dedicated to) making them into one of us.

This also implies differences in the likely representation of the out-group. Competitive collective actions is best served by identifying the out-group as the villain responsible for the in-group's disadvantaged position. Competitive collective action is associated with negative stereotypes about the out-group (Reynolds, Oakes, Haslam, Nolan, & Dolnik, 2000) that justify collective conflict (Stott & Drury, 2004) and may be critical to the development of a politicized identity that leads to collective action (Simon & Klandermans, 2001). As a result of this representation of the out-group, competitive collective action is associated with emotions like anger and resentment. However, conversionary collective action requires a more compassionate representation of the out-group. They must be seen as misguided or naïve and in need of education so they will come to see the error of their ways and come to endorse the "correct" worldview. While patronizing and even sanctimonious, this representation of the out-group is certainly less negative than the one required from competitive collective action. Thus, while conversionary collective actions may be just as passionate and emotionally charged as competitive collective action, negative emotions must be tempered with the extension of an open hand.

Some of the flavor of this idea of conversionary collective actions is reflected in McGarty et al.'s discussion of opinion-based groups. In fact, it may be that opinion-based groups are more likely to have a conversion orientation as their collective identity is build on shared opinions. Presumably, some of these groups would understand that opinions can be changed (group boundaries are permeable), making out-group members potential recruits. However, I do not think this is necessarily so. When opinions harden into ideologies, they can become essentialized in the sense that the out-groups "wrong-headed" opinion are seen to be part of their essence, their character. Those holding these beliefs are seen to be dogmatic, inflexible, immoral, and even evil. They are no longer targets of conversion but rather they must be controlled, defeated, perhaps even eliminated.

These two possible perspectives are vividly represented in historical examples of religious conversion. For example, Spanish Catholics during the early colonization of the Caribbean, attempted to convert the "Indians" to Catholicism. When these attempts failed, dissenting Native People were often killed. The paternalistic perception of the out-group as uncivilized, childlike, and in need of conversion to the in-group's worldview was replaced with a representation of them as subhuman sinners. A less dramatic example of this evolution can often be seen in the contemporary North American political process. As election time nears, members of opposing political parties are first seen as potential converts. Each party engages in conversionary collective actions designed to attract members of out-groups (as well as individual thought to be unaligned) to the in-group. When these attempts have "run their course" competitive collective actions follow and out-group members are vilified and their political beliefs described as defects in their very essence (e.g., they are stupid, selfish, arrogant, tyrannical, even evil).

Forms of Collective Action

We have seen evidence in this volume (and elsewhere) of considerable advancement in our understanding of what leads group members to (or away from) collective action. However, social psychological research to date has given far less attention to the form that collective action might take. Collective action can range from mass protest, to joint action by small ad hoc groups, to individuals acting alone. Behaviors can range from education and consciousness raising, to lobbying, negotiation and voting, to writing a protest letter or signing a petition, to disruptive strikes, violent riots and even bombings. To date, social psychologists have either focused on one specific form of collective action (e.g., participation in a protest) or measured a variety of self-reported actions (or action intentions) and combined them. However, it seems fairly obvious that there should be differences in the antecedents leading one to sign a petition versus burn a flag at a protest, or to attend a rally versus set a bomb. It seems a rather important task for collective action theorists to develop a clearer and more elaborated framework that can capture key distinctions among these many different forms of collective action.

Normative versus nonnormative action. One distinction has received some attention—the distinction between actions that disrupt and violate the rules of the current system and actions designed only to alter the position of groups within that system. Louis provides a very interesting discussion of this distinction and details a number of hypotheses regarding the effectiveness of actions that are rule breaking and those that are rule conforming. Nearly 20 years ago now, my colleagues and I (Wright et al., 1990a) proposed a very similar distinction between actions that conform to the rules of the larger social system and those that do not.

This perspective is consistent with SCT's observation that relations between groups are defined and structured within a larger shared superordinate category (Turner et al., 1987). Thus, relations between ethnic groups are defined and understood within the values and rules of a larger social category—often a nation or collection of nations. For example, the relations between Blacks and Whites are understood in terms of their shared membership in the American nation. It is the norms of this superordinate category that define actions by subordinate groups as normative or nonnormative. Thus, while actors may perceive their actions as appropriate, legitimate or moral based on norms within their subgroup, they will also know when their actions are inconsistent with the norms of the inclusive category. For example, suicide bombings may be legitimate and normative within a subgroup engaged in the practice. However, members of these subgroups also know that this action is outside the norms of larger social system. Note also that this normative/nonnormative distinction is not simply the distinction between nonviolent and violent action. Nonviolent civil disobedience, for example, can be nonnormative, while in some intergroup contexts (e.g., a hockey game) violence is a normative and welcomed intergroup behavior.

Nonnormative actions are, by definition, more disruptive than normative action as they challenge not only the current intergroup status inequalities, but also the structure and the rules (the means) that determine group status. Thus, while normative actions provide tacit support to the social order, nonnormative actions communicate to in-group members, to the out-group, and to third parties a clear message that the actors perceive the current social order to be illegitimate. Thus, participation in nonnormative actions may require firmer convictions about the injustice/immorality of the out-group's actions. Finally, as Louis clearly points out, nonnormative action, because it is novel, disruptive, and questions the broader social order, will draw greater attention from the advantaged out-group and will demand a response.

Normative collective action can also evoke resistance. However, it usually involves less risk of a vigorous and potentially harmful response than nonnormative action. Thus, when a normative avenue is available, it is likely to be engaged first (Wright, 2001). Strong endorsement of normative collective action also seems likely when in-group status is thought to be determined by legitimate means but is also unstable. For example, political parties in a functioning democracy who lose an election are likely to engage in vigorous normative action, because (for the most part) their acceptance of the rules by which group status is determined (the election process), but also believe that the current position of their party can be changed. However, if normative tactics prove ineffective or the advantaged group is seen to be engaging in nonnormative actions to maintain their power (see Drury & Reicher), the perceived legitimacy of the system is compromised and normative actions may give way to nonnormative action.

Drury and Reicher (see also Reicher, 2004) provide a valuable model of the fluid and dynamic relationship between the content of the groups collective identity, the actions of the out-group and the form that collective actions will take. Militancy and disruptive action result from changing in-group norms attached to the group's evolving collective identity, and the specific collective identity that will emerge is, in part, determined by the actions of the out-group. For example, the escalation of crowd behavior to include violence can result because the actions of the police serve to redefine the crowd's collective identity. Arrests and aggressive police tactics define the crowd's actions as nonnormative. Those who were initially moderate protesters may accept this proffered self-representation and respond to police "provocation" with increasingly disruptive actions. However, should the police act in ways that provide an alternative self-definition (as "engaged citizens" perhaps), these same protesters should remain relatively moderate and their actions quite normative. Thus, the actions of the out-group play a major role in shaping the collective identity of the actors and, thus, influence the type of collective action that they take. Drury and Reicher's contribution to this volume strengthens the model by introducing the concept of collective empowerment as a critical mediating process.

These are interesting advances in our efforts to understand how and why different forms of collective action emerge. However, the normative/nonnormative distinction is only one of numerous possible distinctions that might be used to organize the many specific actions that a group member could take. For example, we might consider the psychological underpinnings of collective actions engaged in on one's own (e.g., letter writing) compared to participating in an organized protest event. Similarly, we might consider the example of the lone protester in Tiananmen Square who stood alone in front of the row of tanks. What inspires a single individual (or smaller subgroup) to deviate from the group action and perhaps to alter the course of the group (see Louis, for a related discussion of subgroups within social movements)?

Broadening the array of actions we consider and connecting to other literatures. Social psychology's current focus on a limited set of collective actions may also limit the degree to which collective action research can easily connect to other research domains within the field. As already mentioned, when we consider that many collective actions are actually efforts to influence particular audiences (the in-group, the out-group, or a neutral third party), it may be very useful to consider the large literature on social influence as a tool for considering the particular influence processes that are at work and to understand when and why particular collective actions do (or do not) achieve the goal of enlisting the support of the relevant target group.

Similarly, as mentioned previously, some kinds of collective action, may serve as forms of group-based psychological coping. If this is the case, it may be that collective action theories could benefit from consideration of ideas from the literature on psychological coping. For example, Outten et al. (2009) utilize ideas from Lazarus and Folkman's (1984) cognitive theory of stress and coping, describing collective action as an "intergroup problem-focused coping strategy." They find that use of this strategy partially mediated the positive relationship between in-group identification and psychological well-being among members of disadvantaged group.

In addition, Postmes and Smith point out a very interesting connection that could be made between collective action research and the much larger literature on motivations for discrimination. There is nothing in the definition of collective action dictating that the in-group need be disadvantaged or that the target of the action need be an oppressor. It is certainly true that members of advantaged groups take collective action in response to perceived threats (see McGarty et al.), and that actions designed to maintain the status quo are part of a ritualized pattern of interaction between the powerful and the less powerful. Yet collective action theories have paid almost no attention to the in-group serving actions of the advantaged group. However, the larger literature on discrimination focuses almost entirely on advantaged group members.

It is unlikely, however, that all forms of advantaged group discrimination should be described as collective action. For example, institutional discrimination, although effective at maintaining group inequality, lacks the strategic intent that is usually part of collective actions. Similarly, discrimination that emerges from unconscious or implicit biases, which work below the level of conscious thought, do not seem to fit the definition of collective action. However, deliberative discrimination motivated by an interest in maintaining the superiority of the advantaged in-group seems to clearly fit the definition of collective action. Although there are likely considerable differences between advantaged group and disadvantaged group collective action, a good deal might be learned from the existing literature on discrimination.

The Consequences of Collective Action

I would certainly be remiss if I did not comment on what is the most novel and to my mind among the most interesting contributions to this volume. Louis's compelling question, "collective action—and then what?" calls on collective action researchers to consider the outcomes of collective action, not only the psychological and personal outcomes for individual participants (a question dealt with to some degree by other, e.g., Drury & Reicher), but for the broader social system as well. Certainly, if we are to offer to those interested in creating social change our knowledge of what motivates collective action and the forms these actions can take, it behooves us to have some understanding of whether collective action works. We might want to take seriously whether the knowledge we offer has a meaningful chance of producing the change that is sought.

Final Comments: Minding Our P's and Q's

This is not the forum for a full examination of the breadth of behaviors that might qualify as collective action. However, it appears that a more expansive survey of different forms of collective action will very likely reveal connections with numerous other topics within psychology. However, one outcome of this expansion might also be that we will have to take stock of our own politics (P's) and our particular qualms (Q's) about the kinds of actions that fall within our scope. When we focus on progressive social movements interested in reducing inequality and spreading "social justice," we are rightly invigorated by the importance of translating our research and theory into clearly stated language that can assist activists in developing effective strategies. However, what happens when we consider that some forms of discriminatory actions by advantaged groups are also collective action, or that military action might fall within this purview, or that most of the actions of those described as terrorists fits our broad psychological definitions of collective action, or that many of history's greatest atrocities were committed in an effort to forward the interests of a collective? Finally, even goodhearted progressives sometimes get it wrong.

Of course, I am absolutely not suggesting that I oppose an active effort to connect our work to the work of activists on the ground. We have a clear obligation to do so, and doing so is in the best spirit of the society that publishes this journal. Personally, I am fully committed to the value of making our knowledge of use to those whom I believe are making our world a more just and equal place. The effort of the authors in this issue to translate their work into meaningful practice is evidence of their participation in a responsible contemporary social science. However, we might also remind ourselves that while the topic we study—collective action—can be the vehicle of a progressive revolution, it is also a vessel that brings things far less to our liking.

References

Drury, J., & Reicher, S. D. (2005). Explaining enduring empowerment: A comparative study of collective action and psychological outcomes. *European Journal of Social Psychology, 35*, 35–38.

Fiske, S. T. (1998). Stereotyping, prejudice, and discrimination. In D. T. Gilbert, S. T. Fiske, & L. Gardner (Eds.), *The handbook of social psychology: Vol. 2* (4th ed., pp. 357–411). New York: McGraw-Hill.

Hornsey, M., Blackwood, L., Louis, W., Fielding, K., Favor, K., Morton, T., et al. (2006). Why do people engage in collective action? Revisiting the role of perceived effectiveness. *Journal of Applied Social Psychology, 36*, 1701–1722.

Iyer, A., Schmader, T., & Lickel, B. (2007). Why individuals protest the perceived transgressions of their country: The role of anger, shame, and guilt. *Personality and Social Psychology Bulletin, 33*, 572–587.

Klandermans, B. (1997). *The social psychology of protest*. Oxford: Blackwell.

Lazarus, R. S., & Folkman, S. (1984). *Stress, appraisal, and coping*. New York: Springer.

Mallett, R., Huntsinger, J., Sinclair, S., & Swim, J. (2008). Seeing through their eyes: When majority group members take collective action on behalf of an outgroup. *Group Processes & Intergroup Relations, 11*, 451–470.

Mummendey, A., Kessler, T., Klink, A., & Mielke, R. (1999). Strategies to cope with negative social identity: Predictions by social identity theory and relative deprivation theory. *Journal of Personality and Social Psychology, 76*, 229–245.

Outten, H., Schmitt, M., Garcia, D., & Branscombe, N. (2009). Coping options: Missing links between minority group identification and psychological well-being. *Applied Psychology: An International Review, 58*, 146–170.

Reicher, S. D. (2004). The context of social identity: Domination, resistance and change. *Political Psychology, 25*, 921–946.

Reynolds, K., Oakes, P., Haslam, A., Nolan, M., & Dolnik, L. (2000). Responses to powerlessness: Stereotyping as an instrument of social conflict. *Group Dynamics: Theory, Research and Practice, 4*, 275–290.

Simon, B., & Klandermans, B. (2001). Politicized collective identity: A social psychological analysis. *American Psychologist, 56*, 319–331.

Simon, B., Trötschel, R., & Dähne, D. (2008). Identity affirmation and social movement support. *European Journal of Social Psychology, 38*, 935–946.

Skitka, L. J., & Bauman, C. W. (2008). Moral conviction and political engagement. *Political Psychology, 29*, 29–54.

Smith, H. J., & Ortiz, D. J. (2002). Is it just me? The different consequences of personal and group relative deprivation. In I. Walker & H. J. Smith (Eds.), *Relative deprivation: Specification, development and integration* (pp. 91–118). Cambridge: Cambridge University Press.

Smith, H., Cronin, T., & Kessler, T. (2008). Anger, fear, or sadness: Faculty members' emotional reactions to collective pay disadvantage. *Political Psychology, 29*, 221–246.

Stott, C., & Drury, J. (2004). The importance of social structure and social interaction in stereotype consensus and content: Is the whole greater than the sum of its parts? *European Journal of Social Psychology, 34*, 11–23.

Tajfel, H. (Ed.). (1982). *Social identity and intergroup relations*. Cambridge: Cambridge University Press.

Tajfel, H., & Turner, J. C. (1979). An integrative theory of intergroup conflict. In W. G. Austin & S. Worchel (Eds.), *The social psychology of intergroup relations* (pp. 33–48). Monterey, CA: Brooks/Cole.

Taylor, D. M., & McKirnan, D. J. (1984). A five stage model of intergroup relations. *British Journal of Social Psychology, 23*, 291–300.

Turner, J. C., Hogg, M. A., Oakes, P. J., Reicher, S. D., & Wetherell, M. S. (1987). *Rediscovering the social group: A self-categorization theory*. New York: Blackwell.

Van Zomeren, M., Postmes, T., & Spears, R. (2008). Toward an integrative social identity model of collective action: A quantitative research synthesis of three socio-psychological perspectives. *Psychological Bulletin, 134*, 504–535.

Wright, S. C. (2001). Strategic collective action: Social psychology and social change. In R. Brown & S. L. Gaertner (Eds.), *Intergroup processes: Blackwell handbook of social psychology* (Vol. 4, pp. 409–430). Oxford: Blackwell.

Wright, S. C. (in press). Collective action and social change. In J. F. Dovidio, M. Hewstone, P. Glick, & V. Esses (Eds.), *Handbook of prejudice, stereotyping, and discrimination*. Thousand Oaks, CA: Sage.

Wright, S. C., & Lubensky, M. (2009). The struggle for social equality: Collective action versus prejudice reduction. In S. Demoulin, J. P. Leyens, & J. F. Dovidio (Eds.), *Intergroup misunderstandings: Impact of divergent social realities* (pp. 291–310). Philadelphia: Psychology Press.

Wright, S. C., & Taylor, D. M. (2003). The social psychology of cultural diversity: Social stereotyping, prejudice and discrimination. In M. A. Hogg & J. Cooper (Eds.), *Sage handbook of social psychology* (pp. 432–457). Thousand Oaks, CA: Sage.

Wright, S. C., Taylor, D. M., & Moghaddam, F. M. (1990a). Responding to membership in a disadvantaged group: From acceptance to collective protest. *Journal of Personality and Social Psychology, 58*, 994–1003.

Wright, S. C., Taylor, D. M., & Moghaddam, F. M. (1990b). The relationship of perceptions and emotions to behavior in the face of collective inequality. *Social Justice Research, 4*, 229–248.

STEPHEN C. WRIGHT is Professor and Canada Research Chair in Social Psychology at Simon Fraser University. He received his PhD from McGill University, and was on faculty at the University of California, Santa Cruz, from 1991 to 2003. His research focuses broadly on intergroup relations, with specific interests in: the consequences of membership in stigmatized groups, antecedent and barriers to collective action, prejudice and its reduction, and issues of minority languages and cultures. He is a Fellow of the Association of Psychological Science and the Society for the Psychological Study of Social Issues, and has served as Associate Editor for *Personality and Social Psychology Bulletin*, and on the editorial boards of numerous scholarly journals. His work has been published in scholarly volumes and major social, educational, and cross-cultural psychology journals.

UNITED STATES POSTAL SERVICE — **Statement of Ownership, Management, and Circulation** (All Periodicals Publications Except Requester Publications)

1. Publication Title	Journal of Social Issues
2. Publication Number	0 0 1 – 6 5 2
3. Filing Date	10/1/09
4. Issue Frequency	Quarterly
5. Number of Issues Published Annually	4
6. Annual Subscription Price	$767.00
7. Complete Mailing Address of Known Office of Publication	Wiley Subscription Services, Inc., 111 River Street, Hoboken, NJ 07030
Contact Person	E. Schmidichen
Telephone	(201) 748-6346
8. Complete Mailing Address of Headquarters or General Business Office of Publisher	Wiley Subscription Services, Inc., 111 River Street, Hoboken, NJ 07030

9. Full Names and Complete Mailing Addresses of Publisher, Editor, and Managing Editor

Publisher: Wiley Subscription Services, Inc., 111 River Street, Hoboken, NJ 07030

Editor: Rick H Hoyle, Department of Psychology, Duke University, Box 90085, Durham, NC 27708

Managing Editor: None

10. Owner

Full Name	Complete Mailing Address
The Society for the Psychological Study of Social Issues	1901 Pennsylvania NW Ste 901, Washington, DC 20006

11. Known Bondholders, Mortgagees, and Other Security Holders Owning or Holding 1 Percent or More of Total Amount of Bonds, Mortgages, or Other Securities. ☒ None

12. Tax Status — Has Not Changed During Preceding 12 Months

13. Publication Title: Journal of Social Issues
14. Issue Date for Circulation Data: September 2009

15. Extent and Nature of Circulation

	Average No. Copies Each Issue During Preceding 12 Months	No. Copies of Single Issue Published Nearest to Filing Date
a. Total Number of Copies (Net press run)	4397	4380
b. Paid Circulation (1) Mailed Outside-County Paid Subscriptions Stated on PS Form 3541	1788	1776
(2) Mailed In-County Paid Subscriptions Stated on PS Form 3541	0	0
(3) Paid Distribution Outside the Mails Including Sales Through Dealers and Carriers, Street Vendors, Counter Sales, and Other Paid Distribution Outside USPS®	0	0
(4) Paid Distribution by Other Classes of Mail Through the USPS (e.g. First-Class Mail®)	0	0
c. Total Paid Distribution (Sum of 15b (1), (2),(3), and (4))	1788	1776
d. Free or Nominal Rate Distribution (1) Free or Nominal Rate Outside-County Copies Included on PS Form 3541	388	402
(2) Free or Nominal Rate In-County Copies Included on PS Form 3541	0	0
(3) Free or Nominal Rate Copies Mailed at Other Classes Through the USPS (e.g. First-Class Mail)	0	0
(4) Free or Nominal Rate Distribution Outside the Mail (Carriers or other means)	0	0
e. Total Free or Nominal Rate Distribution (Sum of 15d (1), (2), (3) and (4))	388	402
f. Total Distribution (Sum of 15c and 15e)	2176	2178
g. Copies not Distributed	2221	2202
h. Total (Sum of 15f and g)	4397	4380
i. Percent Paid (15c divided by 15f times 100)	82.17	81.55

16. Publication of Statement of Ownership — ☒ If the publication is a general publication, publication of this statement is required. Will be printed in the December 2009 issue of this publication.

17. Signature and Title of Editor, Publisher, Business Manager, or Owner

Elizabeth Konkle, Associate Financial Manager

Date: 10/1/09

PS Form 3526, September 2006